FREEDOM TO BE
A New Sociology of Leisure

John R. Kelly
University of Illinois

MACMILLAN PUBLISHING COMPANY *New York*

COLLIER MACMILLAN PUBLISHERS *London*

Macmillan Publishing Company
866 Third Avenue, New York, New York 10022

Collier Macmillan Canada, Inc.

Library of Congress Cataloging-in-Publication Data
Kelly, John R. (John Robert)
   Freedom to Be.

   Bibliography: p.
   Includes index.
   1. Leisure—Social aspects.   I. Title.
GV174.K45 1987   306'.48   86-5256
ISBN 0-02-363060-4

Printing 1 2 3 4 5 6 7   Year: 7 8 9 0 1 2 3

ISBN 0-02-363060-4

Preface

How do we go about trying to understand anything that is complex and changing? The fundamental aim of what we call "science" is to develop explanations of what is going on in the world. By dividing the world into arbitrary segments (biological, physical, behavioral, social, and so on), we attempt to reduce the complexity to manageable scope. By basing our explanations on the premises of scientific "disciplines" (biology, astrophysics, psychology, sociology, and economics), we will limit our mode of investigation and explanation to elements that are familiar to us. As a consequence, the tendency in the world of science is to divide the world into smaller and smaller chunks.

We are a bit like the unsober chap who was seen at a street corner on his hands and knees. Asked what he was doing, he replied that he was looking for his lost wallet. To the query, "Is this where you lost it?" he replied, "No, but the light is better here."

Leisure is complex and changing. It is difficult to know just which dimensions are crucial and which means of investigation most useful. So, as good sociologists, philosophers, or whatever we claim to be, we apply the analytical concepts of our discipline. We employ the research methods we have learned, usually as students. We are unsure of the parameters of the object of our inquiry, so we apply limits that are familiar. We look where "the light is better" no matter what is out there in the shadows.

The risk of any other approach is high. When we venture into the bounded fields of other disciplines where others have invested years in gaining competence, we inevitably lack both depth and breadth. When we try to use investigatory methods on the periphery of our experience, we may err even after a period of learning. In general, we find safety and professional approval when we stay within our familiar circle of light.

On the other hand, there are times when risk is required. A divided field of study produces what appears to be a number of complementary explanations that call for synthesis. Or conversely, there are conflicts that need reconciliation. Furthermore, one research method raises questions that can only be dealt with by another. The trend of subdividing a field may have to be reversed—at least for the moment—if we are to *do science,* if we are to try to produce coherent and plausible explanations.

One other metaphor may add to the case. If my computer develops a persistent ailment that inhibits its performance, it would be convenient and economical if I could fix it myself. However, to open the case and "go at it" with the tools *I* know how to use—pipe wrench and pliers—would be unlikely to yield results beneficial to the computer or my repair budget. I will have to acquire new tools and gain new skills if I am to open that grey box and do something useful.

It is no criticism of sociologists to say that for the most part we do what we have been taught. This makes us no better or worse than any other breed of scientist. When a rare sociologist has attempted to understand leisure, the familiar demographic ("structural") variables have usually been employed in a familiar method, survey research. Explanation has been in terms of institutional roles, positions, and socialization. Economists, psychologists, philosophers, and others have also opened their usual toolboxes and gone to work on leisure.

For the most part, representatives of such disciplines have operated well within their normative canonical boundaries. Those venturing into this somewhat eccentric field have tended to play it safe in other ways. Therefore, sociologies of leisure have usually been mainstream rather than innovative or experimental.

In this book I take the risk of operating across several modes of sociology rather than sticking to one accepted model; sociology includes existential as well as structural approaches and interpretive as well as "social fact" modes of analysis. Basic issues raised by political theorists at one extreme and students of consciousness at the other have been accepted on at least the margins of the discipline. Sociology is defined here inclusively rather than narrowly within a single paradigm.

My concern, though, is more to widen the theoretical basis of understanding leisure than to broaden definitions of sociology. If the inclusion of states of consciousness, decision, and models of what it means to be human seem to lead us into social psychology and philosophy, that is tolerable for me. I should admit that I have degrees in other disciplines as well as sociology and can even remember "life before sociology."

The persistent aim of this book is to produce *theory*. The discussion builds on a sequence of theoretical approaches or "metaphors" that have been applied to leisure. Within each metaphor there is a "dialectic" that drives the approach outside itself in an attempt to cope with questions that have been raised. None of the theoretical models is a self–contained dialectic of thesis–antithesis–synthesis; rather, each pushes us beyond itself into another metaphor.

The schema of the book, therefore, is that of a spiral in which each theoretical approach leads to another metaphor where the process of explanation is in turn furthered but not completed. One premise, then, is that the superiority of any single, existing theoretical perspective cannot be presumed. Rather, it is—to use another metaphor—necessary to walk around the phenomenon of leisure quite a bit. We look from different perspectives, from within and from outside. We explore leisure in its variations as well as regularities. At times we even tinker a bit with both concepts and methods. We temporarily suspend prior distinctions that might lead us to an "either/or" exclusion. While attempting to learn as much as possible from others, we risk some critical analysis and synthesis that transforms as well as appreciates the work of others.

Following an introductory chapter on the nature of theory and the outline of the book, there are eight chapters on the explanatory approaches, or models, employed in the dialectical analysis. These models focus on particular elements of leisure: experience, decision, development, identities, interaction, institutions, political forces, and human definitions. Then, there is an attempt at synthesis: the whole is offered as a contribution to a process. No questions are fully answered. No issues are firmly resolved. Many new questions are raised. Yet, there is something more. There is an implicit criticism of simplistic definitions and single-issue approaches to leisure as well as *a priori* limitations to a single discipline or theory. Although science may require countless individual bricks to join into a structure, they have to be shaped to fit together. The process of building theory calls for more than a thousand segregated little projects. There are questions to be answered. This book is my offering to those who will be joining in the common search for understanding. Some may prefer that it all be much neater and one-dimensional. But, as we have all objected at some time, "Who ever said that life was simple?"

I would like to acknowledge the contributions of Neil Cheek, Karen Conner, Mihaly Csikszentmihalyi, Janice Kelly, Douglas Kleiber, Douglas Sessoms, Robert Stebbins, and Robert N. Wilson, each of whom read chapters in an earlier version and offered valuable suggestions for improvement. However, as the saying goes, all final decisions were mine, and I alone am accountable for remaining errors or idiosyncracies.

Looking back further, I would like to acknowledge the influence of Sam Thompson of Monmouth College, who introduced me to the excitement of philosophy, and H. Richard Niebuhr of Yale, who led me into reflexive ethical analysis. Their contributions have outlived them, a mark of real teaching. I would also like to acknowledge the generous support of Joffre Dumazedier, the pioneer, as well as of so many colleagues around the world that it would be folly to attempt to name them all.

JOHN R. KELLY
University of Illinois

Contents

CHAPTER 1

The Play of Theories

ISSUES

Theory may be understood as explanatory metaphor.

The model on which this book is based is that of a *double dialectic:*

1. There is a hermeneutic spiral in which each metaphor is challenged and corrected but not fully negated. Rather, each metaphor advances the analysis to another metaphor.

2. In any theoretical approach there is a negation as well as a positive contribution to understanding. Therefore, theory building is seen as a process rather than a reaching of any final truth.

The model toward which this analysis moves can be called *social existialism* because it includes both the risk of decision and the reality of social forces.

In approaching the question of "What is leisure?" we will identify dimensions rather than delineate limiting parameters. In essence, however, leisure will be understood as a "state of becoming" that is defined more by orientations than by time, place, form, or outcome.

What is theory? To some, theory is what we don't know for sure. To scientists, theory is what we know with a degree of surety that has been subjected to rigorous testing. At the very least, theory is systematic explanation of some repeated phenomena that is based on evidence. Such explanations are not fixed in concrete or held to be sacred and above question. Rather, theories are both created by and subject to "play" in the sense of recognizing that theory is created out of less-than-perfect information and in thought processes that might have taken another course.

One model of theory presumes a rigid system of logical deduction that produces invariable "laws" of predictive accuracy. At the other extreme, theory is seen as a kind of metaphor that suggests that "If you view something from this perspective, it can best be understood as follows." Theory may be defined as lawlike and invariable, as probabilistic and predictive, or as relativistic and partial.

However, all models have in common certain themes:

1. Theory is an act of explanation that is communicated to others.
2. Theory is systematic and discloses it presuppositions and evidence.
3. Theory is always subject to question and criticism.
4. Theory development is something we do whenever we attempt to explain to others the antecedents and conditions of occurrences.

In this approach to understanding leisure, theories are developed by applying these broad themes in a general mode. The aim is simply to present explanations in such a way that they can be examined, compared, criticized, amended, and synthesized into a comprehensive understanding.

Theory as Metaphor

Max Weber, among others, proposed that we never can give a complete explanation of anything. There are always some factors in an event, decision, or occurrence that precede more immediate and recognizable factors. For example, a complete explanation of why I choose to go sailing on a given afternoon would involve not only all perceived alternatives and conscious anticipation of benefits and costs, recollected and subconscious previous experiences, investments in skills and equipment, access to environments and an assessment of their quality, available companions, predicted weather, and available time, but also my full history with that activity and with alternatives. That history, in turn, would have to include not only friends who encouraged me to go, but also everyone who contributed to my interests, and in some infinite regress, all those who contributed to their orientations and opportunities back through history. It might also include a full history of Western culture, value systems, sailing and its technologies, and so on and on.

Consequently, theory development selects some explanatory factors and excludes others. We might assume that the criterion is simply one of importance. But how do we know what is important? Theory, then, begins with some decisions about what will be included and excluded. That set of prior judgments has been variously referred to as "domain assumptions" (Gouldner, 1970), presuppositions, a "paradigm" (Kuhn, 1970), or even a "world view." Whatever the term, the presumption is that we—as explainers—always have some predetermined or preselected way of viewing what we intend to explain, choosing some elements or dimensions as relevant and omitting others. We develop theory from a perspective, not from a blank slate.

One way of understanding such domain assumptions is to view them as a *metaphor*. We approach what we are trying to explain by saying or assuming that it is "something like this." My decision to go sailing is something like a rational weighing of the costs and benefits of alternatives. Or, the decision is the result of having internalized a set of values related to my position in society that directs me to such "elite leisure." Or, my emotional response to sailing is positive and to the alternative of mowing the lawn negative based on previous experiences with both. Or, I merely respond to the expectations of those who are most significant to my role-based identity in my family and community. Each is a metaphor that directs us to a particular way of viewing the same act. Each provides a "shape" for the decision that draws our attention to a particular set of explanatory factors. Each says that in this culture adult decisions to sail are made "something like this."

Of course, we may employ more than one metaphor in explanation. We may combine perceived opportunities, previous history of participation, values and anticipated outcomes, and social pressures into an eclectic analysis. Even so, we tend to give different weights to the various factors—to begin with one model and add in others. In some cases the metaphors may be highly complementary and seem to fit together comfortably. In other cases it may be difficult to reconcile different dimensions or levels of analysis. In research design we may select metaphors and evaluate their compatability as well as their likely importance. In more ordinary explanation we tend to slap metaphors together without concern for possible conflicts between their premises.

Mixing metaphors may not seem too significant in ordinary conversation. However, in the development of theory—systematic explanation that discloses its assumptions as well as evidence—the implications of the uncritical acceptance of a metaphor that focuses on some elements of a phenomenon and excludes others has profound consequences. In one discipline of social study, sociology, there have been a number of analyses of how theory is based on assumptions that are frequently taken for granted by the scientist.

Alvin Gouldner (1970) argued that whether society is believed to be an integrated system or a collectivity of groups with different and conflicting interests shapes a sociologist's theoretical explanations of every institution as well as of history. George Ritzer (1975) based his analysis of theory on the model of scientific transitions and revolutions of Thomas Kuhn. Kuhn (1970) proposed a theory of the history of scientific disciplines based on the idea of dominant "paradigms" that shape both the research agendas and the form of explanation that is assumed correct in a field. The paradigm defines the subject, identifies a community of exemplars, and requires certain acceptable research methods. Such a paradigm is a "ruling metaphor," requiring that scientists within a discipline do their work according to its premises. Further, the exemplars are the "gatekeepers" who decide what will be published, what kind of research is worthy of being awarded graduate degrees, which proposals should be funded, and what accepted textbooks must include.

This approach to science does not preclude the possibility of competing paradigms in a discipline. A discipline tends to change slowly because of the investment of scholars in an established paradigm. Kuhn adds the possibility of a scientific revolution that overthrows the old accepted wisdom when a series of anomalies that challenge the current paradigm have become too significant to ignore.

For a period a field of study may include a number of approaches that cannot be easily reconciled. For example, in sociology Ritzer (1975) proposes that there are three basic paradigms that compete for support. Further, they are different enough—one based on "social facts" that are external to the individual, one based on "social definitions" of actors who interpret their social world, and one based on "social behavior" in which action is determined by the environment—that each remains as a different mode of explaining the same phenomena. Anthony Giddens (1971) takes a historical approach by identifying Emile Durkheim, Max Weber, and Karl Marx as the founding exemplars of three theoretical models that continue to shape research in the discipline. Durkheim's structural model, Weber's assumption of interpretation, and Marx's stress on conflict have led to quite different accounts of causation for the same events.

Structure-functional explanations of leisure, for example, have stressed socioeconomic position variables and the functions of leisure in relation to participation in the economy and system maintenance. Attention has been given to the contributions of leisure to the major social institutions of work and family and to the integrating functions of community organizations. Leisure has usually been operationally defined as residual time secondary to time determined by institutional timetables (Kelly, 1976). Interpretive approaches have contrasted in focusing on the values and orientations of the actor who makes meaning-laden choices based on personal histories and identities rather than structural determinants. Conflict theory has tended to account for leisure patterns in capitalist societies by defining leisure as an instrument of social control shaped by the necessity of maintaining a labor force working contrary to its real interests. In this book, interpretive theory is examined in Chapters 2, 3, 4, and 5, structural theory in Chapters 6 and 7, and conflict theory in Chapters 8 and 9.

No facile amalgamation of items from each vocabulary can produce a single paradigm for the study of leisure. Adherents of each approach do not see the same world even when they look at the same event. An earlier analysis of the state of leisure research proposes that the "structural" model of sociology has been dominant by default, resulting in the neglect of issues and methods significant for the development of the field (Kelly, 1976).

Another possible explanation for the limited development of leisure research is that the field may be "preparadigmatic." This discipline or field of study, like others, may not have developed a consensus on its definition of itself, its accepted wisdom, and its appropriate research methods and measures. In the case of the study of leisure the stage of development may be early enough that a full consensus is premature and conflict among metaphors is inevitable. Too many fundamental explanatory issues may remain unresolved to fasten on a dominant theoretical paradigm.

The initial premise of this book is that none of these approaches to accounting for different explanations accurately characterizes the state of theory building in the study of leisure. Rather, a variety of metaphors have been applied to various segments of leisure behavior and meaning in ways that produce partial accounts of the phenomena. Some of the accounts appear to be conflicting. Others are easily brought into what appears on the surface to be mutually enriching combinations. In any case, the field is becoming increasingly fragmented as scholars design research that begins with an often-implicit premise that leisure is "something like this." Further, unproductive debates over research results and interpretations reach no conclusion because the initial metaphors are never compared.

Underlying the development of this book is the premise that leisure is a complex phenomenon—or set of phenomena. Explanation is not likely to be exhausted by any single paradigm, model, approach, family of theories, or research methodology. Rather, the nature of leisure will be revealed most fully by exploring the various metaphors that have been developed for different disciplines, thus yielding some understanding of both its constituent elements and its overall shape.

Theory Building

However, just a listing, description, or even analysis of a selection of such metaphors is not enough. The aim of science is always to explain, to build coherent theory that can be examined and tested. The aims of this book are to examine a sequence of theoretical approaches in order to build on the strengths of each and to attempt to lay a comprehensive basis for the continuing work of science. At the same time, the level of explanation is intended to be such that it will also serve as an introduction to serious scholarship in the field. Although the disciplines of sociology and social psychology have provided the bulk of research efforts thus far, attention will also be given to old and new possibilities from other disciplines. No metaphor will be arbitrarily ruled out as a possible source of insight, nor will any be assumed to be the foundation of "real truth"—at least not until such a claim is founded on more than assertions of supremacy.

Theoretical Styles in Leisure Explanation _____

On one level of analysis, two basic approaches to explanation have been employed in leisure research. The first was dominant for the decades up to 1980 and probably retains priority outside of North America. It is a *social* model that begins with the assumption that social forces determine behavior. The second approach is *existential* in beginning with the individual actor who makes decisions. Such decisions may be influenced by social forces or other factors. However, explanation is grounded in individual action rather than social structures.

The difference has profound consequences. To begin with, what is the basic problem to be addressed? Various leisure scholars from East and West Europe as well as North America have discussed the issue and have reached a consensus that the farther East one moves from the "mid-Atlantic," the more theory is oriented toward the problem of social solidarity. The fundamental issue is the relationship of leisure to the cultural and institutional factors in social cohesion. The farther one moves West—at least to California—the more scholars are directed toward issues of individual action and meaning, asking first how leisure is related to individual choices and aims. As a consequence, in Eastern Europe research often investigates cultural participation of different kinds of workers, whereas Western research focuses on varieties of lifestyles as expressions of values or developmental periods. What is the "problematic" of leisure—its contribution to social cohesiveness or to personal fulfillment? What questions do we attempt to answer in research? Is leisure fundamentally embedded in the nature of society or in the nature of the human being?

The Social Metaphor. As becomes evident in later chapters, the social, or structural, metaphor includes approaches with critically different premises. Nevertheless, there are also significant commonalities. First, theory is developed to explain group or aggregate behavior. Second, the forces that act on such behavior are collective rather than individual. Third, explanation is sought for repeated events with identifiable commonalities. Fourth, differences among societies are presumed to produce different behavior.

As an example, how do we explain participation in voluntary organizations according to the social metaphor? Voluntary organizations are understood as local expressions of values that tie individuals to the larger society. Those most integrated into the values of the society—for example, the bourgeois middle class—are most likely to participate in the organizations that express and provide a context for such integration. Only voluntary organizations that offer a context for shelter from mainstream social forces or for protest are likely to attract those least integrated into the system. When, in fact, it is found that middle-class Americans are the most frequent joiners, then the explanation is considered supported and a theory of integration through such participation established.

Of course there are variations within the metaphor. Some social theory is deterministic, with a complete explanation expected to identify those factors that control behavior. Some approaches are predictive, with success rates calculated by the percentages of behavioral variations predicted by the model. Some are contextual, with attention focused on immediate factors rather than the structure of the social system. Most often, social models are multivariate and measure the relative predictive power of many factors. Analysis may be stochastic rather than determinative. Nevertheless, whether the goal is nomothetic, seeking behavioral laws, or probabalistic, seeking relative likelihoods, the analysis is of social forces that operate across contexts and on groups of individuals.

The social metaphor includes quite different models of the society and of the salient elements. A *functional* model assumes that the society is made up of a system of institutions that together fulfill the functional tasks that are necessary for a society to exist. From this perspective the fundamental question asked about leisure is "How does it contribute to the integration of the society?" A *conflict* model assumes that the society is composed of two or more groups with different interests and power to impose their will on others. Then, questions about leisure concern its use by those with power to control others and its potential in the formation of effective groups that may alter the basis of such power.

Most often those accepting the social metaphor have asked questions about the relation of leisure to major social institutions such as the economy or the family. To what extent is the nature of leisure for identifiable groups determined by the nature of their work? How does leisure contribute to the family and its functions of reproduction, nurture, immediate bonding, protection, and market consumption? Is leisure itself a social institution with unique functions, or does it only contribute to the economy, family, education, religion, and government? Both the contexts and the purposes of leisure are assumed to be primarily social, to involve the ongoing groupings of human beings in a social system.

The Existential Metaphor. The existential metaphor begins with the individual. Explanation of behavior is based on what individuals do rather than where they are in the society. Theories of the meanings of leisure are oriented toward outcomes for individuals. And, as a result, research agendas and methodologies are different from those seeking social answers to social questions.

The North American preoccupation with personal development and fulfillment has led to a shift in leisure research orientations. In the 1950s and 1960s the social metaphor dominated funded and published research in the field. In the 1970s more and more research began to examine the meanings of leisure participation to individuals. Formats for identifying several dimensions of expected outcomes for participation were developed and refined. The results of such investigation were usually correlated with social position variables but without a prior conviction that the meaning dimensions discovered were essentially the consequence of social factors. Most often a quasi-rational model of leisure decision making was presupposed. The actor was presumed to calculate the likely payoff of leisure alternatives in terms indexed by the scales employed in the research.

One variation of this existential model is no less deterministic than some social approaches. It is assumed that if all decision factors are measured with accuracy, then the information processing and factor sorting of decisions can be predicted and leisure thus explained. A more modest variant of this approach acknowledges that some elements of the decisions always go unmeasured and views predictive levels of 50 percent as acceptable results. However, the metaphor remains intact with its attitudinal assumption that explanation begins in the mind of the individual.

One ongoing debate revolves around the possibility that decisions are more situational than static. That is, although the process is essentially a mental weighing of alternatives, the weight of factors and the alternatives considered is specific to each decision situation. Further, the individual is understood to act in a sequential and cumulative context. Although some values and cognitive systems remain relatively consistent over time, the individual is always in the process of learning and relearning. Therefore, research into decision factors yields a kind of framework of attitudes that are somewhat different in every new situation. This variation of the existential metaphor recognizes that the actor is placed at a person-context interface rather than in a vacuum. Even though the focus is on the information-processing actor, the social context is included in the explanatory model.

As becomes evident in Chapter 3, the approach to the existential metaphor presented thus far omits an entire realm of factors in leisure choices and meanings. Scientific analysis has limited itself to what can, with some consistency, be measured by standard methods. The rational, or information-processing, model of decision making does not exhaust the elements in leisure or any other choice.

The Level of Analysis. The most obvious distinction between the social and existential metaphors is the level of analysis. The social model analyzes either aggregates or groups of people. *Aggregate analysis* takes indices such as income levels, age, and educational attainment to form a statistical number of people who have no real association. That is, there is no necessary interaction or institutional relationship among them. However, the selected measures are presumed to index some common elements that may have an effect on their behavior. In leisure, those with higher income and education levels consistently travel and go to concerts more than those with lower levels. Thus, aggregate analysis forms "statistical groups" based on individual characteristics. Underlying the analysis is the presumption that the indices reflect in some way similar histories, resources, or values that direct behavior.

Group analysis takes real groups—a number of people who share a common experience or institutional affiliation—and analyzes their behavioral or attitudinal characteristics. The unit of analysis is the group whose members have at least one dimension of actual commonality, whether they actually interact directly or not. Such analysis may focus on individual attitudes, action within the group, or action of the group. In leisure, such an approach might be employed to investigate the dynamics of a sport competition, cocktail party, or rock-climbing group.

The existential approach takes the *individual* as the unit of analysis. Various social factors may be taken into account, but it is the actions and attitudes of the person that are examined. Out of such individual attributes may come group action. Individuals may share various characteristics to form a statistical aggregate. However, it is the individual actor who is compared to other actors. The comparison is not of groups or aggregates.

In some research the levels of analysis become mixed and even confused. Complex statistical programs may be utilized to combine such a variety of measures that the total framework becomes blurred in a spaghetti bowl of items and relationships. Such analysis seldom provides a significant contribution to explanatory theory.

One response to all this is to decide that many different metaphors have their value, especially in investigating complex phenomena. Rather than worry or quarrel about metaphors, why not just find out what people do and think and let it go at that? The main problem with this approach is that the results will not lead to real theory or useful explanation. Unless we are clear about our premises, about the context and orientations of our research, we cannot evaluate the results. A photograph of the sun on the horizon does not distinguish a sunrise from a sunset; we must know either the time of day or the directional orientation of the scene. Research that does not know what is included or which direction is chosen cannot even identify what is being studied.

Theory as Explanation

To add to the overall picture, thus far we have been implicitly accepting a metaphor that has gone unexamined: that theory is built on the systematic examination of what is to be explained by observation and measurement. This *empirical* assumption proposes that only through the analysis of some measurable "facts" can we arrive at explanation. However, a number of alternatives have been given serious attention in both Western and Eastern cultures.

One model is that knowledge is produced by the mind. This *philosophical* approach is based on thought rather than on behavioral or attitudinal research. Other metaphors would include the *contemplative,* in which the mind or spirit is said to produce knowledge, and the *revelational,* in which knowledge is believed to be given to the mind from outside.

The Philosophical Metaphor. The history of philosophy is filled with disagreement over both premises and conclusions. The most fundamental conflict is over the means by which knowledge is obtained. The question of the source of knowledge and the processes by which a person "knows"—called epistemology—is basic to all the questions of the nature of existence. In general, epistemological approaches are either *realist* or *idealist.*

Realist philosophers propose that there is some reality "out there" that can be apprehended with greater or lesser accuracy by the human mind. Aristotle's realism took an information-processing approach to the gaining of knowledge. The premises that there is a real world and that the mind is capable of attaining real knowledge of it are only the beginning. Through induction, a process by which the mind takes the instances of apprehension and forms them into general propositions that account for regularities, the mind gives a new existence to the world. (See Aristotle's *De Anima,* Book II, chaps. 6, 7, and 12.) The mind takes perceptions of something that has real existence, reforms the perceptions into mental images, and systematically develops some explanation of the world perceived.

An idealist approach has different premises about the nature of what is real. Plato, who died a decade before Aristotle, did not resolve the epistemological issue. However, his concept of "eternal Forms" that can at least in part be known by the mind implies that knowledge is gained by thought rather than information processing. Employing myths and dialogues rather than a direct exposition of ideas, Plato sought to lead students into truth rather than confront them with his own analysis. Sensory apprehension is distinguished from reason. (See particularly Plato's *Phaedo*.) Sensation is always relative. However, through reason the mind may apprehend some part of the changeless "Ideas" or "Forms" that are the basis for order in existence. There is a necessary order of things that the mind may begin to grasp and that has existence above and beyond the empirical flow of sensory appearance. Truth, then, is found in the touching of the eternal by reason. It is the forms that are truly real rather than appearance. The mind itself produces knowledge through its alignment with the fundamental order of existence.

This fundamental difference between realist and idealist approaches remains at the center of many disputes over the systematic attempts to gain real knowledge that we call science. Those who, knowingly or unknowingly, are Aristotelians seek to gain repeated and accurate perceptions of the world that is external to the mind of the knower. Then, in some implicit or explicit system of logical analysis, those perceptions are arranged into an image of reality. Further, connections among things and occurrences are analyzed so that a scheme of explanation or causation is produced. Always subject to revision, this scheme is formed in ways that can be communicated to others through language or other symbol systems.

On the other hand, those who are either overt Platonists or crypto-Platonists focus on the mind as the fundamental source of knowledge. Either there is a realm of ideas out there that the mind can apprehend, or the only real order is that produced by and in the mind. Sensate perception is only a glimpse, a fragment, or even an illusion of the *idea*—that which is "really real." The idea itself is to be investigated rather than some empirical existence external to the mind.

More frequently, those who attempt to sort out issues about scientific knowledge and epistemology are not so sure that either the realists or the idealists have a hold on all the truth. Rather, knowledge is seen as the product of a process that admits no one-sided understanding. Such a theory of knowledge underlies the theory building of this book and rests on certain assumptions:

- Perceptions of the world external to the mind are always partial and are shaped by the mind that interprets even as sensations are received and processed.
- Whatever the connections among things and events external to the mind, those connections are re-formed in an interpretive process in

the activity of the receiving mind. That is, there is no passive reception of empirical data.

* The process by which the mind engages in such interpretation is learned in a personal history that is embedded in a particular culture with its views and values.
* Further, the interpretation is processed as well as communicated through a language and related symbol system that gives shape to the process. That is, the mind has its "learned logic" that is at the same time culture-embedded and individualistic.
* Therefore, scientific explanation is not made up of "pure data" processed by some abstract system of logical analysis. Rather, theory is produced in an interpretive process that is not only selective but also constructive and reconstructive.

The realist is supported in the analytical production of knowledge by the mind employing the materials of the senses. The idealist is supported in understanding that process as one that is shaped first by the mind rather than anything external to it.

There are several images that offer perspectives on this process. Among them are the circle, the hierarchical ordering, and the back-and-forth of the dialectic. Each image provides part of the approach followed in this book.

The Hermeneutic Circle. The first premise is that there is no uninterpreted knowledge. From that beginning Martin Heidegger (1962) proposed a model of interpretation in which the parts make up the whole in never-ending process. The parts are in turn grasped and interpreted from the perspective of the whole, which is in turn re-formed by the inclusion of new parts. "Any interpretation which is to contribute to understanding, must already have understood what is to be interpreted" (Heidegger, 1966.) Through the mediation of language, products and events are described and explained from a preformed perspective. The interpretation in turn re-forms the metaphor or linguistic framework of the interpretation. The point of emphasis here is that this process is endless. There is no way of breaking into the circle with a new beginning leading to truth. The epistemological circle is one of ongoing interaction of mind and perception in which theory is only a relatively formal and communicated version of the metaphors by which perceptions are assimilated and interpreted.

A Hierarchy of Metaphors. The second premise is represented by a scheme of hierarchical ordering. The fact that the hermeneutic circle is unbroken does not mean that there is no direction within it. At the least, the interpreter may choose a direction in which to go around the circle. Also, the circle metaphor is misleading in suggesting that in time one arrives just where the process began. Rather, there is a spiraling possibility in which the new circle is moved off the old track. Interpretation builds on other interpretation. One metaphor may be employed in the formulation of another. Or a hierarchical scheme may be possible in which the interpretations of one or more metaphors may form a basis for the employment and development of another. Such a hierarchy does not deny the hermeneutic basis of all knowledge but offers the possibility of some direction in the process. In this book the interpretation of individual experience is employed as a base for adding other modes of explanation that expand in scope and content.

Dialectical Theory Building. Another interpretive mode is the back-and-forth scheme of the dialectic. This Hegelian model of thesis–antithesis–synthesis offers an argumentative rather than cumulative approach. In a simplified dialectic an explanatory thesis is offered, countered by a disproving antithesis, and out of the clash of the two a more adequate synthesis is produced. A variant on this classic dialectic suggests that the thesis is tested by some evaluated employment (praxis) that in its less-than-perfect fulfillment calls for revision of the original thesis. What is salient for our approach is the zigzag course of theory development. Unlike the circle suggesting a return or the hierarchy offering a unidirectional building process, the dialectic incorporates conflict and denial into the process. A metaphor may be not only incomplete but also, in at least some particulars, wrong. Being confronted with the strength of other theory or anomalous results from its own practice, an explanation may have to be abandoned or revised rather than simply incorporated into a more inclusive whole. In the analysis of leisure that follows there must be openness to the possibility of conflict among approaches as well as complementarity.

Diagrams of Theory Models _____

How, then, is theory developed? The approach adopted here is based on realist premises and interpretive processes and is the basis of all that follows. The spiral model (Figure 1-1) that is both directional and circular suggests that there is no unbiased starting point. Further, theory building may involve conflicting metaphors and interpretations as well as seek to relate approaches that begin with different premises. The circle is not broken by a presentational convention that begins with data, interprets the data, formulates a falsifiable explanation, tests the formulation, and makes the revisions required by the results. Nevertheless, that ordering for "doing science," however naive, retains the necessary dimension of the dialectic in which nothing is immune from examination. No metaphor is sacred and above question, just as

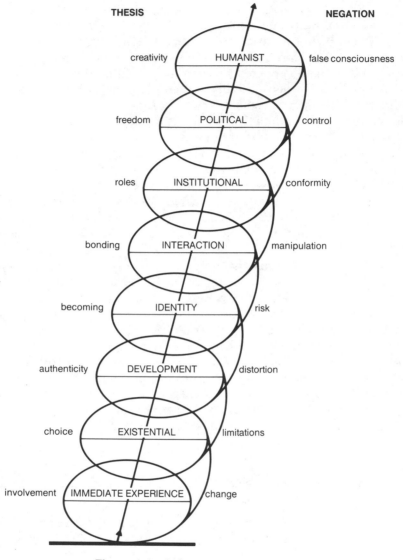

THESIS

NEGATION

creativity — HUMANIST — false consciousness

freedom — POLITICAL — control

roles — INSTITUTIONAL — conformity

bonding — INTERACTION — manipulation

becoming — IDENTITY — risk

authenticity — DEVELOPMENT — distortion

choice — EXISTENTIAL — limitations

involvement — IMMEDIATE EXPERIENCE — change

Figure 1-1 A Spiral of Leisure Theory

no domain assumption can be spared the possibility of a conflicting premise.

A Dialectical Hierarchy

The framework of the analysis of leisure theory and research that constitutes the core of this book takes the shape of double dialectic. The first dialectic is hermeneutic—the interpretive spiral in which theory is continually challenged and corrected by further analysis of data from empirical investigations. Research not only yields the basis for revising explanatory metaphors but also leads to the possibility of having to consider other metaphors. For example, later the argument is developed that any individual-based theory that omits social forces and cultural contexts cannot account for either existential or social manifestations of leisure. However, this does not invalidate the more individual and experiential approaches and what they may offer to an integrated explanation of the phenomenon.

The second dialectic is the negation of every metaphor, either from its own contradictions or from external antitheses. Whether attention is focused on individual experience, developmental outcomes, or political conflict, the potential of meaning and benefit is countered by the possibility of its own negation. Human development may be distorted and interaction inauthentic; freedom may lead to alienation; and cultural celebration may be based on "bad faith." Only when the negating potential of every approach to leisure is included in the overall analysis can the tentativeness and incompleteness of each metaphor be gauged and its contribution to understanding evaluated.

The outline of the analysis—and of the chapters—rests on a model that is not only open to criticism but also subject to some inevitable bias. Although the spiral model of interpretation should be kept in mind, the analysis is given a more hierarchical shape. We begin with the experience of the individual actor in settings and activity that may be identified with leisure and build on that analysis to larger contexts. We move from the most narrowly existential to the most persistently social and structural. Further, the data as well as the context become more complex as foci are widened from discrete individual experience to the meanings and conflicts of the culture and social system. This outline is not intended to imply that later metaphors are superior to the earlier ones or that the "real meaning" of leisure is found only in some final association with conflict or culture. Nor is there a covert assumption that every mode of analysis can in the end be integrated into one grand theory that now and for all time encompasses the "truth" about leisure. The argument developed is that the various metaphors are not as mutually exclusive as might be presumed by their proponents and that each contains a negation that leads to other metaphors without invalidating its own value. The content of this rather high-level analysis should become clear as we zigzag our way through attempts to understand leisure.

The Analytical Framework

The framework/spiral/dialectic that follows introduces the order of metaphors in the convention of chapters:

Chapter 2: Leisure as immediate experience
negated by its transitory character
Chapter 3: Leisure as decision
negated by contextual limits and "bad faith"
Chapter 4: Leisure as human development
negated by distortion and loss
Chapter 5: Leisure as social identity
negated by inauthenticity
Chapter 6: Leisure as social interaction
negated by manipulation
Chapter 7: Leisure as institutional role playing
negated by normative "structures"
Chapter 8: Leisure as political freedom
negated by social alienation and control
Chapter 9: Leisure as creativity negated by conformity and as celebration negated by false consciousness

Theories and a Theory

The final chapter addresses the question of whether or not there is a possibility of some cohesive or integrated understanding of leisure. The argument for the possibility is based on other arguments: that a perspective herein called *social existentialism* provides the basis for such an integration and that the attempt to integrate theory is a process that both informs and alters such a perspective.

Social existentialism is based on the premise that the risk of decision and the reality of social forces are both part of human life. The metaphor offers no break in the circle of interpretation. Life is not fundamentally one or the other—individual or social. Nor is one simply the context for the other, the environment for what is real. Rather, leisure peculiarly demonstrates the dialectical nature of human existence.

The existential dimension proposes that decision—however limited and directed—is real. That is, persons make choices that entail genuine risk and lead to differential consequences. Without taking the extreme view that life is wholly shaped by decision or that decision, indeed, is life, the premise is that choice is not merely illusory or ephemeral. However limited, there are real alternatives that may in some measure be grasped and weighed. Without comprehending all possible alternatives or possible results of those alternatives, decisions are made that lead to consequential outcomes. Any explanation of human activity that omits this existential dimension is neither adequate nor accurate.

On the other hand, decisions are not made in a vacuum. Decision contexts are limited by opportunities, perceived and actual, and by internalized views and values of the culture. Social forces—cultural, political, and institutional—impinge on us all. We are constrained by resource limitations in our social context as well as in ourselves. We are directed by the value systems that we have learned as well as by the concatenations of restrictive norms and sanctions of our social system. We have power to effectuate our preferences only within limits imposed by our place in a system that allocates differential freedom and authority to different groups. When our interests do not coincide with those of others, the institutionalized authority structures give quite specific shape to our degrees of freedom.

Therefore, leisure—like any other designated kind of human action—exists in a dialectic between the existential and the social (Kelly, 1981, 1983). Leisure is not unlimited freedom or choice, nor is it only a manifestation of the pervasive norms and requirements of an integrated social system. It is neither wholly free nor entirely determined. The task of theory building, then, is to attempt to understand how leisure has real existence that is in some way both existential and social.

The Core of Leisure Meaning

Without attempting to offer a full or final definition of leisure, is it possible to identify dimensions that define the phenomenon? To begin with, some concept of freedom seems universal in defining leisure (Kelly, 1982). Such freedom is not necessarily an unconstrained openness. Rather, the freedom of leisure is a freedom to become, some space within the rigidities of life to make consequential decisions. Leisure is at least enough release from obligation to choose activity that may have its own meaning or purpose.

Such self-contained meaning or purpose is the second common dimension. Leisure is chosen with at least some central element of being done for its own sake rather than in response to external demands. Leisure has some integrity of meaning and is, therefore, a phenomenon that can be identified and studied.

The term *play* appears frequently in the chapters that follow. As used, play generally denotes leisure as activity, action that is chosen and has its primary meaning within the event or episode. However, play connotes leisure action highlighting the elements of spontaneity and recognized boundaries that create a nonserious realm of meaning (Kelly, 1982:31). *Recreation,* on the other hand, refers to leisure activity that is organized for the attainment of personal and social benefits. The self-containment and emergent quality of play may be contrasted with the organized and goal-directed dimensions of recreation.

Some of the more specific elements of leisure are examined in the chapters that follow. Is leisure *time* in the sense of filling a durational void? Is leisure *activity* in the sense of willed and purposeful action? Is leisure *experience* in the sense of simple or complex individual interpreted perception? Is leisure affective as well as rational, imaginative as well as physical, role-bound as well as decisive, and cultural as well as creative? Is leisure fundamentally meaning or behavior? Is there a transcultural dimension to leisure even though its forms are always thoroughly ethnic? Is leisure more personal than political? Can the "noninstrumental" individual perception of leisure experience be at the same time the instrument of social hegemony?

The possibility with which we begin is that no single meaning or dimension is likely to exhaust all that we will find under the general rubric of *leisure*. Nor will any single orientation or context necessarily give us the key to understanding all the other meanings or environments. Even a dialectic may prove either too one-sided or too balanced. Even a basic openness to do or become that which does not yet have full reality may be biased toward freedom and away from determinative contexts. First we examine eight metaphors that maintain that to understand leisure you should begin "something like this." Only when we look back at all eight can we try to explore the possibility of another metaphor that catches their essentials.

Theory Building

No development of theory begins from "ground zero." The theory-building enterprise that follows is no exception. There are certain premises about the nature of how such a project can best proceed as well as about the phenomenon to be explained. Some of the most salient can be identified briefly.

Premises About Theory Building. The paradigm is one of "essential Aristotelianism" and holds that theory is to be grounded in some identification and observation of leisure and its contexts. Further, since leisure is a human phenomenon, the biological as well as the social nature of humankind should be included in the analysis. The formulation of theory is to be in accordance with some systematic method open to critical analysis. Therefore, both the materials and the methods of the process of theory building should be examined critically. Nothing that is exempt from falsification (Popper, 1972) can be integral to the process. The design, framework, bricks and mortar, and aesthetics of the building are to be revealed and, insofar as possible, tested by counterevidence and interpretations.

Premises About Leisure.

1. Leisure is a complex rather than simple concept and phenomenon.
2. Leisure is part of the process of existence rather than a static and unchanging idea or phenomenon.

These premises lead to an approach that gives some direction to the theory-building process. Sebastian de Grazia (1965), in his extremely influential exploration of leisure, offers the idea that leisure is a "state of being." It is a condition of existence, however temporary, for the individual. Underlying the following analysis is the conviction that leisure is best understood as a "state of becoming." That is, leisure is more than a present reality. It has future-oriented components as well as existing forms, environments, and meanings. Leisure, then, is defined more by orientations than by time or place, by form or even outcome. Any model that is too static requires the correction of a dynamic view of human existence and its contexts. Leisure is, at least in part, a dimension of becoming as well as of being.

In this spirit, "Let the play begin."

References

de Grazia, Sebastian. 1964. *Of Time, Work, and Leisure*. Garden City: Doubleday/Anchor.

Giddens, Anthony. 1971. *Capitalism and Modern Social Theory*. Cambridge: Cambridge University Press.

Gouldner, Alvin. 1970. *The Coming Crisis in Western Sociology*. New York: Basic Books.

Heidegger, Martin. 1962. *Being and Time*. Trans. by J. McQuarrie and E. Robinson. New York: Harper and Row.

Heidegger, Martin. 1966. *Discourse on Thinking*. trans. J. Anderson and E. Freund. New York: Harper & Row, Publishers.

Kelly, J. R. 1976. "Sociological Perspectives and Leisure Research." *Current Sociology* 22(1974):127–58.

———. 1981. "Leisure Interaction and the Social Dialectic." *Social Forces* 60:304–22.

———. 1982. *Leisure*. Englewood Cliffs: Prentice-Hall, Inc.

———. 1983. *Leisure Identities and Interactions*. London and Boston: George Allen & Unwin Ltd.

Kuhn, Thomas. 1970. *The Structure of Scientific Revolutions*. Chicago: University of Chicago Press.

Popper, Karl. 1972. *Objective Knowledge*. Oxford: Oxford University Press.

Ritzer, George. 1975. *Sociology: A Multiple Paradigm Science*. Boston: Allyn & Bacon, Inc.

CHAPTER 2

Leisure as Immediate Experience

ISSUES ——————————————————————————————————————

Leisure can be approached as *immediate experience.*

Certain elements are abstracted from such experience to identify the qualities that make it leisure. The two most often identified are a sense of freedom and intrinsic rather than extrinsic outcomes.

The mental states that have been associated with leisure are complex. For example, variation in intensity may be highly differentiated in activity engagement as well as social interaction. Intense absorption has been labeled "flow," or a sense of timelessness.

A simple stimulus-response model is modified by corrections such as those incorporating cognitive schema and attitude-behavior analyses. Both internal and external structure render simple state-of-mind models problematic.

The metaphor is negated in its concentration on the thin slice of the process considered immediate and the transitory nature of such experience. Or, a more generalized mental state presumes rational information processing in ways that bias explanation.

Accepting that leisure *is* experience, the question becomes "And what more?"

Experience is such a fundamental term that it is difficult to define. Experience is going through an episode or event as well as processing the perceptions of that time period. Experience is the process of perception and assimilation, mental and emotional, by the individual. It is more than simple feeling. It is an event of action and the interpretive consciousness of that action. It is a mental process related to a particular time-and-place-bounded occurrence.

When we focus on immediate experience, we give attention only to a specified and delimited occurrence and its contemporaneous interpretation. The focus is on the individual's internal process of cognition and interpretation that is produced by interaction with the environment, past or present. Experience is a mental process based on an encounter with the external environment, an apprehension with an external referent.

For our purposes in examining leisure as experience, we concentrate on individual perception and processing based on a processual encounter with the external.

Changes in Leisure Explanation

Most investigation of leisure up to the 1980s has given primary attention to form. *What* people did was assumed to be basic. Even examination of choices was oriented toward the results of the choices rather than processes of decision. One factor in this approach was that the meager funding for such research was usually from government agencies concerned with measuring the demand for their programs and provisions.

There were exceptions. Community studies tended to view leisure as one element of the institutional organization of a town or city. A short-lived University of Chicago center studying leisure and directed by David Riesman was concerned with leisure as a theme interwoven into the fabric of social interaction. But the common approach was to measure participation in some list of activities assumed to be leisure or recreation and to identify conditions under which they were most likely to be chosen. Sociologists engaged in their usual coupling of survey methods with the correlational analysis of aggregate participation frequencies and various social variables such as indices of socioeconomic standing.

The most distinguished exception was the Kansas City Adult Project developed by Robert Havighurst and his University of Chicago colleagues. Their design sought to identify patterns of meaning as well as likelihoods of participation. Although the methods employed were complex and rendered replication unlikely, the questions addressed were fundamental. *Why* do people choose their leisure? How is leisure related to family, work, and community roles? Do leisure patterns vary significantly for different groups who have varying opportunities, resources, and cultural orientations? And, how is leisure related to psychological factors and mental-health functioning? From this sequence of studies came the first inclusive view of the several dimensions of leisure meaning (Havighurst, 1957). The elements of relaxation, social engagement, and self-expression were all found to be part of adult leisure orientations. This was especially important because most previous explanations had tended to stress single dimensions or themes.

Scales were developed and applied to specific activities to measure their relative multidimensionality. Among the dimensions identified were autonomy versus other-directedness, enjoyment versus time-killing, instrumentality versus expressivity, gregariousness versus solitariness, service versus pleasure, relaxation versus arousal, and ego-integration versus role diffusion. Other dimensions identified were creativity, development of talent, future potential, physical energy input, work complementarity, and status and prestige (Havighurst, 1957). Types of activity were examined in terms of required resources, social-role relationships, and dimensions of meaning to the participant. These factors were combined into profiles suggesting the place of leisure in life-styles asociated with various social positions and identifications. This analysis had the potential to provide an agenda for succeeding decades of research on leisure, but its complexity may have propelled most sociologists back to more familiar and comfortable ground.

In 1970 psychological approaches were inaugurated at the University of Illinois with funding from the National Institute of Mental Health. However, the methodology used borrowed from sociological sources as well. Survey methods were enriched by the inclusion of meaning-indexing statements that could be reduced to factors amenable to interpretation and classification. These meaning factors were analyzed along with social-placement variables to add a new dimension to the explanation of leisure participation (Bishop 1970). The three main factors of leisure meaning identified were "active-diversionary, potency, and status." Bishop believed that these dimensions were characteristic of types of activity. The method allowed for comparison of different age groups, in which the meanings as well as the activities of leisure were found to differ when youth were compared to adults in the same community (Witt, 1971).

In the period from 1972 to 1976 the author conducted a research sequence in three communities. The aim was similar: to identify not only what people did but how their choices were related to their life conditions, social ties, and value orientations. Although the methods differed, the results were consistent with those of the Havighurst and Illinois studies. Leisure activities were found to be meaning-laden in the sense of being chosen because certain outcomes were anticipated. These outcomes or satisfactions varied with the social position of the individual, especially with changing work and family roles through the life course (Kelly 1978 a, b, c). Some meanings were found to be intrinsic, involving excitement or expression embedded in the form and environment of the activity. Other meanings were social, focusing on developing or expressing relationships and relating to companionship and communication. Patterns or styles were found to vary through the life course, with family roles generally more salient than work.

In these studies and others that followed the aim was to extract general meanings from individuals who would examine their own understanding of what they did and why. The household locale of the research did not lend itself to investigating what was going on at the moment, on immediate experience. However, other lines of research were developed that took the issues of meaning into the field. One of the most significant investigations was carried out in a U.S. Forest Service research program in which scales were developed to measure the various dimensions of meaning of forest and other outdoor resource-based recreation (Driver, 1976). Using this work as a springboard, a number of scholars produced scales that were then factor analyzed to yield persistent meanings for leisure engagement. A compilation of the findings identified the following factors in leisure engagement (Crandall, 1980):

1. Enjoyment of nature, escape from civilization.
2. Escape from routine and responsibility.
3. Physical exercise.
4. Creativity.
5. Relaxation.
6. Social contact.
7. Opportunities to meet new people
8. Heterosexual contact
9. Family interaction
10. Recognition and status
11. Social power
12. Altruism
13. Stimulus seeking
14. Self-actualization, self-improvement, and feedback
15. Achievement, challenge, and competition
16. Way to kill time and avoid boredom
17. Intellectual aestheticism

Such a listing does not answer a number of important questions: Which anticipated satisfactions are most important and for whom? Do such meanings differ sharply for different activities and in different environments? Are there cultural differences in motivation patterns? In general, comparison of such studies has provided evidence that altering the items in scales, varying samples, and differing methods of statistical analysis yield different results (Kelly, 1983). However, a number of central themes are consistent through the studies: the importance of social relationships, especially family and friends; involvement and expression within the activity context; and a measure of relaxation and withdrawal from routine and obligations.

In all such research there is an assumption that has seldom been addressed. It is that some valid index of meaning can be abstracted from the immediate experience. After all, experience is "going through" an episode or event, not simply analyzing it later. How can we be sure that the meaning of leisure experiences can be captured in a statement or set of statements to which the actor responds at some later time? Further, it is presumed that all the elements can be expressed in scale-type items. Even when the contexts of the experience are identified in terms of activity, time, or place, a quasi-rational structure is imposed on an experience that may be far more complex and processual than is encompassed by such research methods. Are the richness and variability of leisure occasions lost in an abstracting system of interpretation, however advanced over previous assumptions that an activity has *a* single meaning?

The basis of most study of meanings of leisure, then, has been that the individual accumulates a kind of reservoir of experiences that are remembered and interpreted. The immediate experiences are processed at the time and stored in mental memory systems. At some later time these mental data can be combined into a general interpretation and subjected to analysis in meaning-measuring questions or statements. Consistency of meaning across episodes with common features is presumed. At least in a metaphorical mode, the method presupposes that, for example, family picnics or sculpting classes produce outcomes that are "something like this." Whether or not experiences are this consistent and interpretations reliable is explored further in this and the following chapters.

Psychological Models _____

The object of study is the individual in a particular environment. The model has usually been some variation of the stimulus-response (SR) design. The premise is that by varying some salient aspect of the environment an altered behavior will result. In an experimental design only one stimulus is changed while all others are controlled or concurrently measured. The consequence, whether behavioral or attitudinal, is measured before and after the stimulus. The environment, then, is presumed to be the major determinant of whatever is being investigated. Some fundamental sameness of information processing is assumed among all subjects, with individual differences labeled "error."

Research into the play of children has frequently been based on this model (Iso-ahola, 1980:26–27). The flexibility, variety, spontaneity, persistence, and social preferences of play have been examined in terms of the nature and complexity of stimuli. The aim has been to isolate those factors that influence play. However, much of this research has been from the perspective of education, with attention on learning rather than expression.

One of the earlier studies in this mode (Bishop and Witt, 1970) sought the sources of variation in leisure behavior using hypothetical rather than actual situations. Employing a method parallel to one used to examine hostility and anxiety, the analysis of choices compared the various leisure patterns in the hypothetical situations as factors prior to patterns of response. Some support was found for a choice orientation, in which leisure is defined as free and unobligated activity chosen for reasons within the psychological makeup of the actor. However, situational factors external to the actor were also found to influence the mental state in which the choices were made. Neither psychological nor situational factors accounted for a major proportion of the variance.

It was inevitable that paper-and-pencil modes of research would be employed by social psychologists to investigate attitudinal factors in leisure. If the stimulus-response approach had the limitation of treating the mind making choices as an unknowable "black box," some method of dealing with the information-processing system was an obvious next step. If environments do not account for as much variance as the stimulus-response model might have anticipated, then what about the processes by which the stimulus is received and used?

From an information-processing perspective attitudes are formed about the attributes of an event or experience. The attributes are combined with beliefs and evaluations to form attitudes toward the behavior. However, attitudes alone are not enough to predict decisions (Fishbein and Ajzen, 1975). Rather, subjective norms consisting of beliefs and applied values also contribute to behavioral decisions. Therefore, a decision concerning a possible leisure engagement is made out of the materials of past experience that are processed and evaluated to form a behavioral intention (Fishbein and Ajzen, 1975). The model links environments and behaviors with attitudes in a mental process of receiving stimuli and processing them in a cognitive and evaluative sequence that leads to decision. The general model now becomes:

$$\text{Environment} \rightarrow \text{Attitudes} \rightarrow \text{Behavior}$$

However, the more precise Fishbein and Ajzen model specifies the components of attitudes and adds normative beliefs and intentions:

Attributes
Beliefs $\rightarrow$ Attitudes
Evaluations
$\rightarrow$ Intentions $\rightarrow$ Behaviors
Normative beliefs $\rightarrow$ Subjective
   and evaluations   norms

Focus remains on the individual actor who processes the information of experience and develops an interpretation that leads to future behavior. However, the intervening "black box" is now opened a crack with the analysis of cognition and the formation of attitudes. Then the question becomes "What are the attitudes that characterize leisure?" It is this question that has occupied the attention of most psychologists interested in leisure.

Defining Attitudes of Leisure. The early work of John Neulinger (1974) presented a model of leisure that consists of three attitudinal dimensions. The primary dimension is "perceived freedom." The others are attitudinal: intrinsic motivation and final rather than instrumental goals. Leisure, then, is characterized by attitudes related to perceptions of freedom and desires to act for the experience rather than for reasons or purposes outside the experience. Neulinger thus defines leisure as a "state of mind" rather than activity or time. Leisure is neither the environment nor the behavior but the attitude accompanying the behavior. Leisure is not defined by its where, what, or when elements; it is a mental state for that episode, event, or period of time. Even though the state of mind exists in time and space and is transitory, it is the mental condition that distinguishes leisure from other states. A decision to participate in a particular activity, then, is made in anticipation of that desirable mental state. Such a state can be found in almost any context since there is no necessary condition for the perception outside the individual.

Special Environments for the Experience. Mihaly Csikszentmihalyi of the University of Chicago identifies certain conditions under which the leisure experience, among others, may be heightened (1975). He returns to the activity context in which there is something to do, a task or challenge. When that task is perceived as too difficult for the actor, a condition of anxiety is produced. When the task does not challenge the skills of the actor, the resulting state is one of boredom. Only when skill and challenge meet does the actor become absorbed in the experience to the extent that the externalities of time and environment seem to disappear. The actor is wholly "into" the experience for at least a brief period of time. Csikszentmihalyi has found the possibility of this experience in many contexts, but proposes that certain kinds of demanding activity are most often the environments of such absorption.

Although primary attention remains on the attitude of the actor, on individual experience, the first element of the psychological model is reintroduced. "Autotelic" activity that incorporates the mental states of freedom and being done for its own sake occurs in environments that engage the actor rather than simply stimulate the senses. The stimulus factor of complexity returns to corroborate the findings of some of the earlier research on children's play (Ellis, 1973). Csikszentmihalyi labels the absorption experience as "flow." It is the optimum condition between boredom and anxiety. Further, there are certain environmental factors that tend to foster the experience. Level of challenge is one. Others are structural, such as regularities or rules that permit the actor to concentrate on doing the activity rather than negotiating what is appropriate or permissible. When there is agreement on aims and forms, then all attention may be given to execution.

One implication of this model is that environments conducive to the "flow" experience can be constructed almost anywhere. The issue is not the context—whether work or leisure—but the conditions of action. Therefore, the analysis of autotelic activity is not a definition of leisure or even of elements peculiar to leisure. The environmental conditions are not restricted to any situation, physical or social. Rather, the experience is a special joining of the aesthetic and the ecstatic, of form and affect. It is a kind of symmetry of action and engagement that produces an intensity of experience that gives heightened meaning to related times and activity. In theory, at least, the context can be one of physical or mental effort or of intense interaction that results in a kind of "social flow."

The Question of Persistence of Attitudes. If "flow" is transitory and the state of mind of leisure an occasion-based attitude, then how is it possible to measure leisure by reference to persistent attitudes associated with types of behavior or settings? Are the states of leisure relatively stable over time or quite transitory? One answer is that the question is one to be investigated, a researchable issue. For example, are the immediate states associated with specific activities, settings, or companions quite consistent? Is the intensity level of a competitive sport with a well-matched opponent much the same from event to event, or does it vary in relation to other factors? Is reading highly variable in the likelihood of engrossment, and, if so, what are the conditions that cause the variation? Are they more environmental, situational, or attitudinal?

One approach to the variability issue is to solve it by definition. Attitudes may be defined as relatively stable with both cognitive and evaluative components (Iso-ahola, 1980:73). The employment of retrospective attitude scales assumes a rather high degree of stability. On the other hand, personal experience suggests that the affective state of any kind of activity—work or leisure—may range from exhilaration to lethargy and from rapt attention to ennui. In fact, the mental state may even pendulum back and forth within an event or episode. There may well be more variation within an event or episode than between occurrences. Is it possible to refer to the state of mind of cocktail parties or of reading in general? Are there general leisure attitudes abstracted from a series of experiences with similar forms or environments? If leisure is a mental state, it may be moment-by-moment rather than bound to an entire action or event.

Summary of Psychological Models. The three elements in psychological models are the environment, or stimulus; attitudes, or mental states; and behaviors. The usual assumption is that they are sequential. The actor forms attitudes toward the stimuli that are processed, resulting in action. For the most part, psychologists concerned with leisure as a phenomenon to investigate and explain have concentrated on the attitudes and mental states of the actor. Since the mental states tend to be complex and involve both cognition and evaluation, the term *experience* might connote better than *state of mind* both the mental process and its environmental basis. Experience is a situated condition produced in the individual by what has been undergone and interpreted. It is such experience, made up of the sequence of more momentary mental states, that is formed into persistent attitudes.

Other Attitudinal Models ————————————————————

The dimensions of leisure experience identified thus far are those of perceived freedom and intrinsic motivation. Also, the concept of "flow" suggests an absorption in the activity during the experience, which implies another dimension—intensity. Is there something about the nature of the experience as it is going on that either identifies leisure or is critical to its meaning?

One common attitude toward the concept of leisure in Western culture is that it must be "leisurely." The element of relaxation is often considered central, even to the extent that demanding activity is excluded from the defined realm of behavior. To the disciplined athlete, for example, leisure is often seen as physical rest but not the strenuous acquisition of skills required for the sport. One problem with this bias is that it tends to exclude from leisure many of the kinds of engagement that actors consider most important to them—demanding activities in which they become most absorbed and in which they find their own identities (Kelly, 1983b).

Leisure, then, is commonly referred to as disengagement. But is it engagement as well? One model that attempts to cope with this question has been proposed by B. G. and Nancy Gunter (1980). The two primary axes of the two-by-two scheme are the relative levels of freedom and involvement. A high level of involvement (engagement) is presumed to contain a high level of pleasure in such activities as creative hobbies, the arts, sports, and community roles. Low involvement, on the other hand, may provoke antipathy rather than pleasure. It includes the alienated activity of overload or obligations as well as the anomic activity of participation without meaning or aim.

The second dimension, that of freedom or choice, is rendered difficult to interpret by the inclusion of time and structure. The Gunters assume that a high degree of freedom is correlated with a minimum of institutional structure. Here the sociological approach is combined with the psychological as social norms and expectations are introduced into the analysis. The institutional context removes the qualifying "perceived" from the freedom of leisure. Now choice is said to have a reality apart from perception.

Nevertheless, the introduction of the experiential dimension of intensity can be accepted on the psychological level. Intensity is part of the experience of the individual actor in the episode or event. As suggested by Csikszentmihalyi (1975), the level of involvement may be that of a mental state of almost total absorption. The intensity may be at an incomparable level at least for a moment. At the other extreme, a low level of intensity may characterize those episodes in which the requirements are minimal and the expectations oriented toward rest and recuperation.

The Gunter model is not purely psychological. When they classify leisure as institutional, pure, alienated, and anomic, they include in the model the elements of social setting and institutional structure. Role expectations impinge on the activity in ways that alter the psychological perceptions and interpretations. Attitudes are shaped by social factors.

The approach to intensity developed by the author (Kelly, 1983b:148–49) focuses more consistently on the experience of the leisure actor. The level of intensity of the experience varies along a continuum from flow to involved to relaxed to time-filling. Then, the nature of the social setting is added on a continuum from solitary to parallel to joint activity to communion. The social context dimension also incorporates intensity in the interaction itself. The model in Figure 2-1 displays intensity as a mental state that has the dual dimensions of involvement in the action and in the interaction. Therefore, an episode may be of relatively high or low intensity on either dimension at the same time.

Doubly casual leisure, such as much TV watching, is relaxing in its low levels of intensity of attention, demand, and interaction. Socially intense activity, such as a spirited conversation, offers a high level of communication or interaction without a demanding activity context. Activity-intense leisure focuses on the demands of activity that is rigorous mentally or physically, such as writing or practicing solo

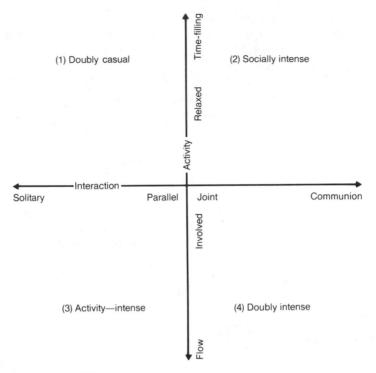

Figure 2-1   Intensity of leisure experience.

crosswind landings. Doubly intense activity would include some team sport situations that require high levels of intensity in both interaction and the activity.

Focus is on the level of intensity. Two dimensions of the environment, however, are considered to be factors in that intensity: the social context and the form of the activity. The stimulus or stimuli affect the nature of the experience for the actor. The leisure experience, then, may be disengaged or highly involved in both dimensions. Leisure is concentrated on the experience itself. That experience, however, may be differentiated by levels of intensity in engagement, both in the activity and in social intercourse. If that is the case, then other elements of the experience may also be identified and distinguished.

Properties of Leisure Experiences

Leisure experience, even from the seemingly simple perspective of the mental state of the individual, would appear to be more complex than some models suggest. As soon as the intensity dimension is introduced, then considerable variety in mental states is possible. Further, the variety may be related to environmental factors including the form of the activity and the social context. The original model of environment influencing attitudes that shape behavior remains. However, the mental states are more complex than undifferentiated perceptions of freedom and intrinsic motivation.

There have been a number of compilations of possible kinds of mental states that may be associated with leisure. Although not held to be the defining factors in the sense that all must be present if leisure is to exist, these kinds of states may be said to characterize many leisure experiences.

One line of research has employed a series of scales to measure dimensions of leisure experience (Beard and Ragheb, 1980). Six components of perceived meaning have been identified. These components are abstracted from immediate experience and generalized as recollected outcomes:

1. **Psychological:** a sense of freedom, enjoyment, involvement, and challenge.
2. **Educational:** intellectual challenge and knowledge gains.
3. **Social:** rewarding relationships with other people.
4. **Relaxation:** relief from strain and stress.
5. **Physiological:** fitness, health, weight control, and well-being.
6. **Aesthetic:** response to pleasing design and environmental beauty.

Such a list tends to confuse outcomes such as educational and physiological factors with immediate experience. The approach is limited by its degree of abstraction from the actual mental states of a leisure experience. The premise that there is a commonly understood realm of behavior called *leisure* is open to question. Nevertheless, Beard and Ragheb have provided a useful framework for identifying possible properties of leisure experiences.

Another such list is based on a review of literature in the field rather than empirical research (Gunter, 1979). In Gunter's analysis the experiential qualities are somewhat more tied to traditional writings in the field. These potential qualities of leisure include the following:

- Choice: Choices in leisure may include the acceptance of constraints and parameters of participation. However, in some way, the engagement is selected from alternatives.
- Self-containment: The meaning of the activity is primarily within the episode or event. It has its own integrity of meaning.
- Intense involvement and enjoyment: The event has a high level of affect to the extent that it fully occupies the participant.

- Timelessness: A suspension of awareness of the passing of time. Some would maintain that such a state of mind is the best indicator of the value of leisure.
- Fantasy: Some separation from the ordinary routine of life. Leisure is, to some extent, its own world.
- Creativity: The possibility of producing something new.
- Spontaneity: Openness of response rather than prescribed actions in defined situations.
- A sense of exploration, curiosity, and adventure.

One problem with such a compilation is that it tends to be based on what various persons have hoped that leisure might be or become rather than on an empirical reality. For example, proponents of both physically active recreation and of the arts tend to decry leisure that has a low level of intensity and aims chiefly to entertain. However, such relaxation is one consistent element of leisure. For most people leisure would seem to have orientations of both engagement and disengagement, whatever the preferences of a recreation professional. Although several of the elements listed have been found in research on the mental states of persons engaged in chosen activity, they are far from being either a complete list or even an identification of the most common kinds of attitudes. They do, on the other hand, suggest some of the dimensions that may draw individuals into leisure engagements.

A research approach more grounded in actual leisure experiences has been supported in the United States by the U.S. Forest Service. The focus has been on leisure experiences in outdoor recreation environments. Although this is only one kind of leisure, the varieties of meaning identified suggest something of the probable complexity of other experiences of leisure as well. Further, since much of this line of research has been carried out on site, it is somewhat less dependent upon methods that call on respondents to reflect back on kinds of activity engaged in at other times and in other places. There is still a mixture of outcomes, some abstracted from the immediate process and some describing consequences.

This U.S. Forest Service research has been conducted by B. L. Driver and his colleagues for a decade. The researchers have developed hundreds of items for scales, analyzed responses, evaluated the scales for validity and reliability, and compiled the results to produce a number of consistent factors (Driver and Brown, 1978). They have found that the salience of the elements of outdoor recreation experiences differs as environments, social groups, orientations, and activities vary; there is no monolithic outdoor recreation experience. Engagement with the environment, interaction with companions, and the forms of activity all shape the nature of the experience. Further, individuals come to the environment with different aims and expectations that affect the outcomes.

One summary of outcomes based on several studies offers seventeen such outcomes. When measured in relation to activities such as wilderness backpacking, hiking, camping, fishing, hunting, river running, trail skiing, and use of offroad vehicles, only a few are consistently found across the activity spectrum. Those outcomes include being with one's recreation group, escaping from physical and social pressures, learning and exploring, exercising and improving fitness, and relating to the natural environment. Meanings reported for only a few of the activities include achievement and challenge, independence and autonomy, reflection, recollection, risk taking, excitement, meeting other people, use of equipment, family togetherness, privacy, security, and physical rest (Brown, 1981). In general, the orientations of the actor, social contexts, and environmental and activity settings all contribute to the nature of the experience. The experience, then, is situated in its environments as well as being a product of the information processing and evaluation of the individual.

From such lines of research, both those specific to environments and those generalized to kinds of activity and even to leisure in general, are there common themes or defining elements? Can certain properties be identified that define an experience as leisure? Out of all the elements that have been proposed or measured are there a critical few that make an episode or event leisure?

The persistent social factors of valued companionship and the expression and development of relationships may be a prominent feature of much leisure, but they can also be found in the common tasks of work and maintenance. The same is true of experiential factors such as emotional release, excitement, and deep involvement in what is occurring. Conversely, some relaxation and recuperative elements may be found in such an activity as driving to work and are not exclusively the properties of leisure. In fact, even the perception of freedom and attention to the activity at hand may be experienced in almost any setting. One possible conclusion is that there is no clearly defined leisure experience at all. Leisure as a state of mind is nothing more than a convention for referring to an attitude characterizing activity that did not have to be done and is done largely for its own sake. If so, then the defining elements are freedom of choice and intrinsic meaning that are measured by a relative absence of coercion and instrumental intent.

Leisure, then, could incorporate a number of the experiential elements proposed. Leisure that involves disciplined effort might be especially expressive and creative. Leisure that includes intense interaction with others might yield experiences of closeness, sharing, and even a joining of minds or bodies. Leisure that begins with a withdrawal from ordinary settings would produce mental states of relaxation and release from pressure. Leisure that immerses the individual in a created world of literature or music might elicit states of fantasy or timelessness. However, none of these likelihoods would be exclusive to leisure. They are dimensions of human experience that might characterize particular episodes or events in a wide range of settings.

Another question emerges out of the emphasis on perception. Granting that perceived freedom involves processing and interpreting an experience through learned frameworks and categories of the mind, is the relative freedom of leisure something more than perception? Is there a requirement that the engagement was a real alternative, an actual choice? Or, is a feeling of freedom enough? So far, it would appear that the seemingly simple model of leisure as immediate experience is less transparent than first appeared. If episodes or even moments taken to be leisure vary widely in their experiential elements, is this approach either misleading or inadequate?

Leisure as Immediate Experience _____

Leisure as immediate experience is more than perception. Rather, the mental state incorporates the information processing that receives the sensory perception and forms it into an impression that selects aspects of the total perception for attention. Further, the mind processes the impression according to previously processed experiences. The mental state is at least this perception-impression-selection process. For most experiences the processing continues into evaluation, in which the experience is categorized according to preformed attitudes of meaning. According to some models, such an evaluation may also incorporate a disposition to take action in regard to the experience. The mental state, then, is not a neutral reception of stimuli but a processing and evaluating activity. Immediate experience is more complex than simply being in sensory range of some occurrence. It is going through the episode as an interpreting actor. Mental or physical distance may vary, but the process of reception and interpretation goes on at some level of attention and intensity.

Experience and Structured Interpretation. Experience occurs in time and space, situated in a world that has form and shape. Even though the individual does not know this world directly, without the processing of the senses and mind, it is still the context of the processed experience. Further, there is an activity context. The state of mind is produced through the engagement of the individual in intentioned action, in activity. The form of that activity is one factor in the mental state produced. There are differences between reading and hiking, between softball and sexual intercourse. The situation of the experience includes the environment and the activity context as vehicles of the meaning of the experience.

This does raise the question of the immediacy of the experience. How direct is a state of mind that is processed and interpreted? How independent is a mental state that incorporates a selected and reconstructed interpretation of an event or episode shaped by a complex environment? From one perspective, the issue is one of the level of abstraction. Any mental state is distanced from the immediate to a greater or lesser degree. Further, the experience is processed out of a history of interpretation that has been learned in a culture with its ideational forms and analytical categories that are part of the language with which the individual accomplishes the information processing.

All this places the perceived freedom and intrinsic motivation elements of a leisure experience in a somewhat different light. Simply saying to oneself "I feel free" presupposes the linguistic categories of *feeling* and *freedom*. Not only is the statement a qualified one, but it signifies a complex set of meanings. At least, the statement would signify something like "I am experiencing an affective state that I identify as relative lack of constraint." Such a statement can come only as the result of an analysis and evaluation of the time-bounded episode that has been identified for such processing. More accurately one would say, "Utilizing the analytical conventions I have learned to apply to such perceptions, I find the affective state of relative lack of limitation to be greater than I have experienced in the other situations that I have selected for comparison."

Note as well the rational bias of this description. The affective state is presumed to be amenable to such analysis employing the culture-embedded categories of the language. There is no "pure" emotion or state that is communicated or on which we reflect. Rather, all is subject to interpretation. We cannot even communicate to ourselves, much less anyone else, apart from this learned process. To maintain that this rational interpreting process is all there is to an experience diminishes the totality considerably. We raise the issue of the subconscious and deep emotions, the Freudian question, in a later chapter. However, for this section the bias of the Aristotelian assumptions of the nature of a human experience must be noted. The wholeness of any experience, leisure or other, may be curtailed by concentration on a mental state that can be abstracted from the event and encapsulated in any statement of relative freedom or another meaning dimension.

Structure and Experience. The term *structure* is used in many ways to refer to elements of regularity in the context of experience. Social structure consists of the norms, conventions, rules, role expectations, and so on that give predictability to social interaction. Such structure may be complex in its institutionalized forms or relatively simple in the mutual expectations of an interacting dyad. To a large extent, science is the systematic study of structure, of regularity. Contemporary science, physical and social, is now attempting to cope with the likelihood that there is no invariant structure in reality but rather systematic regularities in a process of existence that is always in movement.

In relation to a social phenomenon such as leisure, the context of activity yielding an experience of relative freedom and contained meaning also contains some structure. This structure may be seen as a limitation on the freedom element of the experience. If leisure is entirely a mental state, perhaps a product of the imagination, then limitations are minimized. They exist only in the mind. However, even then, the imagination creates out of the learned and interpreted experiences of the past.

Within the mind there is no pure or undifferentiated perception. Rather, a "schema," or cognitive representation of the social situation, selects and shapes the perception. In the schema a kind of structure is imposed on the phenomena, and any action taken is based on that interpreted formulation of the situation.

External to the mind, any ongoing episode has a number of limiting factors, regularities that may be labeled structural:

- Time, however conceived, gives some shape to any experience.
- Space imposes limits on activity.
- The activity itself generally has accepted forms. Many have quite specific rules that enable more than one participant to engage in synchronized action.
- A larger social context permits certain kinds of behavior within the bounded activity, regulates who may participate, and gives meaning to the event.
- A history of meaning exists for the activity and for each participant.
- An initial set of factors influences the choice for or against participation and makes such choices relatively predictable.

One critical question concerns the inevitability of structure. Is there not always some such regularity endemic in any experience? Such regularity exists in both the context of activity and in the interpreting schema of the individual. Every event or experience incorporates this duality of structure, of regularity that makes any new occurrence in some sense a subset of previously existing categories of experience.

From this perspective no state of mind is completely new. Any mental state is the product of the processing mind that draws on already-stored and meaning-laden experiences in its ongoing interpretation. The perception of freedom, then, is always relative to other evaluated perceptions of lack of constraint. The separateness or autotelic nature of any occurrence is always relative to its connectedness to other realms of meaning. Nothing stands totally independent from the learned meanings of previous experience. Even fantasy employs previous experiences in its construction of a mental event. As a consequence, the immediacy of any experience is mitigated in the very act of assigning it meaning. We cannot have a mental state without importing into the experience all sorts of learned categories and implicit analytical frameworks. To say, then, that leisure is a mental state or experience is to refer to a complex process rather than a simple and momentary state.

The Negation of Leisure as Experience

The introduction of negation in this and every chapter presenting a theoretical model does not imply that the thesis offered is invalid, nor, within its own framework, is the theory necessarily incomplete. However, no explanatory model can be allowed to rest comfortably only in its selected analytical context. Rather, questions of meaning and explanation refer back to the phenomenon being explained. No theoretical approach can dismiss from consideration all dimensions and issues that challenge its credibility. The approach employed here is one of a dialectic, at least one counterthesis to every model is assumed. Further, because of the order of presentation, some of the negation of each theoretical approach provides an introduction to the succeeding theory. An analysis of the limitations of each metaphor provides a springboard into the subsequent approach.

The Transitory Nature of Immediate Experience. The most evident negation of the model is the transitory character of such experience. Whether the unit of analysis is an episode of action within a larger event or a time-defined event with a beginning and end, the mental state of actors may vary within the time period. Within a single conversation an individual's affective state may go from gaiety to anger to disappointment and back to some elevation. An event may be begun as a means to an external end and become totally engrossing during the participation. An engagement may be freely chosen in the beginning and then become a duty. Only moments within an event are likely to be "purely" anything, in mood or meaning.

Further, there are many factors in the changing nature of such experience. An episode or event is processual, developing and changing in complexity and content. The total experience, then, is composed of many elements that rise and fall in salience. Unless leisure is defined as momentary, an immeasurably thin slice of time and experience, then no single state of mind can encompass its meanings. As already presented, social psychologists meet this problem through some directed method of abstraction. The processual meanings and moods are·to be evaluated and weighed in a way that enables the subject to ascribe general meanings to the event or activity. Further, the most common research approaches require that such an evaluative and ascriptive process be conducted for a whole series of engagements labeled for the purposes "golf," "swimming," or "window-shopping."

This method may be quite acceptable as a research tool approximating actual experience. The unstated premise is that "in general the experience found by X number of subjects engaged in window-shopping includes these elements in a mental scheme that is something like this." As long as the research model does not claim to be reproducing the actual mental state of the actor going through the event, the method is quite useful. However, experience is "going through" some activity, not just categorizing and reflecting on it later. Maintaining that I "feel relatively free in general while walking in the Custer National Forest" is not the same as having the experience step by step.

What begins as a focus on the immediate awareness process of the actor in some kind of environment becomes a delayed information-processing and -evaluating mental event. The experience of leisure is not as immediate as first claimed. Rather, it is abstracted out of the actual "going through" process. The experience is not so much immediate as reflective. The mental state is attitudinal, constructed by the mind out of the materials of immediate perception and all the learned apparatus of a being with a history and a culture.

Environmental Contexts of Activity. Further, the model itself suggests another aspect of its own negation. Immediate experience is not discrete or self-contained. Rather, environmental factors have impacts on the experience. Not only may an extraneous noise break concentration and attention, but the environment affects how the actor anticipates, enters, and participates in an activity. Immediate experience is more than a mental state. It is also response to the environmental conditions of action. Because most leisure engagements are processual, the environment usually changes during the experience.

Certainly in activity that involves interaction with other people or response to a changing stimulus, the mental state of the individual may be in a continual state of change. As indicated in research on children's play and on autotelic activity by Csikszentmihalyi, complexity and structure of the stimulus activity or context may alter both the attitudes and behavior of those interacting with the environment. Further, as the environments are altered, the mental states as well as behaviors also are likely to change.

There is no model of explanation of leisure that excludes contextual factors. The immediate experience approach admits contextual elements, but only as they have some impact on the state of mind of the individual. They may be influential, but they are external to the phenomenon. The problem with this is that the mental states are then accounted for at least partly in terms of the context. The form of activity, the nature of the social relationships, and the dimensions of the environment are all factors in the experience. Also, the experience is apprehended in a mind that has learned its processing forms and schemes. The state of mind exists in more than a mental context. If that is the case, then explanations require more than attention to the mental states—either immediate or abstracted. Leisure may be experiential, but it is experience in a life context that is both individual and environmental. An exclusive concentration on immediate mental states truncates the nature of that experience. It is negated by its own nature. In fact, such a self-limiting focus raises the question of a state of mind that is induced by some stimulus other than engagement in activity. If leisure were to be defined as a mental state of perceived freedom and separation from external aims and purposes, then it could easily be induced by chemical substances. In fact, a drug-induced state might well be the purest as well as most convenient form of leisure. If that view of leisure is unacceptable, then those elements that render it incomplete must be introduced into the theoretical approaches that claim to deal with its nature.

Leisure as Experience. The negation offered here does not deny that leisure is experience. Nor is there any demonstrated necessity to exclude mental states from any understanding of leisure. Leisure *is* experience. It is, at least in part, the mental states accompanying the process of going through an episode or event. It does incorporate perception and mental processing that leads to attitudes and related behavior.

The negation is not a denial of experience but calls for a full accounting of that experience. What more is there to leisure? The state-of-mind model is not only limited to internal processes but in research tends to be limited to rational information processing. It is only one element of total experience—that inclusive process that cannot be wholly encompassed in any language of analysis or communication. Leisure is this kind of experience . . . and more! The *more* is what we explore in the subsequent chapters.

However, later focus on affective states, social processes, and political structures should not lead us to abandon the fundamental experience base of leisure. The possibility that leisure has meaning that draws us beyond the immediate for explanation does not deny the immediate or its mental apprehension. The question to which we now turn builds on the experiential model: What gives meaning to the experience?

References _____

Beard, J. G., and Mournir Ragheb. 1980. "Measuring Leisure Satisfaction." *Journal of Leisure Research* 12:20–33.

Bishop, Doyle W. 1970. "Stability of the Factor Structure of Leisure Behavior: Analysis of Four Communities." *Journal of Leisure Research* 12:55–68.

———, and Peter Witt. 1970. "Sources of Behavioral Variance During Leisure Time." *Journal of Personality and Social Psychology* 16:352–60.

Brown, Perry J. 1981. "Psychological Benefits of Outdoor Recreation." In *Social Benefits of Outdoor Recreation,* ed. J. R. Kelly. Champaign: Leisure Behavior Research Laboratory and Washington, D.C.: U.S. Forest Service.

Crandall, Rick. 1980. "Motivations for Leisure." *Journal of Leisure Research* 12:45–54.

Csikszentmihalyi, Mihaly. 1975. *Beyond Boredom and Anxiety.* San Francisco: Jossey-Bass, Inc.

Driver, B. L. 1976. "Quantification of Outdoor Recreationists' Preferences." Proceedings of Symposium on Research, Camping, and Environmental Education. University Park : Pennsylvania State University Press.

———, and Perry Brown. 1978. "The Opportunity Spectrum Concept and Behavioral Information in Outdoor Recreation Resource Supply Inventories." Rocky Mountain Forest and Experiment Station. Ft. Collins: U.S. Forest Service.

Ellis, Michael J. 1973. *Why People Play.* Englewood Cliffs: Prentice-Hall, Inc.

Fishbein, Martin, and I. Ajzen. 1975. *Belief, Attitude, Intention, and Behavior.* Reading: Addison-Wesley Publishing Company, Inc.

Gunter, B. J. 1979. "Properties of the Leisure Experience." In *Leisure: A Psychological Approach,* eds. H. Ibrihim and R. Crandall. Los Alamitos: Hwong.

Gunter, B. J., and Nancy Gunter. 1980. "Leisure Styles: A Conceptual Framework for Modern Leisure." *The Sociological Quarterly* 21:361–74.

Havighurst, Robert. 1957. "The Leisure Activities of the Middle-aged." *American Journal of Sociology* 63:162–82.

Iso-ahola, Seppo. 1980. "Toward a Dialectical Social Psychology of Leisure and Recreation." In *Social Psychological Perspectives on Leisure and Recreation,* ed. S. Iso-ahola. Springfield: Charles C. Thomas, Publisher.

Kelly, J. R. 1978a. "Leisure Styles and Choices in Three Environments." *Pacific Sociological Review* 21:187–207.

———. 1978b. "Situational and Social Factors in Leisure Decisions." *Pacific Sociological Review* 21:313–30.

———. 1978c. "Family Leisure in Three Communities." *Journal of Leisure Research* 10:47–60.

———. 1983a. "Leisure Styles: A Hidden Core." *Leisure Sciences* 5:321–38.

———. 1983b. *Leisure Identities and Interactions.* London and Boston: George Allen & Unwin Ltd.

Neulinger, John. 1974. *The Psychology of Leisure.* Springfield: Charles C. Thomas, Publisher.

Witt, Peter. 1971. "Factor Structure of Leisure Behavior in High School Age Youth in Three Communities." *Journal of Leisure Research* 3:213–19.

CHAPTER 3

Existential Theory

ISSUES ——————————————————————————————

Leisure is also existential when understood as decision and action.

Existential sociology deals with the everyday world composed richly of emotions and decisions.

Decision creates meaning. An existential metaphor is based on action and a self-definition of "I am able" rather than an ontological "I am." Knowledge is created as an act rather being an apprehension.

Leisure from this perspective is situated decision, action, process, and even creation.

One negation of such existential action is "bad faith," in which the "given" is accepted as reality and the dialectical nature of knowing denied.

In play there is a becoming of the "not yet." Within structured constraints, play is creation that produces meaning.

Freedom, then, is an act rather than a state. It is the situated possibility of meaningful action. Such freedom may be negated in the acceptance of arbitrary limits as final or through a repression of creative activity.

Leisure, in the existential metaphor, is an actualization of situated freedom in the world.

Every approach to defining leisure incorporates some element of freedom or decision. However, freedom has different meanings for those who approach leisure in different ways. Psychologists who focus on the experience tend to refer to a feeling of freedom from coercion. Structural sociologists refer to lack of constraining factors related to socioeconomic position in the social system. In both approaches freedom is a state in which the leisure actor exists either during the leisure episode or as a condition of life. What is bypassed is the actual act or process of decision.

It is assumed that leisure involves some decision to engage in the act or activity. Although choice may not be absolute or unconstrained, at least there is the option of *not* doing the activity and of selecting some other use of the time. One of the elements missing from the experiential model is just this dimension of choice. Leisure becomes a state rather than an act, a perceptual condition rather than a process.

Further, freedom becomes defined as a perceived absence of limit rather than a possibility of action. Freedom is freedom *from* rather than a freedom *for* action. When leisure is defined purely as a mental state, then freedom is reduced to a feeling rather than an actual condition or possibility. In a more existential approach freedom would become a condition of action or even the exercise of that possibility. *Existentialism* stresses decision and action rather than conditions and states.

Three Themes of Existentialism

Existentialism as a philosophical movement has a history associated with a number of persons of conflicting perspectives, and several key figures are considered in a later section. However, the movement has been united in its insistence on the centrality of decision in human life. Existentialists have insisted that to be human is to decide.

The first theme of existential approaches to life is that decision creates meaning. Meaning, in general or in the particular instance, is not given from the outside. Rather, meaning is created in the act of decision. For Jean-Paul Sartre (1943), the French philosopher and writer, such meaning is created out of chaos or even the absurdity of existence. His novels and plays dramatize the anxiety produced when the human being experiences the "trapped" nature of life from which there is "No Exit." On the other hand, for an existential theologian such as Paul Tillich (1952), there is a possibility of meaning grounded in existence. However, that meaning can only be apprehended and made concrete through the courage to act decisively. There is no general meaning apart from the human decision to take action. Action, then, creates existential meaning, meaning that has concrete reality for the actor.

The second theme is that such decision is not necessarily solitary in its setting or consequences. While some existential thinkers stress the fundamental aloneness of the self and of real decision, there is also the possibility that decision may lead to or even create community. Martin Buber (1937) was a Jewish philosopher who emphasized that decision may transform the partial and secondary relationships of much institutional life to primary relationships of communication and sharing. "I-it" relationships may become "I-thou" relationships with the reality of community. However, this possibility of community is rejected by many of the most radical of the movement who insist that each person remains essentially alone.

The third theme stresses that decision is actually an act of creation.

That which did not exist now comes into being through the act of decision. In fact, there is no other creation. One modern philosopher has taken the existential theme and grafted it onto a concept of play in which necessary creation occurs (Hans, 1981). It is through the openness of play that the old limits and structures are subjected to novelty and change.

In this book there is only a very limited attempt to present the history and varieties of existentialism as a philosophy. However, various elements of the movement are employed as a basis for a model of leisure that focuses on freedom as found in decision. Further, the drawing out of the philosophical themes in social analysis and explanation are applied to leisure in ways that renew the ancient centrality of freedom and decision for current attempts to understand leisure.

Existential Sociology

Existential sociology, though not a direct offspring of the philosophical movement, adopted the label to provide a distinction from other approaches that deal with everyday life. The themes, however, are consistent with those of the philosophy. Human action is seen as having a central component of decision; it is not determined by external forces, social or other, to the extent that the actor is no more than a product of the environment. Rather, the social environment is produced in a dialectical process in which the actor both acts and is acted upon. The "social experience of daily life" (Douglas, 1977) is the focus of sociological enterprise. Further, this social experience includes dimensions of emotion and feelings as well as reason and analysis.

Traditional social and behavioral sciences, seeking to explain what people do in terms amenable to the accepted research methods and theoretical premises of their fields, have all too often overlooked the dimensions of emotion and feeling. For example, academic social psychology has wrought a kind of "bloodless revolution" that has come to account for human behavior in terms of ratiocination, information processing, and evaluation. People interact without emotion. There is no anger or fear, no desire or repulsion. Freud and all the evidence of the significance of the nonconscious and irrational in shaping behavior have been ignored. In development of research designs such elements are inconvenient or inadmissible. Presumed dictums of "science" do not admit data that cannot be replicated or interpretations that are not "objective." The unique and the problematic elements in social interaction are abandoned in favor of factors of structure and information assimilation that are much the same from one episode to another.

Existential sociology takes a different stance and begins with the question of "What is human action?" (Douglas and Johnson, 1977). Action presupposes the actor who takes intentioned action in the context of daily life where many of the elements are not repeatable. Decisions are made both out of some assessment of what is possible and in response to what is desirable. Analysis of action does not begin with a set of premises that dictate the framework of explanation but with concrete experience in the world. This experience includes the reality of feelings as prime components of action. Existential sociology begins with actual situated experiences and attempts to build more general understandings of social life only on the basis of such data.

This approach denies any objective knowledge in the positivist sense as well as the dualism of subject and object. Building general accounts of social action based on consistencies of behavior and of interpretation does not require uniformity. Nor are all the factors in any explanation amenable to quantification. Statistical analysis is but one investigative tool among others and is not considered superior. Rather, the problematic and situated nature of all human experience calls for research methods and theory building that take into account the richness and complexity of such experience rather than rule out whatever cannot be incorporated into a set of numbers presumed to index the salient elements of the experience. Existential sociologists recognize the unique and contingent elements in an event or episode as well as the consistent and structural. They agree with those who focus on the symbol systems of language for interpretation and evaluation as well as for communication, but they do not limit nonmaterial factors to the linguistic. It is true that shared meaning is essential to social action, but in a pluralistic and problematic situation there is always the possibility of conflicting interpretations and uses of the symbols. Shared meaning may undergird the regularities that we term structure, but those meanings are also subject to change and distortion in the situation.

Premises of Existential Sociology

Phenomenological models of sociology begin with the social actor's consciousness *in* and of the perceived and interpreted world. Existence is not eternal or necessary but is contingent on the social world. The world is neither made up of simple facts to be processed and related (realism) nor of an independent system of ideas (idealism). Rather, the social world is complex and interdependent. It is contingent rather than necessary, with regularities that can be shattered by a break in communication or an action counter to expectations.

The historical origins of existential sociology do not offer a clear and orderly sequence of development. However, several precursors provided ingredients for the approach. Fundamental to all "interpretive" sociological approaches is the work of Max Weber (1964), who distinguished between "understanding" *(verstehen)* and explanation *(erklaren)*. *Verstehen* is an imaginative reconstruction of the thought and experience of other persons in such a way that crucial elements of their decision processes are understood. For Weber, *verstehen* is not only a method of social research, but also a day-to-day process of social interaction. In order to make sense of and anticipate the actions of others, we mentally "take the place" of those with whom we interact. We assume that their action, like ours, is "meaningful" rather than random. "Interpretive sociology" begins with the presumption of meaning and seeks understanding of the decision-action process. Although Weber's approach may have been overly rational and analytical, its blending of practical and scientific *verstehen* has led to sociological analysis that incorporates thought and emotion as well as action.

A second foundation of existential sociology is the symbolic interaction model of behavior developed by George Herbert Mead (1934). Mead must be considered basic to any sociology that gives prominence to day-to-day social interchange. Mead stressed the symbolic context of the social order as well as its learned substance. Generalized role expectations are abstracted from the symbol systems associated with social contexts such as games. From this approach, some have focused on the problematic nature of the society, given that it is changed as such symbols are defined and redefined. More commonly, however, functional sociologists have stressed the role-learning and personality aspects of Mead's work rather than its more radical implications for the problematic nature of social regularities.

Phenomenological sociology also has evident parallels with existential models. Alfred Schutz (1972) has been given credit for providing the basis for a sociology that "brackets" the question of what is real and concentrates on what is observed. The attempt to make sense out of social situations as they are experienced is an everyday occurrence for social actors; it is the social world as perceived and interpreted to which the actor responds. In much the same way, the sociologist should identify indices of the meaning of the situation rather than impose a predetermined framework of interpretation. Meaning is drawn out of the situation in which those engaged in action are employing a variety of signs as signifiers of meaning. The issue is not what is "really there" but what is selected out of the overall context as the basis for decision and lines of action. In this process of seeking and summarizing meaning, social actors develop "typifications" that lend a kind of quasi structure to the situation and serve as a basis for relatively regular interaction. Actors behave "as if" they can rely on the regularity even when it is being continually negotiated and renegotiated. Seeking meaning in the situation is a requirement of action as well as of explanation. However, that meaning is always relative—for us in that time and place—rather than objective and unchanging.

A paradox of phenomenological models is that they frequently have been employed to search for the hidden structures of social action rather than explore its problematic character. There is a certain fascination in being able to demonstrate that seeming openness is actually shaped by a normative consensus woven into the fabric of the situation. As a consequence, the negotiated and meaning-producing aspects of inter-action have been subordinated to "revelations" of implicit structure. Especially the work of Erving Goffman (1967) has been oriented toward explicating the hidden rules and regularities of a variety of social situations, including leisure episodes. Nevertheless, there is also a consistent orientation toward intentioned action that is based on interpretations of meanings within the social situation.

One of the most influential modes of phenomenological sociology has been the "ethnomethodology" of Harold Garfinkel (1970) and his compatriots. Again the emphasis is on the order that is produced in social settings by the cognitive symbol systems ("accounts") employed to provide a basis for action. Order is constituted of those accounts that are indices of the situation. Language itself is a form by which such order is created and shared. In the situation actors behave as though there is a reality of "deep rules" (Cicourel, 1970) that govern behavior and have the appearance of structure. Actors implicitly share such frameworks of meaning in ways that allow them to interact with generally reliable expectations.

Peter Berger and Thomas Luckman (1967) presented an argument that so-called "reality" is in actuality the construction of this interaction process in which common symbols are used to anticipate the actions of others and develop lines of action. The social consensus, while not complete or absolute, consists of a shared universe of meanings that is pervasive enough to be a basis for common action. However, the problematic nature of this consensus is concealed beneath a cloak of acceptance disguising its fragility. For the most part, members of a social system prefer to rely on the stability of the consensus under-girding the system rather than cope with its continual creation and re-creation. The task of sociology should be to discover and explain the constructed cognitive elements that provide a basis for social action rather than to add to the illusion of the reality of fixed structure inherent in social phenomena.

Maurice Merleau-Ponty (1964) produced one influential attempt to give a relatively systematic description of sociology from an existential and phenomenological perspective. The beginning point is always the perception of the self embodied in the world. Such bodily existence is experience as the possibility of action rather than as self-conscious thought (Descartes) or as being. Merleau-Ponty follows Martin Heidegger in presenting self-perception as existential, as "I can" or "I am able" rather than "I am." This expression of effectuality means that the environment is defined as possibility, a space for action in the world. Existence, then, is action in the world.

This action is perceived in the process of doing. The phenomenology of perception occurs in a *gestalt,* or complex field in which the world is perceived in a process of give and take, a dialectic of action and interpreted perception. The perceived world is all we have. While perception is a nonintellectual act, we understand it in a context to which we ascribe meaning. The field of perception is not simple and yet is not created by the perceiver. Perception is always an act of relationship, of *being in the world* as an actor. Being is interaction in the perceived world.

Interpreting perception in this process is also complex. No aspect of the world can be reduced to a single dimension. For example, sexuality is more than biology and more than philosophy, yet both the animal being and definitions of human relationships are part of understanding human sexuality. Rational analysis is integral to any interpretive act, but emotions are also endemic to human action. Further, it is in the world as perceived that we take action, a world from which we have selected out certain factors as relevant to our action possibilities. Action is embedded in the perceived world of possibilities as well as directed by a shifting set of self-defined aims and resources.

Leisure and Existential Sociology

What does this imply for understanding leisure? First, leisure cannot be reduced to any unalloyed set of motives, satisfactions, orientations, or defined elements. Leisure, rather, is action in the perceived world of possibilities. Human beings are not monodimensional—reason or emotion, mind or body, will or reflection. Second, an essential element in understanding any human act is in the decision. The decision to act in the milieu of the complex perceived world, the exercise of freedom, creates the reality of leisure. Leisure is found in the action, not in the locale or the time. Leisure must be enacted in order to be. Third, analysis of this action requires some dealing with the data of the perceived world in which the action occurs. Research, then, involves investigating the context of possibilities for action in which the action is decided on and carried out. Methods of gaining indices to this perception and the process of decision are necessary in order to begin to assess the consistencies of such action. The existential nature of leisure does not require that each decision be made *de novo* without a history of learned interpretations of possibilities and consequences. Fourth, however consistent their form, the action and its contexts are always a construct of the actors, an agreed-on set of behavioral expectations. The process of agreement or situational definition is also part of the action.

It is not necessary to agree totally with the existential sociologists in order to incorporate into our explanation of leisure those factors that they highlight. Decision in the sense of relative freedom to choose among alternatives is implicit in leisure and play. We explore limits of that freedom later. However, those limitations do not warrant bypassing the reality of situated decision. Further, the emphasis on emotion and feeling is also essential to comprehending the nature of leisure experiences and of the decisions that lead to them. Leisure is a part of daily life. It is situated amidst the realities of the push and pull of social interaction. It is more than abstracted elements of meaning, more than social symbol, more than rationally evaluated variables in a decision matrix, and more than articulated elements of a coherent lifestyle or socially determined pattern.

The initial question for anyone who would attempt to explain any social phenomenon is "What is it?" What is the experience to which the symbols refer? For our purposes, then, the question begins with leisure experience as it is situated in a variety of social settings. However, we cannot assume that there is some invariant entity that exists in a fixed social context to which we can apply the label of "leisure." Rather, leisure is a construct, based in experience and compounded out of the communication of countless experiences. Leisure is a phenomenon that is experienced as it is constructed and yet with elements that permit its identification in shared communication.

A contribution of an existential mode of analysis is to highlight the notion that experience is decision. Further, the experience labeled leisure is not a fixed and immutable "thing" to be analyzed with the assumption that its nature can be defined once and for all. Rather, leisure—like all social experience—is constructed in the concrete situation with problematic elements that call for continual reconstruction of the order essential for interaction and communication.

Leisure, then, from this perspective is experience with a variety of components that can be identified and analyzed. However, every leisure experience is also a new creation with the following elements:

- Leisure is decision, an act as well as a state. Decision is not external to the phenomenon but integral to its nature.
- Leisure is creation, a product of decision and action.
- Leisure is process, not fixed but developing and created in its time and place.
- Leisure is situated, constructed in an ever-new context.

- Leisure is production in the sense that its meaning is always reproduced in its situation rather than appropriated from some external source.
- Leisure is act, whole and complex with its history, emotion, interpretation, episodic development, and telos.

An existential approach, however it may deviate from any party line of exemplars who claim the label, maintains these orientations in any attempt to understand leisure. Leisure is situated action with its uncertainties, feelings, interpretations, and episodic lines, and, as the history of leisure philosophy has insisted, it contains the existential theme of decision as part of the act.

Existential Philosophy _____

Existential philosophy, like its sociological counterpart, offers a number of themes that contribute to our understanding of leisure. All focus on the centrality of decision in the creation of meaning. All begin with opposition to realistic and idealistic approaches to knowledge. From a realistic perspective knowledge is gained by apprehending what exists "out there" in some regular form. Learning is some form of information processing. From an idealist perspective the basis of knowledge is found in the ideas themselves, which have some systematic correspondence with reason or a logic of the mind. Aristotle's realism is the basis of empirical science, which presumes that the mind can apprehend what exists external to it. Plato's idealism is the basis of philosophy that presumes that reason itself is the source of knowledge.

Existential modes of thinking deny that there is any preformed and preexistent reality either "out there" or in the mind. Rather, whatever exists is the result of action. There is no ultimate meaning given from above or beyond. There is no form to which life must correspond. There is no structure that must be apprehended. Rather, that which has relevant existence for humankind is known through decisive action. Essence does not precede existence. Rather, existence is created over and over through decisive acts of human beings.

Without becoming enmeshed in the technicalities of existential philosophy, we can examine emphases associated with key thinkers. This review of themes is important to the development of an understanding of leisure.

Sartre. Jean-Paul Sartre (1943) in the period following World War II wrote a number of novels, plays, short stories, essays, and books that revolved around the theme of chaos. Life is not only chaotic; it is absurd. It is not only devoid of meaning; it has become an encompassing trap of absurdity that is masked by the learned lies of the culture. Sartre's political bent led him to Marxism and a support of radical socialism. His more philosophical orientation is expressed in novels such as *Nausea* and plays such as *No Exit* in which the misery of human existence is dramatized. Whatever is given is false. Therefore, the sole way even to begin to have meaning is to create it. Amidst absurdity and chaos the only meaning for a life is created by decision that may lead to some moment or approximation of authenticity. This authenticity is not a model for others s but is real for the one who takes the action in that time and place.

Kierkegaard. Soren Kierkegaard, a Dane who lived in the mid-nineteenth century, was also a radical, but he was a radical Christian whose passion was an existential view of faith and a loathing of institutionalized religion (Bretall, 1951). Kierkegaard, like Sartre, wrote more indirectly than in an expository style. He believed that to communicate the necessity for radical action he must draw the reader into a recognition of entrapment by the culture and especially by those who benefit from society's institutions. He employed his own life as a parable of the journey that must be undertaken before the great "leap" of belief. Kierkegaard strongly opposed any view of life—be it the accepted wisdom of the church or the philosophy of Hegel—that was based on belief in the reasonable nature of existence. Rather, life is fundamentally paradoxical. It is decision that cuts through the paradox to meaning, that exposes the shallowness of assent to the common culture. It is the leap of faith that creates the true person, enabling him to let go of the ordinary and trite and seize meaning.

Nietzsche. Friedrich Nietzsche, also writing in the 1800s, espoused an atheistic and Dionysian approach to gaining understanding and to living. In opposition to Hegelian idealism, Nietzsche (1888) believed that the old values must give way to a "revaluation" in which will supercedes reason as the way to knowledge. Life is to be affirmed rather than analyzed. In a spirit of Dionysian joy rather than cold reason, the spirit comes alive in affirmation. The wholeness of life cannot be grasped by adding up bits of knowledge but by saying "Yes" to its fullness—both joy and sorrow—and by acting decisively to create a self that can become real. One becomes "what one is" by grasping freedom. Freedom may be realized in "play" that acts and creates, in which one realizes in the self the "eternal joy of becoming" (1888:81). Music and the arts are vehicles toward decisive immersion in becoming because they are filled with the Dionysian element of life, emotion rather than pedantic reason and reasonableness.

Margaret L Driscoll

Tillich. The violently atheist Nietzsche is partly balanced by the Christian philosopher Paul Tillich, who came to New York from Germany just before World War II. In *The Courage to Be* (1952), Tillich presented the core of his existentialism. He maintained that life is defined by the courage to decide, that being is not a given but the consequence of the ethical act of self-affirmation. Rather than an ontology of being, life is grasped by the affirmation that in spite of limitations and imperfections there is the possibility of fulfilled life. Where Tillich differed from Sartre and Heidegger is in the affirmation of a "ground of being" rather than the alternative of nonbeing. Being is prior to nonbeing and encompasses it. Anxiety at the possibility of nonbeing is overcome in the courage to affirm the being of the self—both in the concrete present and in the possibility of what the self may become.

The dominant theme identified by these and other existential thinkers is the necessity of decision. Life is a creation. Only the possibility is given, and even that is problematic. Freedom is not some absolute principle but the possibility of action in the midst of the distortions and absurdities of life as it is. In decisive action, whether toward affirmation of self or of self-embodied meaning, life is created. Without the exercise of freedom there is only meaningless routine and acceptance of the given. In Nietzsche's writings there is even a hint that in the openness of play the ecstatic element of affirmation may have particular opportunity and fulfillment. Music especially embodies the richly emotive as well as creative potential of being human.

Leisure and Contemporary Philosophy

One strand of modern philosophy has been labeled *post-Nietzschean* because of the premises of absurdity and the creation of meaning through affirmation and act. It is also existential in the premise that meaning is created by action and communication rather than given in some structure of existence. However, of special interest here is the use of concepts of play as fundamental to the creation of knowledge. Continental development has contrasted with American and British reverence for logic and linguistic analysis. Some Continental philosophy that has returned to the premises of Nietzsche from various "structuralist" models has also been called *deconstruction*. It shifts attention from the implicit structures of existence to the creation of meaning in communication processes.

One starting point is the "hermeneutic circle" of the existentialist Martin Heidegger (1962). Objective knowledge based on directly apprehended data is rendered impossible by the inseparable connection between the whole and the parts. Neither can be understood without the other. There are no simple objective data apprehended outside a framework of meaning, nor is there a ruling concept or ideal with existence apart from its constituent parts or data. Rather, the circle of interpretation takes us around and around from whole to parts to whole and so on. One possible approach to this dilemma is to develop a dialectical model of gaining knowledge. However, the search for "truth" in the sense of final and unquestionable information is destined to remain unfulfilled. Every dialectical accounting is relative to the particularities of the observed and interpreted data of the situations under study.

The first questions, then, from this perspective are epistemological: How can knowledge be obtained? Is there any method for gaining or formulating reliable knowledge in this deconstructed world? One contemporary thinker, Hans-Georg Gadamer (1975, 1976), argues that there has been a shift in Western culture from verification by "common sense" (the sense of the community) to variations of scientific method. Consensus, authority, and prejudgment have given way to science. As a consequence, those activities and sources of knowledge not amenable to scientific verification have lost status. The aesthetic, for example, is relegated to a realm of taste rather than of a discipline.

It is not necessary to depreciate science to argue that there are other ways in which knowledge is developed. For Gadamer one such source is "play." Play has prejudgments in the sense of guiding orientations. However, it produces meaning out of experience. For Heidegger the hermeneutic circle does not destroy the possibility of meaning but rather makes it possible. Interpretation is possible in the dialectic, not precluded by it. Gadamer builds on this a "playful" theory of knowledge:

1. Play is the purest form of self-presentation in which the actor becomes absorbed in the activity. The focus is on the action rather than on the subjects and objects of the activity.
2. However, play does involve prejudgments that give an orientation and structure to the activity. These prejudgments are recognized as being for that play rather than possessing some ontological permanence. Therefore, play experience is not bound to the forms forever, but plays with them in the context of the action.
3. Such play is noninstrumental, even though the results will affect future play.
4. Play, then, is one mode of interpreting and trying out the "givens" of the world, of adjusting and manipulating "structure" because it is recognized to be a temporal construction.
5. In play experience the actor possesses the experience to the extent that it can be interpreted reflexively (Gadamer, 1975:317). This experience can be understood in a way that can produce new meaning. Play is discrete enough in form that it can be utilized to test and produce meaning.

James Hans goes on from this basis to argue that play actually "produces" meaning (*The Play of the World,* 1981). It is in play that the seeming structures or givens of existence can be moved around, tried in differing configurations, and experimented with in ways that may yield new understanding. Play for Hans is a central activity in the world of work as well as leisure, in science as well as aesthetics. Play is activity with a dialectical back-and-forth flow between the whole and the parts. There is an ongoing dialectic of action and interpretation. Although the constructed nature of the activity is known, the dialectic can yield different and alternative interpretations. Play is experience yet is not so embedded in given meaning that it cannot be subjected to contrived change and subsequent interpretation. Play occurs—it happens—and yet is meaningful. It is meaning producing just because it is not limited to a single set of prejudgments or method of analysis. Play creates meaning—that is, it is existential—because it is not strictly instrumental. In any setting play may be enacted with both an openness to unanticipated outcomes and an acknowledgement of the constructed nature of the forms employed. Therefore, those forms can be altered and outcomes evaluated. This "playing with play" yields new interpretations, explanations of the regularities of occurrence given those forms and orientations.

The idea that play produces meaning is associated with the French philosopher Jacques Derrida (1973, 1976). Derrida employs the term "freeplay" to refer to action in a world that has no fundamental foundation of structure or knowledge. Knowledge is not "out there" to be apprehended but is the product of action. For Derrida the chaos of existence is rendered interpretable through an acceptance that the only agreement for linguistic communication is developed through the freeplay of language usage. There is no Being, only the action of freeplay with its meaning for the moment that is created in the action. What passes for a foundation is actually the fragile network of linguistic meanings in which communication is attempted.

Our interest here is not that of ontology (being) or epistemology (knowledge), but of the understanding of play as creating and created. Hans, particularly, is in touch with previous studies of play in his stress on its noninstrumental orientation as well as the construction *for the episode* of a structure that is recognized as made rather than given. He also emphasizes that playful activity can take place in any realm of life and is not segregated in a secondary sector labeled *leisure.* He deviates from others such as Huizenga, however, in his stress on the productive nature of play. Precisely because it is not caught in having to produce a predetermined product or outcome, play may be the environment for the creation of the novel. Not only in the aesthetic realm but in ordinary life it is play that offers the possibility of producing what did not exist before. This activity, crucial to any civilization, places play at the center of life rather than the periphery. Further, although linguistic creation is central to understanding play as production, linguistics does not exhaust the material or methods of productive play. Play is, from this perspective, the openness in all of life.

Although these philosophers prefer not to assign to themselves the existentialist label, they are closely related to the approach that holds that meaning is created by decision and action rather than given from some external source. Further, although they are dealing with play as a kind of action rather than leisure as a social space, they would agree that some domains of social life are more amenable to decisive action than others. Leisure is not necessarily free of distorting ideologies and structural constraints. However, insofar as leisure is the possibility of relatively free action, it may provide special opportunity for play, for creative activity. Further, play is understood as experience that is not so enclosed and constricted by prejudgments that its potential for real action is lost.

The Existential Freedom of Leisure _____

Existential approaches to leisure are experiential. They begin with the actual concrete experience as it is perceived in the world. Any analysis of that experience that rests on the perception of the actor contributes to understanding the phenomenon. The state of mind or consciousness of the actor is essential to the act. The ways in which the actor defines both self and environment are integral to any understanding of leisure from a phenomenological perspective. However, the state of consciousness does not exhaust the action or its context. One limitation of modes of analysis that deal only with mental states is that they tend to bypass the dimension of freedom. Some action perspective is necessary to incorporate the central theme of freedom. A perception of possibility or lack of constraint is a beginning. However, freedom is actualized only in action. Freedom is more than an illusion of possibility; it is the exercise of that possibility through intentioned action. Leisure from an existential perspective is the actualization of some facet of the perceived possibility, not the perception alone. Leisure is action, not just the feeling-state that accompanies it.

To explore this addition further takes us back to existential philosophy and sociology. Sartre not only described the misery of a failure of nerve that exists without real action but also offered a basis for such failure. *Bad faith* is a definition of life that denies the possibility of freedom, that takes the givens of the social situation as final. When *what is* is accepted as the best that is possible or all that is possible, then such bad faith stifles the possibility of decisive action. A life may be trapped in a truncated view of what is possible. Real action is defined out of the realm of perceived possibility. In this way, leisure as bad faith would entail a perception of freedom and meaning in an action context that is limited to instrumental activity. If the actor believes that freedom is simply following the norms and dictums of some external authority or guide, then leisure may be a prison as much as any other domain of life. In fact, an illusion of freedom would be the very heart of such leisure bad faith. A perception of freedom would serve to shield the actor from really decisive action.

Jack Douglas (1977) is quite explicit about the negation embodied in such leisure. It is necessary to recover a concept of the whole self—mind and body, reason and emotion—in order to create an authentic self and a new world. Such a self is found in action that breaks open the bonds of self-deception and cuts through the facades of social oppression. Leisure may be one of the most insidious instruments of fraudulence when it becomes defined as expression without fulfillment. TV, movies, spectator sports, drug use, pornography, and other kinds of escapism are designed to produce a feeling of gratification without the risk or costs of real action. Precisely because they yield a feeling of freedom, they may stand in the way of the exercise of freedom (1977:18). Leisure becomes a passive being "done to" rather than a seizing of the possibility of openness to act and create. Play is escape rather than initiative that is productive in the sense of creating a new facet of the self or the world. Leisure reduced to a mental state may be the basis of bondage rather than an act of freedom.

Existential phenomenology does not offer a simple path to leisure or to any kind of meaning. The social theory of Alfred Schutz (1972) focused on the "typifications," or shared experiences that have been transmitted in linguistic symbols and have the force of structure. Decisive action is not easy in a social world in which such definitions are enforced and reinforced by institutional agreements. The realization of freedom, in leisure or any other mode of action, requires acting on a definition of self and environment that sees the possibilities beyond those presented by the social consensus. Nevertheless, the fact that this world of predefined activity and pseudo decision is a creation of defining actors means that its rigidities can be cracked. It is not fixed, an external and eternal given. Within that structured world there is the possibility of play. And play redefines the world!

From this perspective leisure is the action-possibility of play. It is decisive action, freedom, in a world that is created by symbol-using actors who have—albeit unknowingly—made it. Leisure is the actualization of meaning-producing action that is not instrumentally determined by the social forces of a consensual or power-shaped system.

Essential to such action is an existential phenomenology that recognizes the possibility within the *gestalt,* presupposing that action produces meaning as well as responds to social forces. Nor can leisure be reduced to any single dimension of existence; it is emotion, intellect, will, physiology, value, culture, and all that makes up the perceived field of action. Leisure, then, is *the actualization of situated freedom.* It is act more than being, action more than feeling. However, the feeling-perception is integral to the act. There is no either/or of emotional perception versus decisive act. Perception and feeling states, both before and during the acts, are integral to the experience. However, the experience of leisure does not just happen as a consequence of certain conditions; it is possible in certain environments but is produced by the exercise of freedom.

From one perspective there is a flow from perceived openness to choice to action:

Perceived possibility → choice → experience

From another perspective social definitions of linguistic symbol systems defining possible action are the context of existential decision that leads to a leisure experience:

Social definitions → action → leisure experience

Both perspectives are part of the reality. Social contexts, however symbolically constructed, are real in their power over individual actors. What is perceived—or not perceived—is the context of decision and action. Freedom *is* perceived. However, such perception may also be a delusion fostered by the institutional interests within a social system. Freedom is real only when it is tested by action and found to yield some creation, something or some condition that is new.

How does leisure occur? With the warning that we are still in the initial stages of the overall conceptualization, from the experiential and existential modes introduced thus far, leisure occurs when perceived freedom is actualized and found productive. Leisure, then, is

- processual, with decision and action in a dynamic context rather than a single entity,
- inaugurated in decision,
- situated in a dialectically perceived and interpreted context.

Furthermore, leisure is

- more than either feeling or thought,
- an occurrence in a perceived social *gestalt,*
- the actualization of a possibility.

Leisure is both understood and studied in a dialectic. There is a necessary back-and-forth flow between experience and context, between action and outcomes. Always the experience is being perceived and interpreted in the process so that meanings change rather than remain static. Research that does not encompass this processual character of the phenomenon touches only its edge. There are many metaphors that express some of this dialectic process. Leisure may be referred to as "encounter," "exchange," "conversation," or "play." The point is that the phenomenon is not exhausted in either the thesis or the antithesis of the dialectic. It is not *just* feeling or act, experience or decision, perception or outcome, immersion or interpretation. Leisure is not wholly determined by the thesis of perceived possibility nor by the antithesis of the limitations of the social context.

In subsequent analysis more attention is given to outcomes and contexts and the negations of false consciousness and institutional and political limitations. However, the existential dimension should not be lost in concentration on developmental, institutional, and social division elements of the context. Rather, experiential and decision themes are fundamental to any attempt at theoretical synthesis.

References

Berger, Peter, and Thomas Luckman. 1966. *The Social Construction of Reality.* New York: Penguin Bks., Inc.

Bretall, Robert, ed. 1951. *A Kierkegaard Anthology.* Princeton: Princeton University Press.

Buber, Martin. 1937. *I and Thou.* Trans. by R. G. Smith. Edinburgh: T. and T. Clark.

Derrida, Jacques. 1973. *Speech and Phenomena.* Trans. by D. Allison. Evanston: Northwestern University Press.

———. 1976. *Of Grammatology.* Trans. by G. Spivak. Baltimore: Johns Hopkins University Press.

Douglas, Jack, and John Johnson. 1971. *Existential Sociology.* Cambridge: Cambridge University Press.

Gadamer, Hans-Georg. 1975. *Truth and Method.* Trans. and ed. by Garrett Barden and John Cumming. New York: Seabury Press.

———. 1976. *Philosophical Hermeneutics.* Trans. and ed. by D. Linge. Berkeley: University of California Press.

Garfinkel, Harold. 1967. *Studies in Ethnomethodology.* Englewood Cliffs: Prentice-Hall, Inc.

Goffman, Erving. 1967. *Interaction Ritual.* Garden City: Doubleday & Co., Anchor Books.

Hans, James S. 1981. *The Play of the World.* Amherst: University of Massachusetts Press.

Heidegger, Martin. 1962. *Being and Time*. Trans. by J. Macquarrie and E. Robinson. New York: Harper & Row, Publishers.

Mead, George H. 1934 (1967). *On Social Psychology*. Chicago: University of Chicago Press.

Merleau-Ponty, Maurice. 1964. *In Praise of Philosophy*. Trans. by John Wild and James M. Edie. Evanston: Northwestern University Press.

Nietzsche, Frederick. 1964 (1888). *The Portable Nietzsche*. Ed. by W. Kaufmann. New York: The Viking Press, Inc.

Sartre, Jean-Paul. 1943. *L'Être et le Néant*. Paris, Gallimard.

———. [1943] 1953. *Existential Psychoanalysis*. Trans. by Hazel E. Barnes. New York: Philosophical Library.

Schutz, Alfred. 1972. *The Phenomenology of the Social World*. Evanston: Northwestern University Press.

Tillich, Paul B. 1956. *The Courage to Be*. New Haven: Yale University Press.

Weber, Max. 1964. *The Theory of Social and Economic Organization*. Trans. by A. M. Henderson and Talcott Parsons. New York: The Free Press.

CHAPTER 4

Developmental Theory

ISSUES

In developmental theory leisure is viewed from a longer-term perspective. It is a process of becoming through the life course.

Socialization *in* leisure is intensified because of the concentration on immediate experience.

Socialization *into* leisure through the three main life-course periods takes place in a context of intersecting role sequences.

The dilemmas of development in the shifting contexts and aims of the life course express a basic security versus challenge conflict.

In the life journey, decisions produce development.

Negation of development occurs in failures to complete developmental tasks due to blocks, traps, and diversions.

An existential approach to leisure stresses decision and the freedom to become. One danger of concentrating only on the experience and decision is that the process may appear to be like the selection of a flavor at an ice-cream store. Only the remembered and anticipated tastes are the objects of the decision. The outcomes sought are based entirely on what is available in the showcase. Decision is reduced to the selection of a peppermint stick or chocolate ripple experience in the immediate episode. In Chapters 4 and 5 we explore two more internal and lasting dimensions of leisure: the outcomes for personal development and for self-definitions. The existential theme of becoming, of the actor who is making decisions about the self, is offered as a response to two questions:

1. What personal change do we anticipate in leisure experiences?
2. What do we hope to become in and through leisure?

The Theme: Continuity and Change in the Life Course

Developmental theory is based on the inevitability of change that is integral to individuals and societies. The fundamental theme is that of *becoming,* not only in decisive action but also in personal development in the changing contexts of the life course. Continuity is expressed in the idea of a self that moves through the life course with some persistent identity. Change is always built on the self that has already come into identifiable being. At the same time, the self is always developing into something more than currently exists. Further, many contexts and themes of that development are common to those who make their way through life at the same times, a cohort. They enter and leave major periods of life at about the same ages and experience much the same major historical events simultaneously. Developmental theory may focus on individuals, but it is profoundly social and historical as well.

In general, the life course in contemporary societies consists of three bio-social periods: preparation, establishment, and culmination. In the preparation period learning and growing are the central tasks as the young person is getting ready for adult or productive life. In establishment the themes are productive contribution to the society and securing a place in the social system. In the final, or culmination, period, the end point of death is anticipated in ways that make meaning and a passing on of life's outcomes significant. Life is seen as a journey in which the human actor seeks to have some continuity of meaning and identification rather than just a series of experiences. In short, we attempt to become persons with satisfying lives and persistent meanings. Our immediate decisions are made in the context of that becoming as well as of discrete elements of experience. Further, leisure is an integral part of this process, not a "time out" from meaning.

To understand leisure developmentally we must approach it from dual perspectives. Leisure itself is learned behavior, attitudes, and meanings. We are socialized *into* leisure through our histories of experiences and choices. *Socialization* is the acquisition of the knowledge, attitudes, skills, and communication and interpretive competencies to act effectively in social institutions and roles. Leisure socialization is first learning how to be leisure actors.

However, there is also socialization *in* leisure (Kleiber and Kelly, 1982.) There is more to the experience than the moment. In leisure events and episodes we are in the process of becoming. We are learning, developing, and acting. We act in ways that elicit responses from the context, as in a game, and from the others engaged in the activity. This learning is both positive and negative. We may become stronger and more competent persons through our socialization in leisure, or we may develop fears and inhibitions that block growth. In the past, sociologists have been most likely to investigate socialization into leisure and educators and developmental psychologists socialization in leisure. In this chapter, we attempt to deal with both issues.

Leisure and Learning

We now have over a decade of research on the question of how leisure interests and investments have been learned. The earliest studies focused on outdoor recreation and the persistence of patterns learned in childhood. In general it was found that familiarity with natural resources and sited activities, such as camping and fishing, in formative years increased the likelihood of adult participation. However, the increasing rates of participation in the 1970s also suggested that some people begin such engagement as adults.

A very general approach queried adults on the timing and social context of their first involvement in a wide range of leisure-type activities. Overall, samples in three communities reported that the activities in which they currently participated were as likely to have been begun in postschool years as in childhood. Further, some family context was the inaugurating community for 60 percent of such activities, with 40 percent begun with friends or in some institutional setting. Only cultural activities such as music or drama were generally started in school (Kelly, 1974, 1977). Further research has elaborated this picture without altering the basic findings. First, although early life opportunities and contexts are important, adults may add new activities through the life course up to years of serious health impairment. Second, the most common social contexts of learning are familial. However, peer groups such as neighborhood and school companions in student years and friends in later years are also significant. The percentages for the various inauguration contexts are biased by the kinds of activities included or omitted.

Two additions need to be made to this relatively simple approach to socialization into leisure. The first is that employing activities and types of activities as the substance of the analysis may obscure the sense of competence and ability to learn that carries over from one activity to another. Especially when required skills are perceived as similar to ones learned in the past, an actor may be more ready to try a new activity. Second, the sequential quality of such learning is lost when activities, contexts, and events are examined in terms of one-time beginnings. The process of becoming interested in some form of leisure, sampling it, being encouraged and taught, finding a group of companions, securing access to required resources, experiencing relative success or failure in acquiring skills, and gaining feedback from significant others about the appropriateness of the engagement cannot be reduced to a single time or place. In fact, some such socialization may be happenstance, as when a new neighbor or business associate is seeking a companion for an event that opens the door to a new interest.

Further, such interests occur in a social context that changes through the life course. The association of sport participation with student years is in part a response to both opportunities and expectations. On leaving school, people must exert more organizational effort to continue team sports that were available and encouraged in and after school. Further, learning opportunities and standards of performance that allow for learners are the rule in school programs. A skill level with the violin that is acceptable for the junior-high orchestra may be scorned in the community symphony.

As roles proceed through their life-course sequences, leisure socialization may develop in relation to new roles. In the early establishment years leisure has been found to change in relation to the assumption of family roles of spouse and parent (Kelly, 1978a) and employment roles with attendant social expectations (Rapoport and Rapoport, 1975). Participation in family activities, especially those with solidarity and child-development aims, are expected of young parents. Joining certain community organizations may be strongly encouraged for those in local businesses and professions. Even the friends selected may vary according to the perceived norms of acceptability for social positions and strata.

Along with changing social expectations and opportunity contexts, the value systems and world views of individuals may be altered as they advance through their life spans. The journey of life involves the adoption of different perspectives on what is important, appropriate, and satisfying. The kinds of parties sought by students may be avoided by the same persons five years later as they seek to find accepted places in the adult social world. Styles of participation in the same activities may change when locales, attire, and companions deemed suitable at one age may be seen as damaging to a social identity at a later period in life. We may alter earlier views of the country club or the concert hall as new interests develop or new reference groups lead us into valuing what had earlier been ignored or even scorned.

Further, learning is more than taking on new interests and attitudes. Individuals may change in the deeper sense of learning. They may come to discover new dimensions of their own selves, to find enrichment and satisfaction in the development of new competencies, associations, or investments. Leisure previously ignored may be found to open possibilities for the self that had never before been considered. Travel may begin an interest in architecture that leads to the acquisition of skills as a photographer. A spouse, child, or friend may coerce entry into a leisure investment that is found to yield a return of undreamed excitement. In the process the self may be redefined as new dimensions of life are realized.

Along with this process of socialization into leisure, there are a number of factors that may limit such learning. The time frames for leisure and education may be reduced for a cohort by requirements to give a number of years to military service, especially during wartime. The economy may offer entry to fewer completing school for some cohorts, with lasting impacts on work trajectories. The ethnicity of leisure, especially leisure that consists primarily of social interaction, shapes both contexts and associations. Opportunities and expectations are differentiated by social stratification. The costs of leisure in terms of money, time flexibility, and access to resources mean that possibilities taken for granted by some are never considered by others. Further, all leisure experiences are not positive. Sometimes others do laugh when we "sit down at the piano." Sometimes we are left out rather than included, derided rather than applauded, and blamed rather than rewarded. Feedback is not always positive. There are more losers than winners in some leisure events. As a consequence, youth may drop out of a sport (Snyder and Spreitzer, 1976), or an aging adult may decide that former satisfactions are no longer possible.

Socialization into leisure is a dialectical process that continues through the life course. As we learn leisure interests and skills, we also learn something about ourselves. Further, we may learn that the costs of some kinds of leisure engagement are too high for the experienced or anticipated benefits. We make decisions, but we do so in the framework of both perceived opportunities and expectations externally and what we perceive ourselves to be internally. We learn in engagement and redefine our aims and investment in the process. New promises are envisioned and old ones found unfulfilled. We are always *becoming,* selecting life contexts from a changing base. In this process there is not only continuity with the past but also the possibility of at least a slightly different future.

Learning in Leisure

As already introduced, leisure socialization is more than adding and subtracting activities. In leisure as in all life we are in the process of becoming—sometimes in recognized ways and often in ways we do not perceive at the time. Mihaly Csikszentmihalyi (1981) has argued that it is in leisure experiences that we are most likely to develop criteria for the rest of life. Expressive activities may be those in which experiences of the highest quality become the standard by which other experiences—as in work or education—are judged. Gratification in the event, environment, or interaction may be highest in those times in which we have exercised the fullest choice. Work enrichment, for example, may involve enhancing the leisurelike elements of the work setting by maximizing control over the environment and increasing feedback of effectual control over outcomes. Dissatisfaction with events that are chiefly instrumental and devoid of intrinsic interest and meaning occurs partly because in leisure socialization we have learned that it is possible to become engrossed in the experience of certain expressive activities.

One major transition expected of young adults in industrial societies is that they be ready and willing to devote a central place in their lives to productive activity with little meaning beyond instrumental rewards. Experiences that are "just for the moment" and that immerse adolescents in sensual stimuli are in part a refusal to move into the "real world" of extrinsic rationales. And part of the distress of parents may stem from the fact that they have come to terms with such reality by settling for instrumentality.

The issue is that of learning *in* leisure. When we are able to choose, at least within a range of possibilities, what we will do and whom we will be with, then the probability is increased of experiencing some of the elements that yield meaning then and there. In such "high" experiences, the possibility of significant learning is also heightened. When we are most fully caught up in meaning and are receiving feedback that is reinforced by affective components, we are most likely to change (Csikszentmihalyi, 1981). We learn most compellingly who we might be and what we may become.

There is, then, much more to learning in leisure than the enjoyment of the moment. Intrinsic meaning is developmental as well as situational. In experiences to which we devote high energy and attention, we receive attitude-altering response. In the leisure of games, with their discrete and measured outcomes, we learn on the spot how well we are doing. With companions we have chosen we receive feedback that is most salient. Competence is given an instant rating. Initiative is both possible and rewarded. Children try out their abilities and their hopes in play. Adults seek to demonstrate what they would like to be in their leisure, and when it works, their self-definitions are changed. The nature of the experience is developmental just because it is focused within the episode.

Learning interpersonal skills may also be enhanced in leisure. Many of the institutional settings in which we interact with specified others are quite prescribed. The roles that we are given permit only a narrow latitude of discretion in our enactment. Leisure, on the other hand, may be less rigid. In general, parties or vacation trips allow for more variation than production lines or sales meetings. Our options for trying out somewhat different portrayals of selfhood may be greatest in leisure events. Therefore, the learning potential is also greatest. Lines of action or self-expression that are found viable in leisure may then be transferred to other role portrayals. In the next chapter we explore personal and social identities as they are developed in leisure. The critical issue is that leisure may be central to our *becoming* through the life course (Kelly, 1983). Life is more than *what* we are (roles); it also encompasses *who* we are (identities).

The Life Course

There are a number of models that offer a framework for analyzing life as journey. Each focuses on one or more dimensions of continuity and change, and each is a metaphor that may be useful for our analysis.

The Family Life Cycle. Perhaps the most familiar model from traditional sociology is that of the family life cycle based on role shifts. Earlier versions presented "stages" of life with the implication that each was different and identifiable (Hill and Rodgers, 1964). Later revisions tended to refer to periods rather than stages and continuities as well as change (Rapoport and Rapoport, 1975). However, the model has proved useful for differentiating the central tasks and expectations associated with being in sequence a child, launched child, courting young adult, newlywed, childbearing parent, child-rearing parent, launching parent, postparental adult, grandparent, and widow. Note that the adult roles presume having an intact marriage and becoming a parent. There is little attention to disruption, traumatic change, or choice of a different pattern. The model deals with the normative sequence of family formation, reproduction, and nurture. Despite this limitation, attention to the different expectations, resources, and responsibilities related to family roles has proven to be one valuable perspective on adult life.

The Life Span. Psychologists, on the other hand, have tended to give their attention to age-related change in the individual. Chronological age is employed to index changes in patterns of interaction, personality, mental preoccupations, and identified problems (Baltes and Schaie, 1973). Usually the life-span metaphor is combined with another model when used to explain behavior or psychological variables. Historical change and social conditions have been included as the other end of the dialectic of development (Riegel, 1976). A particular contribution of the life-span approach is that it has incorporated biological as well as psychological factors in explanation. There is variation in just which elements in the metaphor are considered central as well as debate over whether or not the approach tends to be "ontogenetic" in emphasizing a prescribed and inevitable course of development (Dannefer, 1984).

The Life Course. Some social psychologists have expanded the family-life-cycle model in ways that correct some of its deficiencies (Neugarten, 1968; Riley, 1979). First, the idea of discrete stages is ameliorated with more stress on the continuities of the journey. The life course consists of periods linked by transitions that enable the individual to learn coping devices that may be adapted to multiple changes. Second, primary focus on the family is widened to include other major roles. Work roles of preparation, inauguration, establishment, and retirement are added to the model (Rapoport and Rapoport, 1975). Productivity is a dimension found to permeate family and leisure as well as work. Further, the intersections of work, family, leisure, and community roles allow for a more complex and variegated analysis. No one institutional context, either work or family, is presumed to be central throughout every life journey. Third, the life-course perspective has been enlarged to encompass more variety. It is recognized that neither traditional family sequences nor a simple work sequence of school–apprenticeship–career–retirement will characterize the life course of most adults today. Rather, different patterns of both the paths of life and ways of responding to those paths are likely to be found in any comprehensive study over time.

The Crisis Model. Recent attention has been devoted to an approach that emphasizes identifiable crises that have to be dealt with in the life course. Daniel Levinson (1978) has proposed that a series of crises occur more or less on schedule. Especially in the "midlife crisis," fundamental commitments may be questioned and radical reorientations undertaken with decisive consequences. Both values and institutional roles may be realigned in a traumatic upheaval of the contexts of life. While it may be argued that the kinds of crises identified are specific to particular cultures and even positions within social systems, we incorporate some of this metaphor in the life-course analysis of leisure that follows. Life does frequently involve crises as well as predictable transitions for which we are somewhat prepared.

The Developmental Model. Erik Erikson (1963, 1968) proposed a series of stages of psychosocial development that have had wide and pervasive influence across many disciplines. His neo-Freudian approach gives a central place to the development of sexuality and sexual identity. This model incorporates complex interrelationships of sociocultural factors with stages in which sequential "tasks" have to be accomplished in order for the personality to move forward to the next set of requirements (Havighurst, 1958). This approach has had significant impacts on most subsequent formulations. Research and theory referring to adult development have most often attempted to unite the series of social roles expected in a social system with the continuities and changes in the individual through the developmental journey (Neugarten, 1968). One formulation of this psychosocial framework that includes leisure and play was presented by Chad Gordon and employed in a cross-sectional study in Houston. In this model nine periods of life are identified, and the major "dilemmas" of development are suggested (Gordon, Gaitz, and Scott, 1976). The dilemmas are all based on the drives toward both security and challenge that characterize the life course. Social contexts of significant others also change both as resources and sources of relational requirements. As an illustration of the developmental metaphor, an abbreviated outline of Gordon's approach appears in Table 4.1.

Note that this model shifts from social contexts and meanings to those based on changes in the individual required to negotiate the later life course successfully. Further, the life course is not analyzed as a simple series of tasks but as something of a struggle in which both previous development and new role expectations may pull and push in opposite directions. Further, the shifts in significant others as the social world expands in childhood, stabilizes for some periods, and then contracts at the end alter both the resources and the pressures of the environment. Both differentiation ("Who I am") and integration ("Where I am in the social system") are elements in the sequence of developmental dilemmas.

In the presentation that follows only three major periods of life are used in the analysis, although the dilemmas from Gordon's model will be included (Kelly, 1983). *Preparation* incorporates the first six periods from infancy through adolescence. *Establishment* includes young adulthood through maturity. *Culmination* actually begins in later ma-

TABLE 4.1   Life Course Development and Dilemmas

Period and Age	Dilemma of Development: Security vs. Challenge
1. Infancy: 0–12 months	affective gratification vs. sensorimotor experiencing
2. Early childhood: 1–2 years	compliance vs. self-control
3. Oedipal period: 3–5 years	expressivity vs. instrumentality
4. Later childhood: 6–11 years	peer relationships vs. evaluated abilities
5. Early adolescence: 12–15	acceptance vs. achievement
6. Later adolescence: 16–18/20	intimacy vs. autonomy
7. Youth: 19/21–29	connection vs. self-determination
8. Early maturity: 30–44	stability vs. accomplishment
9. Maturity: 45–retirement	dignity vs. control
10. Retirement: to disabling event	meaningful integration vs. autonomy
11. Disability: to death	survival vs. acceptance of death

turity and continues through retirement and disability. For each life period we highlight a number of the developmental themes that are most closely connected to play and leisure. The aim is to add to the previous analysis of experience and decision a grounding in how the individual is *becoming* as a person and social actor.

The Salience of Leisure

For decades intermittent scholarly efforts to deal with leisure as a phenomenon of some significance were rendered marginal by a general social-science assumption that leisure was both secondary and residual. Leisure was usually presumed to be "what adults do when everything important is finished." Further, it was seen as largely the result of other social factors, especially economic ones. One of the contributions of developmental approaches has been to draw leisure into a more central position in understanding contemporary life.

A variety of early community studies, including the "Middletown" research (Lynd and Lynd, 1934), gave considerable attention to leisure as part of the social fabric of the community. However, this attention was not incorporated in mainstream sociology textbooks and course outlines. A different approach was required on which to develop a perspective that incorporated leisure as an important element in social analysis. One of these approaches has been provided by developmental psychology. Beginning with attention to the play of children, developmental approaches brought the experience-centered activity of play into the overall set of environments in which significant things happen that affect growth and learning. Despite an educational bias in most such research, the issue of outcomes that have lasting and important effects began to attract attention.

The book that provided a basis for the extension of such work to the entire life cycle was written by Rhona and Robert Rapoport and entitled *Leisure and the Family Life Cycle* (1975). Despite the title, the authors offered a model in which the continuities of the life course were balanced with analysis of the changing roles of work, education, family, and community. The approach combined the sociological life-course model with a developmental set of themes. The patterns of roles changed as the developmental tasks and social contexts changed. Leisure was found to be much more central to the working out of a number of developmental tasks than had usually been recognized. The salience of leisure to adults was not reserved for the retired. However, leisure does change in orientations as well as settings as students leave school, begin to establish families, attempt to find a place in the economic world, and move on through the life course.

The approach adopted here is not a rigidly developmental one that presupposes a fixed set of tasks driving all aspects of life. Such an ontogenetic model is based on the concept of an ordered sequence of developmental requirements that must be accomplished by all members of a species. Variation is considered failure. The ontogeny of the individual is seen as *the* driving force in the journey of life. Counter to this narrow model, we will assume that cultural, social, and historical contexts shape both the aims and outcomes of any individual's life-course development. Not every individual will become the same when developmental tasks are accomplished. Even in the most prescribed roles, we develop our own *identities* that give a special flavor to how we enact our roles.

Role Careers: The Social Context

Any social system is made up of some combination of institutions with roles or positions with reciprocal expected behaviors. These roles have some pattern of assumption and release related to age. The roles of any individual form an age-related "role career" based on the functional requirements and authority system of the society. This role career is the institutional social context of a life course. For example, preparation roles include those of child and sibling in the family, student in school, learner in childhood leisure and prime participant in some adolescent leisure, and marginal contributor and secondary consumer in the economy. Those roles change in the establishment period in interrelated ways. The roles intersect so that assuming a parent role in the family, for example, has impact on everything else.

The framework of role careers includes the following:

- Both continuity and change characterize the individual. The evidence does not justify any assumption of radical discontinuity from one period to another or of complete determination of later stages by earlier ones.
- Both continuity and change characterize the social context. Old roles are left behind and new ones assumed. However, there are transitions that enable us to anticipate and prepare for new roles. The changes are real, but they are seldom disjunctive.
- The historical context is significant. Major events such as wars and economic shifts do have impacts that make each cohort different from any other.
- Most lives contain traumatic events. Only a minority of people move through the life course with only the predictable transitions of establishment, parenthood, launching, retirement, and the like. Less predictable disruptive events have powerful effects on both the contexts and the personal development of most individuals. These traumas alone are ample evidence that there is no immutable ontogenetic scheme that determines everything important in every life course.

- As roles change and shift, both orientations and resources change as well. Therefore, any presumption of a single-factor determination of the life course must be addressed critically rather than used to interpret everything else.

Preparation: The Anticipatory Period

Of course, there are several different subperiods within what we are calling preparation. However, they have in common a forward orientation, with at least some of the meaning of most experiences and learning directed toward the future. For the child a play or leisure experience may have all its meaning in the moment. A child does not play a game in order to grasp the concept of role expectations associated with designated positions. A teen does not "hang around" with his crowd after school in order to explore the dilemma of autonomy versus acceptance. Nevertheless, these developmental consequences are part of the experience. Learning takes place in leisure whether intended or not.

The descriptions and analysis that follow are in no way exhaustive or complete. Rather, they are intended to offer an introductory glimpse of ways in which developmental theory adds to the overall picture of meanings and contexts of leisure. Also, the life-course framework is employed in order to illustrate its value in following the continuity and changes in leisure associated with role sets and sequences.

Infancy: 0–12 Months. In the Gordon outline that we follow, the developmental dilemma for the infant involves affective gratification versus sensorimotor experience. The infant is primarily responding to sensed conditions of the environment and internal factors. In the affective responses the infant begins to experience a trust of significant others (Erikson, 1963). Play is developed in response to recognized others (e.g., peek-a-boo) and as an aimless manipulation of external objects such as crib toys. Sensory gratification is found in affectionate warmth when being held as well as in initial acting on elements of the environment that produce perceivable outcomes. Security in affection and challenge in motor activity may be combined. Both affective bonding and effectual action are inaugurated in this period in experiences that have only immediate meaning. It can be argued that immediacy in both social bonding and action-response is based on the experiences of infancy as the environment is gradually differentiated. Play is *the* form of action by the infant that tries out possibilities and outcomes. In such play the infant is also developing motor control and, in a basic form, social skills. Pleasurable body sensations may be experienced in conjunction with actions initiated by the infant, a fundamental existential element of development.

Early Childhood: 1–2 Years. The learning dimension becomes more explicit in the compliance versus self-control dilemma of this period. The security found in parental bonding, especially with the mother, is reinforced by rewards for several forms of self-control. However, some sense of efficacy is also stirred by the experience of being able to act and get results. Play in this period is more immediate than the culturally based forms of later childhood. However, learning occurs as problem solving is incorporated into simple interaction with others and in directed action on play instruments (Piaget, 1952; Sutton-Smith, 1971). Such learning is a forerunner of the sense of competence of later development (Caplan and Caplan, 1973). Perhaps more important are two more immediate elements: a sense of self as actor on the environment and a sense of rewarding and pleasant states associated with both initiated and responsive play. Certainly the expansion of motor and social skills through playful action and interchange is fundamental to development. At the same time, the reward and sanction systems of the culture are being experienced as behaviors are tried and evaluated as acceptable or unacceptable by significant others. The "autosphere" of the infant is expanded into the "microsphere" of the young child through the experimentation of play (Erikson, 1963).

Oedipal Period: 3–5 Years. Both the complexity and emotional loading of the social environment are increased in the period in which the expressivity versus instrumentality dilemma comes to the fore. Sexuality is only one dimension of interactions with significant others that have their impacts on the development of self-definitions. In this period there is an extension of the proactive play of the child, who more and more creates situations in which outcomes may be experienced and tested (Erikson, 1963). The social world of the child is beginning to expand beyond the family to the neighborhood. This increased complexity is reflected in the nature of games as well as negotiation of social relationships. Also, community institutional opportunities of preschool care, recreation, and learning have become increasingly common and complex since most of the earlier developmental research was done. The situational relationships of day care, extrafamilial nurturing programs, extended and reconstituted families, and substitute mothers have added many factors to both the play environments and learning requirements. Expressivity and instrumentality are held in some tension in many play settings as the child increasingly has ends in mind for episodes and interactions. Intentioned behavior may require choices between immediate affective outcomes and longer-term goals. In this period gender differences found in older research may be lessened as girls are encouraged to engage in physically demanding and socially complex activities. In general, the uncertain outcomes within some accepted framework of interaction provide both excitement and opportunities for learning about the rules and roles of game playing (Opie and Opie, 1969). Recently there has been more interest in the relative values of adult-directed play and child-initiated activity (Devereaux, 1976). Certainly the socialization of adult expectations requiring fairness, inclusion, and order has considerable impact on the organization of play even when adults are absent.

Later Childhood: 6–11 Years. The dilemma of peer relationships versus evaluated abilities is given its major contextual shift in school. The child is graded in so many ways, including cognitive, communication, motor, and social abilities. Competence in learning is given structured evaluation that is both competitive and public. The effects on the child's self-definitions are both profound and complex. Further, the differentation of leisure, or play, from more institutionalized roles and expectations now has elements of time and place, as "recess" and after-school become designated for such activity. Families may remain the primary context of socialization into leisure (Kelly, 1977), but the school institution as well as organized programs for sports, the arts, and other activity take more salient places in the overall scheme of time and resource allocation. In this period the question of skill emerges more prominently, with comparative ability governing inclusion in activity. Competence as assessed by others is central to being chosen and in turn affects the choices of the child. Further, the consequences are cumulative, as those who are included are most likely to develop the higher levels of ability required for further participation. In this period there is also the power of the media, especially television, to introduce opportunities and to present styles of action that may or may not be appropriate for the developmental readiness of the child. Cognitive and emotional changes allow the child at this age to engage in considerable perseverance in lines of action, negotiate rather complex social situations, and abstract multiple meanings from a series of experiences (Erikson, 1963). The "Who am I?" question is always salient, with learned answers now including sexual identification, activity-specific and generalized competence evaluations, and a rich set of imagined conceptions of possibility. Peer relationships are becoming increasingly central to development and are now differentiated from the expectations of significant adults. Also, those adults whose evaluations are not tempered by familial ties are emerging as significant gatekeepers of opportunities and rewards. One function of games is to provide a comprehensible context for grasping that all evaluation is not personal but is based on agreed-on criteria and formats. As in the earlier periods, play is a critical context for the dialectic of learning that moves from action to perceptions of the responses of others to revised lines of action and identities. The consistent findings of gender differences (Lever, 1978) in form and group composition in play also suggest that social norms and values are learned differently by males and females (Gilligan, 1982). For girls, value orientations of affective bonding provide a different basis for judgment from the negotiated action system of boys. Children develop in and toward a concrete social system that is permeated by value systems prescribing and proscribing action in every arena of life and at every age. The competition and cooperation found in the forms and reward systems of sports, games, and other modes of learning reflect the sex-differentiated value orientations of the society. As children advance in age they increasingly are being socialized into a particular culture that permeates every aspect of their lives.

Early Adolescence: 12–15 Years. The dilemma of acceptance versus achievement is primarily peer-oriented. In this period an adolescent may concentrate on a small circle of close friends, usually of the same sex. However, the school is escalating the evaluation of performance and the differentiation of opportunities and rewards. Future orientations of postsecondary education selection and employment preparation may clash with present orientations of pleasure seeking with a group of intimates. Sexuality becomes more central to identities and choices but is as much a source of bewilderment and discomfort as identification and integration (Csikszentmihalyi and Larson, 1984). A number of themes are interrelated in this critical transition period of development:

- The maintenance of independence from parents through leisure choices and involvements (Friedenberg, 1959; Gordon, 1971). The symbols of leisure engagement, especially music and clothing, often refer to independence and rebellion.
- The domination of values and choices by a peer group that has in some way adopted particular symbols and settings to specify their social identities.
- A fascination with the forbidden, especially when joined with explorations of sexuality and intimacy.
- A pull toward the immediate and a resentment of all the norms and pressures to prepare for the future, in which pleasure is to be subordinate to duty (Csikszentmihalyi, 1971).
- Some tension between those engagements that are evaluated and yield prestige, such as sports, and those that are primarily expressive and immediate in meanings.
- The primacy of leisure in developing heterosexual attachments and self-definitions of acceptability and attractiveness. Leisure episodes and settings are where much critical action takes place. Emergent excitement may be converted to developmental growth in peer in-

teraction and ability-challenging activity with strong affective dimensions (Csikszentmihalyi and Larson, 1984:261–84).

Self-expression and social integration are not necessarily in conflict for the young adolescent. Rather, in leisure settings apart from the family and school the peer group with which a young man or woman identifies will engage in expressive activity together that cements the feeling of acceptance and integration. For some teens such integration may be found in a performance-oriented group such as an athletic team, arts group, or religious community. Some remain firmly enmeshed in their families, by choice or by enforcement. The desire on the part of many parents to protect as well as nurture maturation often adds to the tension of the social context with its forces of security and freedom pulling at the individual. Also, gender differences in both opportunities and expectations have strong influence on development in this period. Encouragement of exploration for males is often in contrast with the shielding of females from environments in which they may be at risk physically, sexually, or even emotionally. Leisure choices may be reduced for females due to such restrictions as well as learned inhibitions.

Later Adolescence: 16–18/20 Years. The developmental dilemma, an extension of the previous period with greater power and specificity, is between intimacy and autonomy. However, the institutional context has become much more complex. School is less a world to itself and more the beginning of a transition. For some the evaluation schemes of the school are a prelude to the testing of employment seeking and employer decisions. *Adolescence* itself is a label that would be rejected by most in this age group. It connotes immaturity and a lack of sexual competence. For those who are completing secondary education or entering the work force, higher education, the military, or the great reserve of unemployed youth, self-identification as *adult* is preferred. yet, from a developmental perspective, the tasks appear more like extensions of the previous period than those of establishment. What changes is the urgency and immediacy of the tasks. The desire for peer acceptance and the common same-sex group now changes focus to particular partners and the development of sexual competence as well as identity. On the other hand, the institutionalized need for achievement also becomes more specific and individualized. This is the time of transition into the reward structure for which all this preparation has been a prelude. Evaluations have a consequential salience that in some cases causes late teens to pull back from the evaluators and events in which performances are compared. It may appear as the last time for some autonomy in which life may be lived for its own sake unencumbered by all the constraints of adult life. Exploration and autonomy may be combined in some attachment to a leisure activity or series of events. Leisure may become even more than before the last best chance for freedom. The themes often express the basic dilemma:

- Leisure includes both the desire to develop intimacy and to maintain some vestige of independence from a net of obligations.
- Leisure may begin to be oriented toward establishment settings and yet demonstrate the pull of being free and autonomous.
- Intimacy in the sense of relationships of some depth and commitment are balanced by personal uncertainties about the risks of such attachment and the loss of freedom to shape one's future life without encumbrances.
- Contexts that allow for a demonstration of competence are less common for those in this transition than those that permit expression and emotional release.

The indefinite age termination of this period is partly a result of extended education for many and of the barriers to any employment for others. Life in this period is both future-oriented and present-based. Leisure, as always, expresses the fundamental dilemmas of development as well as the opportunity structures that are based on gender, age, social status, and culture.

Establishment: Production and Position

Two themes predominate in this central period of the life course: (1) productivity in work and family, and (2) placement in the social system. The central orientations of life tend to begin with the establishment and maintenance of a place in the society through developing work and family roles with demonstrated products that are socially valued.

The Transition to Establishment. Despite all the attention given to preparation and anticipation in the previous years, the transition to establishment is dramatic and often traumatic. Now the evaluation components of the social system are more than indicators of the future. Entry into the economic sector in what is expected to be a work career lasting thirty-five years or longer begins with an entry level with both present and future consequences. The courtship games may become real negotiation in the marriage market. Expectations turn from being well prepared to producing, especially in the work and family spheres of life. Now the struggle for independence becomes a norm rather than a struggle. The exploration of intimacy makes the transition to commitment one often enmeshed in a concatenation of joint responsibilities.

This does not mean that leisure disappears while the "serious business" of establishment is begun (Kelly, 1983:67–68). Rather, leisure is changed in its orientations and settings to complement the new positions and goals of life. In an intensive study of former university students making the transition (Kelly and Masar, 1970) six themes were identified:

- The extraresidential leisure of student years was largely moved to at-home entertainment and interaction.
- The sexual exploration of late preparation turned to commitment and the building of a new nuclear family. This family then became the focus of most leisure.
- Becoming parents had the most significant impact on the resources and aims of leisure, especially when it required the mother to relinquish a work role.
- Some leisure became oriented toward establishing a *place* in the community by joining appropriate organizations or activity contexts.
- For those intent on beginning a work career rather than just having a job, leisure that was in conflict rather than complementary was laid aside or reduced.
- Different leisure styles were based on an intersection of resources and expectations in work, leisure, and family as well as on preestablished leisure investments and interests. Leisure was adapted in the transition but in continuity with previous styles and salience.

A number of social and economic trends have tended to extend the transition from student to establishment. The educational preparation for many economic positions has lengthened due to higher technical requirements. Competing in a world-market economy has tended to move considerable low-skill work away from North America and reduce the number of entry positions in production industries. Redefined economic roles and opportunities for women have delayed both marriage and childbearing timetables for many women seeking to begin their own careers.

Nevertheless, the central theme remains *productivity*. Social expectations center on reproduction of the society and securing a recognized contributing place in the economy. Social identities are most often based on family and economic roles. Personal identities are generally consistent with those assigned by others. Usually in early establishment, leisure identities are complementary to the more central family and work roles. However, there are many exceptions as individuals choose to make some leisure investment—most often in the arts, sports, or a resource-based activity set—the hub around which life revolves (Stebbins, 1979).

As central roles and self-definitions are developed in this period, the establishment of social identities in which there is some consensus among significant others is critical. Whether the central identity is as wife and mother, advancing junior executive, community theater performer, political activist, or some combination, achieving agreement between the self and others as to who we are is a central task. However, when that central social identity is leisure-based, there may be the question of appropriate maturity raised. A man who postpones other investments to remain a nonprofessional baseball player is accused of not growing up. Establishment expectations exert a powerful force on what we expect of ourselves in both timing and transitions.

One way of viewing life in the establishment period is as a set of nesting roles. Familial roles are the center of intimate acceptance, support for maintenance, economic consumption and management, social position, group interaction, and gender-role investment. The family is most often the base for leisure participation and the chief external purpose for economic engagement. The residence is more than shelter; it is a symbol of having a *place,* of being located in the society. Even when relationships are less than had been hoped, home and family are most often the core of the role complex of establishment adults. The tendency to reconstitute a nuclear family after one has been broken by divorce or death is evidence of its social salience even when fewer marriages survive the entire life course.

Gordon (1980) divides the establishment period into three substages with their own developmental dilemmas. On the security side of each is some variation on the theme of social identification, of securing an agreed-on place in the society. On the challenge side the developmental theme is some kind of production or recognized accomplishment. The negation in this period is the failure to achieve such recognition in ways that shape both the rewards received and self-definitions. It is no wonder that in a society where most adults have a series of jobs rather than a progressing work career most look for meaning in more proximate domains of life in which some evidence of having taken effectual action may be found.

Further, the pervasive influence of differential sex-role expectations comes to fruition in this period. As long as most women are expected to bear children and to be the primary nurturers of the children they bear, then choices will have to be made that call for relinquishing some other opportunities and investments. As long as men are expected to weight the compromise between intimacy and economic production one way and women another, then this period will demonstrate gender differences with lifelong consequences. It is deceptive to discuss establishment in ways that do not take such differences into account.

Young Adulthood: 19/21–29 Years. The more specific dilemma of this time is connection versus self-determination. The young adult has to "get in," to cross the multiple thresholds into adult life and get things under way. Wide discrepancies in resources and opportunities may be recognized in general, but some connection or reciprocal engagement with the "real world" is expected. This is one reason why high rates of unemployment for youth are especially damaging. Gaining a foothold on establishment is a serious challenge for many with a limited resource base. Failure to make that initial connection comes at an especially vulnerable time. On the other hand, the challenge of self-determination is also present. Now the former ambivalence of independence changes to an expectation. The pressure to demonstrate responsible autonomy runs through all the domains of life.

There are still many crosscurrents in the life of the early-establishment adult. Gordon (1976) locates some in leisure, in which the desires of youth for expression and sensory experience conflict with more "settled" expectations. This tends to be most true prior to marriage. If the marriage commitment is accepted as a symbol of the transition, then it may also include a change of leisure orientations to what is now appropriate. Such expectations are differentiated both by gender and by socioeconomic background. Sex-role socialization toward distinct and separate orientations for males and females is often clearest among status groups with the lowest education levels and occupational aspirations.

Getting started in occupational positions may call for considerable adjustment of schedules and nonwork relationships. Now the employment schedule has to take precedence regardless of whether or not the work proves satisfying or holds promise for advancement. Some initial occupational positions require extraordinary investments of time and attention during apprenticeship periods. If such requirements are combined with a central "career" orientation, then work tends to be the central factor in early establishment (Goldman, 1973).

However, for most young adults, the transition revolves around intimacy rather than work. Starting work tends to be more instrumental than all-defining. A job yields income and an economic base to widen participation in the social system. The consumer role is related closely to both leisure and family. A car, a place to live, some leisure instruments, clothes, entertainment fees, and other consumer items are part of the new independence. They are also part of a revised system of obligations. Not only consumer credit but anticipated needs are dependent on some regular rewards in the economic system. Income is more than spending money; it is the possibility of a new life-style. And leisure resources purchased on the market are then a symbol of social identification and family formation.

Nothing changes life like the marriage-parenthood package. As marriage is increasingly predicated on a decision to become parents rather than a desire for sexual access, the two become even more closely related. Not only do the contexts and resources but also the aims for leisure change. Within marriage orientations of the development of intimacy in companionship may be radically redirected by the birth of a child. Soon nurture and child development move into a central place in the leisure decision scheme. The demands of parenting are so intertwined with changed self-definitions that it is difficult to separate the two elements. What is certain is that for most young parents life and leisure will never be the same. In a matter of months or years the relative autonomy of the period is changed to a new set of limitations and obligations. In more traditional families the shock of loss of independence is much more radical for the wife than for the husband.

At the same time, there is the continuing need to demonstrate competence in the various life domains. Intimacy may be focused on courtship and marriage, but other kinds of competence are to be manifested and recognized in work. When such opportunities and meanings are blocked, some leisure investment may come to the fore as salient to definitions of worth and ability. In one analysis of motocross racing by blue-collar young men, the context for demonstrating masculine competence and courage, which is absent in most jobs, is found to be at the heart of the appeal of the demanding sport (Kelly, 1982a:170–71). Levinson (1978) also sees this period as one in which a "dream" for the future is developed. When opportunities to move toward the realization of the dream are lacking, young adult years may also be acutely damaging to a sense of worth and an anticipation of the future. The possibility of leisure identities becoming central during this period is one that requires careful research. It is evident, however, that for some young adults, leisure is the dominant theme of their lives. The extent to which this is compensation rather than a freely chosen dream remains to be investigated.

Early Maturity: 30–44 Years. Stability versus accomplishment are proposed as the poles of the developmental struggle for those who have moved into their establishment roles. This might be seen as the "central" period of life. From the perspective of economic and family roles this is the time toward which preparation and early adult years have pointed and from which later periods may be seen to decline in productivity. In the economic sphere careers have usually demonstrated a likelihood of success or never will. In the family domain, childbearing is completed and the offspring are being evaluated in school and as they are launched into worlds of independence. It is a time of greatest investment in roles and of maximum demands. It is also a time in which the negations of failure, dissatisfaction, and alienation may be recognized.

Stability is sought regarding investments that have been made. If traditional family roles have been accepted, the husband-father is likely to devote time and attention to consolidating his work position as well as supporting his family. The wife-mother deals with increasingly complex household management tasks as well as child support and nurture. Leisure is defined primarily in relation to family cohesion, child development, and community solidarity. Traditional values support such orientations through community institutions and organizations. Such an integrated life-style has been labeled "conventional" in terms of values or "balanced investment" in terms of commitment of resources (Kelly, 1985). Leisure tends to be home-and family-centered and vacations designed for common family participation.

The other side of the supposed dilemma is accomplishment. However, it might be argued that for conventional individuals and households, stability and accomplishment are complementary rather than opposed. This is the period in which results are supposed to be realized. Children may show promise of future ability and accomplishment. Occupational investments demonstrate the likelihood of rewards in status as well as income. Community participation is rewarded with a series of offices and honors in organizations. Accomplishment, so much a goal for the career-oriented in young adult years, now is expected to provide some payoff in institutional settings.

Some research indicates that the dilemma may be between different life-styles and orientations. The traditional combine goals and investments in stable roles that are expected to yield symbols of accomplishment. The unconventional may begin to question both the stability and the significance of traditional signs of success. Daniel Levinson (1978) has not been supported in his claim to have discovered an inevitable and universal "mid life crisis" in America. On the other hand, he has identified elements of negation in this period. As major life investments are stable enough to demonstrate their outcomes, cracks may appear in the hull of life's journeying ship. Children are seen to be limited and even recalcitrant. Marriage partners are less than exciting and sometimes appear to have been lost as companions. The escalating technical requirements of much employment as well as changes in occupational markets may shunt a once-promising career to a sidetrack from which there is no evident way back to the fast main line. Limitations may be more fully recognized by oneself and others. Rather than offering new heights and vistas, midlife may disclose a set of dead ends and limited possibilities.

For some these negations lead to precipitous change. Divorces, affairs, new marriages, and even different sexual styles are the choice of some who locate their frustrations in that domain. Children may be subjected to considerable pressure to achieve. Environments may be changed by moving to another residence, community, or region. Work conditions may be altered by seeking a transfer, a similar job with a different employer, or a radical change. Some corporate employees cut loose to begin their own businesses, often in quite different areas.

For women many of the same dilemmas of role losses and shifts occur at about the same time. However, they have quite a different context of expectations, identities, and values (Rubin, 1979). Becoming a person of recognized productivity in her own right rather than as one who nurtures others requires considerable change in orientation as well as a willingness to cope with the conflicting definitions of others. Housewives-mothers take up dropped careers or prepare for new ones. And for some, new or recovered leisure investments may be employed to seek significant change in life. Physical fitness, an artistic discipline, a craft, travel, or immersion in some community enterprise may become central to identities as well as the allocation of time and other resources.

It would appear that more people adjust than revolt. More find ways of coping with problems that do not call for radical change or risk than abandon established investments to begin anew. For such people leisure engagements that offer some promise of newness in self-definitions, social relationships, or status rewards may take precedence. For others negative evaluations in major roles may lead to withdrawal from active engagement and a retreat into smaller and safer worlds. Leisure may offer stability and a lack of competence evaluation as well as opportunities to develop new interests and abilities. Some will seek "role comfort" (Kelly, 1983) rather than challenge, low intensity engagements rather than those that may produce stress (Gunter and Gunter, 1980).

Whether or not life is radically restructured in the later middle years, it would seem that reevaluation is a common theme (Rapoport and Rapoport, 1975). Choices between stability and change may lead to undramatic revisions rather than personal revolutions. In any case, the transitions of the period are important to leisure:

- Childrearing responsibilities change from primary care to more distanced support and then to launching. During the period, children change from leisure constraints to objects of planning, to companions, and sometimes to resistant or deviant family members.
- As children enter school and in time leave the residence, mothers who did not remain in the labor market may return. Often the main motivation is related to increasing household costs or the need to be the main financial supporter of the family. For single-parent families time and resources for leisure may be quite restricted. For dual-career families with higher incomes schedule conflicts and time constraints may be partly balanced by greater financial latitude.

- Although children remain a focus of meaning and investment through most of this period, toward the end parents may be reevaluating many of their orientations, including leisure. Their own personal development and satisfaction may become more salient in leisure choices for adults who believe that as workers and parents they have earned the right to do some things for themselves. This fosters interest in many kinds of self-development activity as well as travel and other costly leisure.
- In some cases, the interests of children may provide a resocialization experience for parents who learn while supporting school or after-school activities.

In general, the interweaving of the resources and expectations associated with role careers is seen as the context for leisure in this period. The age and developmental engagements of children have considerable impact on parents. The rise and fall of intimate relationships is central to social contexts, goals, and meanings of much adult leisure. Developing and expressing relationships remain central, but the significant others may change. Work roles are salient to leisure in the provision of resources, the imposition of schedules and other constraints, and the waxing or waning centrality of the work career. Life in this highly institutionalized period is integrated with almost every enterprise in some way shaped and directed by an individual's set of roles. However, those roles change continually and often dramatically during this period, which is less stable for many than traditional views suggest. Withdrawal, reengagement, and even experimentation in leisure may characterize some phases of the middle years.

Both work and family may provide basic identities for men and women in this period. Identification with an occupation or a workplace is more obvious than identification with a family unit or residence, but probably no more common. Leisure, on the other hand, may be more variable. For those experiencing disruption in work and family roles, leisure may offer substitute identities as well as opportunities for associations with congenial and communicative others. In the time of preparation for later maturity, the reevaluation process may lead to more attention to personal fulfillment, social integration, or experiences of pleasure. The transition that takes a limited future into account may refocus attention on the self and satisfaction that may be lost if not seized now.

Full Maturity: Age 45 to Retirement. Gordon (1980) labels the developmental dilemma of this period as dignity versus control. The precipitating factor seems to be a consciousness that the remaining years of life are limited. Life is down to the last third of its span. Life's meaning, if not already established, must formulated for the individual. The age of forty five is probably arbitrary. Later maturity may occur earlier for some who experience disruptive events that require a serious reevaluation and reconstituting of life. For others whose lives develop more or less on schedule and as expected, there may not seem to be any real transition in late maturity at all. They go on toward the final periods with considerable continuity. The values and investments that have worked for them in the past remain viable. Life is "ok"—if less than perfect.

However, there are changes. Women experience menopause with associated physical change. Men also find that their metabolic systems are different. For some, physical appearance becomes a major concern when these changes are manifest. Occupational advancement may level off for some and even recede for others. Those whose technical or physical proficiences are no longer competitive with younger workers may be released from long-held positions and find reentry into the labor market on an acceptable level difficult or impossible. Although launching of children seldom means the cessation of all parental opportunities and obligations, the focus of time and meaning on parenting responsibilities may be lost for some for whom care and nurture had been life's central meaning. At the same time there may be a loss of control over goals, decisions, resources, and environments. Life seldom turns out just as expected. In late maturity the evidence is mostly in, and there may seem to be little a person can do about the outcomes. Children, work, community, and other significant elements of life cannot be determined by the decisions or desires of the mature adult. The lack of further work advancement may be a major factor in a shift from work to leisure as the major context for achievement (Veroff, 1980).

A study of orientations and life investments by Wolfe and Kolb (1979) locates significant shifts in salience during the middle years. Men in their early forties often experience a sharp drop in their investments in work careers and the personal relations associated with the workplace. Some increase their attention to family and especially marriage. However, for many the new preoccupation is with the expression and development of the self. Women's patterns, however, were found to be quite different. Seeing their investment during their twenties to have been focused on the family, many attempt to reach out to a career. Women's personal investment in family while nurturing young children may be followed by greater investment in career. In their forties, both family and career are given major attention, with the division probably reflecting different life-styles and orientations. Wolfe and Kolb found that midlife women often believe that they have not been able to devote adequate resources to their own development. Both men and women were likely to seek affirmation of their worth and competence externally, from the significant others related to their primary social roles. The major shift in later maturity is away from the primacy of the work career and toward investment in the self and in intimate relationships. However, the post-midlife period also tends to be one in which adults seek a balance among the life investments of family, self, work, and leisure. Both self-expression and the "generativity" of contributing to the lives of others emerge as goals along with those related to central roles.

Gordon suggests that leisure in this period may be reoriented to fulfill some of the developmental needs that arise. Leisure may be an environment for expressive relationships in which the aim is responsive warmth and acceptance rather than achievement of instrumental goals. Further, leisure may help alleviate the despair that Erikson holds to be the demon of later middle age (Erikson, 1950:98). Leisure may also yield some structure to life when the reduction of some roles opens unfilled spaces. There may be a reinvestment in some forms of leisure, especially by those with discretionary time and income increased by the reduction of parental obligations.

Family-life-cycle analysis reveals a profound change since the 1880s. A period that did not usually exist at that time, the postparental preretirement stage, is now the longest in the family life cycle. A century ago, one parent usually died by the time the last child left home. Now the postparental period averages about twenty years. Except for the lowest-income households, it may be the time of fullest discretion over resources. For some it may be a time of reinvestment in leisure. For others it is a period of entrenchment in what remains of work, family, residential, and immediate community contexts. Some travel and some reroof the garage. Some begin painting again and some watch more TV. Some seek new friends and some discard many old ones.

The place of leisure in this time of consolidation and review varies from person to person. Some look back, settle for where they have been and what they have become, and seek security and acceptance. Others want something more in the limited time remaining and prepare to make changes in their priorities and allocations. Dignity may most often be sought in what is known and safe. Autonomy may be sought in some new context, investment, or enterprise. What is evident is that leisure may rise in salience as options in other roles are closed off. When employment is largely playing out the string and children are establishing their own lives, leisure may be the domain remaining somewhat open. Waiting to be a grandparent and weeding the lawn may not be enough.

One critical element in later maturity is the quality of intimate relationships. Communication and sharing with primary others is a major resource for enhancing pleasure and coping with problems. Therefore, a major function of leisure is to provide a context for the expression, maintenance, and enrichment of intimacy. Whether focused on the traditional family gatherings or ongoing sharing, life may be oriented more and more toward leisure that brings together those for whom one really cares, both friends and family. The shift toward intimacy may be more dramatic for men than women, with their growth related to events more than relationships (Ryff, 1985).

Culmination: A Time of Consolidation

Gordon divides the final period of life into two parts: active retirement and disability when health problems limit activity. Referring to this final period as "Culmination" emphasizes the positive aspects of drawing together the themes of the life course, the process Erikson (1950) calls "integrity." Retirement is not seen as a relinquishing of meaning and accomplishment but rather as a developmental period with its own tasks and possibilities. The analysis that follows will be limited to the active period, to those often referred to as the "young old." Gordon identifies the developmental dilemma as meaningful integration versus autonomy.

One aim of most of the "young old" is to maintain their independence in both the maintenance functions and meanings of life. They prefer to have control of their own lives, to be able to continue to choose how they invest themselves and their resources. Fear of eventual dependence haunts those who look ahead to a possible time of disability in which they may become a burden to others. Therefore, some time and effort are given to making arrangements and preparing environments in which they can be independent as long as possible. In order to accomplish this task the older person has to begin to accept the inevitability of death and the probability of some decline in functions. Coming to terms with the limits of life, however, does not mean that retirement adults are just waiting to die.

The other side of the dilemma is the attempt to pull life together, both in meaning and in shaping some outcomes from life investments. Gordon refers to "meaningful integration" as the sharing of life with the persons who are most highly valued. Affective involvement may be combined with weighing and interpreting the meaning of the life course in terms that place family and close friends at the center. This means that the "Who am I?" question is still salient. A valued identity, which others too may appreciate, may involve components such as past work roles, contributions to the development of significant others, social integration with informal and formal groups, and leisure accomplishments (Havighurst, 1973; Gordon, Gaitz, and Scott, 1976). Looking back is more than reminiscence: it is a putting together of events and outcomes in ways that yield an interpretation of life that has demonstrated competence and worth.

Expressivity in personal relationships may become more important (Rosow, 1967; Cherlin, 1983). There is a melding of companionship and helping in later years. Those friends and kin with whom an older person has the strongest affective bonds are also most likely to be confidants, provide emotional support, and share leisure activities (Kelly, Steinkamp, and Kelly, 1986). They are also frequently those who live close by and are readily available (Lawton, 1985). As a consequence, meaningful integration with primary others is a central dimension in every domain of life—household maintenance, leisure, intimacy, support and counsel, and continued identity as a person of worth and ability whose life has counted for something. Social integration is closely related to an integration of meaning in the final active years.

The recognition that life will not go on forever is frightening for some people and liberating for others. Such a recognition may lead to a reevaluation of life that involves appreciation of persons and investments that have proven most rewarding, an acceptance of the limiting contexts and possibilities of life, and an integration of what has been with what is still possible. People look back for meaning and also look ahead to ask, "What does life mean now that the peaks of productivity and performance are past?" A reassessment of investments often leads to a voluntary disengagement from responsibilities and relationships that no longer afford rewarding outcomes or experiences. It may also lead to a concentration on those possibilities of highest priority. In this realignment it is common for the permeable distinction between leisure and expressive relationships with family and friends largely to disappear. However, leisure may also be a context for the demonstration of continued competence and autonomy. The two dimensions of an interior integration of meaning and an exterior concentration on social integration run through all aspects of adaptation in the culmination period.

Leisure, then, is not just a way to fill empty time (Kelly, 1982b). Shifts in role salience have been identified throughout the life course. Formal retirement is only one event in the usual process of turning attention toward intimate others, self-development, and the expressive engagements of leisure. Although retirement may require a structural adjustment of timetables and schedules, an older person's priorities and purposes have usually been directed away from occupational meanings for some time (Atchley, 1976). Leisure is one life domain in which meaning may be found. For most retirees continuity with engagements previously found to be satisfying characterizes their restructured social time.

Gordon (1980) suggests that leisure may afford opportunities for both continuing investment in self-expressive activity and for exploration of new possibilities. It can provide a context for trying engagements for which blocks of time were not previously available as well as for greater focus on investments known to be satisfying. Leisure socialization does not end at any age but may continue as long as there are the resources for participation.

In a study of older adults in Peoria, Illinois, leisure was the dominant life interest for only a few of the 400 in the sample (Kelly, Steinkamp, and Kelly, 1986). Rather, the most common pattern of life investment for those coping well with the changes of later life was that of the "balanced investor" who had built up lines of involvement with family and close friends, productive roles, and expressive engagements. For most with such a pattern, the balance had shifted through the life course, with productive investments giving way in the second half of the life span to those of personal bonding and meaning. However, there were also those who were clearly family-centered, work-focused, or leisure-invested. Leisure, then, for most was found to be one element of life, not separate from personal development or central relationships but integrated into a whole and varied fabric of life. Most of the exceptions were persons whose resources were drastically limited by poverty, health, or some traumatic set of events.

For older adults experiencing a gradual rather than sudden loss of abilities and resources for activity the last period of life may be characterized by geographical and social constriction. Social integration is more and more with immediately available others. Leisure engagements at a distance are reduced and the residence becomes the primary leisure locale. The world is constricted in size and reduced in social complexity. Finally, if there is a period of acute limitation, the main issues are survival and coming to terms with death. However, even then learning continues and the mind may reach out to what have become truly ultimate issues.

Becoming in the Life Course

In tracing the argument thus far, we began with the composition of immediate experiences in leisure. Then, the need to place such experiences in a context of decision that is more than simple choice was analyzed. Existential theory was added to explore how leisure experiences become a part of the decision processes through which persons try to become more of what they believe they might be. The freedom dimension in leisure is more than an idea: it is a necessary element in human becoming.

In this chapter we have gone a step further in analyzing contexts for leisure experience and decision. Still focusing on the individual, we noted that the changing roles of the three major periods of the life course provide one framework for enriching the analysis of leisure's meanings. Leisure was found to be a major social space in which the tasks of human and social development are carried out. The play of childhood, the exploration of adolescence, the intimacy building of young adulthood, competence and personal expression in middle years, and social integration in later life are only a few of the central themes of a developmental view of leisure. Leisure through the life course is a persistent and often central arena for development. It is not separate from the main network of roles and investments but is most often integrated with the whole in some kind of balance that shifts through life's journey. Appropriately, the metaphor of a journey provides an apt approach to the personal openness and freedom that may be sought in leisure. Developmental theory presupposes a dynamic view of life as *becoming*.

The dilemmas outlined also suggest the basis of negation in development. Even within the framework of the model, there is failure to complete central developmental tasks. The child may experience crucial disappointment in playing at productive roles and be inhibited from risking later productive efforts that will be evaluated. An adolescent may suffer such rejection in seeking heterosexual exploration and establishing gender identity that later intimacy development is blocked. The contests of childhood games may inculcate self-definitions of loss rather than success. Failure in preparation for adult roles and identities may truncate development and lead to a life course shunted into a dead-end spur. Such experiences would seem to be common to those who become resigned to their lot in life and deal with change in a mode of accepting adaptation.

Further, the context of the developmental journey has many traps for those who are unaware or ill-equipped. The consequences of poverty, persistent health problems, or other handicaps in the early stages of the journey may persist. Failure to develop may be more a result of externals—socialization, opportunities, and resources—than of some failure to engage in the tasks of personal maturation. Any social system has traps laid in which some are caught and prevented from going on to succeeding roles and opportunities.

In the next two chapters we examine learning and becoming in immediate social contexts. Development is more than a matter of passing through a sequence of roles. We actively engage others on our life journey in ways that have consequences for the kind of persons we become as well as for future role settings. Then, in Chapters 7 and 8, the limitations and distortions possible in the structures of the social system are analyzed. Decisions leading to developmental outcomes—both anticipated and unknown—are a real part of leisure. However, both the dilemmas and the contexts of development may slow, block, or divert those making their way through the complex maze of life.

References

Atchley, Robert. 1976. *The Sociology of Retirement.* New York: Schenkman Bks., Inc.

Baltes, Paul B., and K. Warner Schaie. 1973. *Life-span Developmental Psychology: Personality and Socialization.* New York: Academic Press, Inc.

Caplan, Frank and Theresa. 1973. *The Power of Play.* Garden City: Doubleday & Co., Anchor Books.

Cherlin, Andrew. 1983. "A Sense of History: Recent Research on Aging and the Family." In *Aging in Society,* eds. M. W. Riley, B. Hess, and K. Bond. Hillsdale: Erlbaum, Lawrence, Assocs., Inc.

Csikszentmihalyi, Mihaly. 1981. "Leisure and Socialization." *Social Forces* 60:332–40.

———, and Reed Larson. 1984. *Being Adolescent.* New York: Basic Books, Inc., Publishers.

Dannefer, Dale. 1984. "Adult Development and Social Theory: A Paradigmatic Appraisal." *American Sociological Review* 49:100–116.

Devereaux, Edward. 1976. "Backyard vs. Little League Baseball: The Impoverishment of Children's Games." In *Social Problems in Athletics.* ed. D. Landers. Champaign: University of Illinois Press.

Erikson, Erik. 1950. "Growth and Crises of the Healthy Personality." In *Identity and the Life Cycle,* ed. E. Erikson. New York: International Universities Press.

———. 1963. *Childhood and Society.* New York: W. W. Norton & Company, Inc.

———. 1968. "Identity and Identity Diffusion." In *The Self in Social Interaction,* eds. C. Gordon and K. Gergen. New York: John Wiley & Sons, Inc.

Friedenberg, Edgar. 1959. *The Vanishing Adolescent.* New York: Dell Publishing Co., Inc.

Goldman, Daniel. 1973. "Managerial Mobility and Central Life Interests." *American Sociological Review* 79:119–25.

Gilligan, Carol. 1982. *In a Different Voice.* Cambridge: Harvard University Press.

Gordon, Chad. 1971. "Social Characteristics of Early Adolescence." *Daedalus* 100:932–60.

———, C. Gaitz, and J. Scott. 1976. "Leisure and Lives: Personal Expressivity across the Life Span." In *Handbook of Aging and the Social Sciences,* eds. R. Binstock and E. Shanas. New York: Van Nostrand Reinhold Company.

―――. 1980. "Development of Evaluated Role Identities." *Annual Review of Sociology.* California Annual Reviews, Inc.

Gunter, Billy and Nancy. 1980. "Leisure Styles: A Conceptual Framework for Modern Leisure." *Sociological Quarterly* 21:361–74.

Havighurst, Robert. 1958. *Developmental Tasks and Education.* New York: David McKay Co., Inc.

―――. 1973. "Social Roles, Leisure, and Education." In *The Psychology of Adult Development and Aging,* eds. C. Eisdorfer and M. P. Lawton. Washington, D.C.: American Psychological Association.

Hill, Reuben, and Roy Rodgers. 1964. "The Developmental Approach." In *Handbook of Marriage and the Family,* ed. H. T. Christensen. Chicago: Rand McNally & Company.

Jung, Carl. 1954. *The Development of Personality.* Princeton: Princeton University Press.

Kelly, J. R. 1974. "Socialization Toward Leisure: A Developmental Approach." *Journal of Leisure Research* 6:181–93.

―――. 1977. "Leisure Socialization: Replication and Extension." *Journal of Leisure Research* 9:121–32.

―――. 1978. "Family Leisure in Three Communities." *Journal of Leisure Research* 10:47–60.

―――. 1982a. *Leisure.* Englewood Cliffs: Prentice-Hall, Inc.

―――. 1982b. "Leisure in Later Life: Roles and Identities." In *Life after Work,* ed. N. Osgood. New York: Praeger Publishers, Inc.

―――. 1983. *Leisure Identities and Interactions.* London: George Allen & Unwin Ltd.

―――, and Shelley W. Masar. 1970. "Leisure Identities in the Student-Establishment Transition." Champaign: Leisure Research Laboratory, University of Illinois.

―――, M. Steinkamp, and J. Kelly. 1986. "Later Life Leisure: How They Play in Peoria." *The Gerontologist* (in press).

Kleiber, Douglas A., and J. R. Kelly. "Leisure, Socialization, and the Life Cycle." In *Social Psychological Perspectives on Leisure and Recreation.* ed. S. Iso-ahola. Springfield: Charles C. Thomas, Publisher.

Lawton, M. Powell. 1985. "Activities and Leisure." *Annual Review of Geriatrics.* New York: Van Nostrand Reinhold Company.

Lever, Janet. 1978. "Sex Differences in the Complexity of Children's Play." *American Sociological Review* 84:471–83.

Levinson, Daniel. 1978. *The Seasons of a Man's Life.* New York: Alfred A. Knopf, Inc.

Lynd, Robert and Helen. 1956. *Middletown.* New York: Harcourt Brace Jovanovich, Inc.

Neugarten, Bernice, ed. 1968. *Middle Age and Aging.* Chicago: University of Chicago Press.

Opie, Iona, and Peter Opie. 1969. *Children's Games in Street and Playground.* London: Oxford University Press.

Piaget, Jean. 1952. *Play, Dreams, and Imitation in Childhood.* Trans. by G. Cattegno and F. M. Hodgson. New York: W. W. Norton & Co., Inc.

Rapoport, Rhona and Robert. 1975. *Leisure and the Family Life Cycle*. London: Routledge and Kegan Paul.

Riegel, Klaus F. 1976. *Psychology of Development and History*. New York: Plenum Publishing Corporation.

Riley, Matilda W. 1979. *Aging from Birth to Death: Interdisciplinary Perspectives*. Boulder: Westview Press.

Rodeheaver, Dean, and Nancy Datan. 1985. "Gender and the Vicissitudes of Motivation in Adult Life." In *Motivation in Adulthood,* eds. D. Kleiber and M. Maehr. Greenwich: Jai Press, Inc.

Rosow, Irving. 1967. *Social Integration of the Aged*. New York: The Free Press.

Rubin, Lillian. 1979. *Women of a Certain Age*. New York: Harper & Row, Publishers.

Ryff, Carol. 1985. "Adult Personality Development and the Motivation for Personal Growth." In *Motivation in Adulthood,* eds., D. Kleiber and M. Maehr. Greenwich: Jai Press, Inc.

Snyder, Eldon, and E. Spreitzer. 1976. "Socialization into Sport: An Exploratory Path Analysis." *Research Quarterly* 47:238–45.

Stebbins, Robert. 1979. *Amateurs: On the Margins Between Leisure and Work*. Beverly Hills: Sage Publications, Inc.

Sutton-Smith, Brian. 1971. "Children at Play." *Natural History*. Special supplement on play, pp. 54–59.

Veroff, J., and J. Veroff. 1980. *Social Incentives*. New York: Academic Press.

Wolfe, Donald, and D. Kolb. 1979. "Career Development, Personal Growth, and Experiential Learning." In *Organizational Psychology: a Book of Readings*. 3d ed. ed. D. Kolb. New York: Prentice-Hall, Inc.

CHAPTER 5

Social Identity Theory

Social and personal identities are one mode of analyzing what it is we are becoming in life-course development. We become who we are in a social dialectic of existential and contextual elements.

Even community, in the risk of an "I-thou" relationship, is an existential act as well as a social context of development.

Leisure styles incorporate a common core of accessible activity as well as a balance that changes through the life course.

In enacting social roles we learn social identities—how others define us in those roles—and create our self-defined personal identities.

Intimate bonding is explored, developed, and expressed in leisure. Such leisure requires a freedom *for* community-creating action.

Leisure, then, is one context of identity creation and expression, a process with both continuity and novelty. The relatively open social space of leisure may enhance novelty and change.

Leisure is one life domain in which the creation of identity may be negated and distorted by the pressures and repressions of a mass society.

The concept of social and personal identities provides a transition from individual to social perspectives on leisure.

The previous chapter outlined how leisure has a part in our development through the life course. Not only do role changes affect leisure opportunities and orientations, but our socialization *in* leisure changes focus. The sequence of developmental tasks and dilemmas reorients both the associations and aims of leisure. In the "becoming" process of the life course we develop new attitudes, skills, and self-definitions in leisure as well as in other engagements. Primary attention in the previous analysis was given to the ways in which leisure offers contexts for working out one or both sides of the sequence of developmental dilemmas. In this chapter the focus is more directly on the dialectic between the self and society in the crucial process of identity development.

One theme of the chapter is that of community. *Community* is defined as the set of ongoing relationships in which there is reciprocal inter-action, communication, sharing of tasks or regular activities, and a history of such common enterprise. When such community is on a deeper and more sustained level, it is referred to as *intimacy*. Intimacy is primary community in which the levels of trust and sharing are sustained and include elements of vulnerability and lack of defense against possible hurt and attack. Intimacy may include sexual dimensions; however, just as there may be sexual interaction without intimacy, so there may be intimacy without intercourse.

The first assumption of this approach is that human beings are social animals. The biosocial nature of humankind presupposes conception, nurturing, and development *with* as well as by others of the same species. We develop toward our maturing potential in social contexts. There is no identifiable "real self" that waits within the organism for release. Rather, our means of understanding and communicating what we are and might be are learned from others. Through the life course we are always "becoming" through interaction with others. We become persons in a society.

The second assumption, however, is that we are also existential beings. We act as well as are acted upon. What we become is not just a social determination. We act toward other beings as well as toward the environment in ways that have consequences for what we are becoming. In this process of becoming there is both continuity and change, the persistent and the novel. Therefore, one of the primary requirements of analyzing any identifiable set of social actions and interactions such as leisure is to deal with the dialectic of existential action and social contexts.

One common problem of social analysis has been that only one side of the dialectic is considered. Traditional sociological approaches have tended to ignore the existential. The forces that shape behavior and attitudes are the sole object of research. On the other hand, existential philosophies and behavioral sciences so concentrate on the inner elements of decision that external factors are neglected. This chapter is intended to serve as something of a bridge between the previous attention on the developing and deciding individual and the social context factors that are an integral part of learning and becoming.

Leisure Patterns: Behavior and Meaning

Until the last decade most leisure research had dealt almost exclusively with behaviors, with what people did. More recently issues of meaning have been given greater attention. The integration of the two dimensions is now leading to quite different generalizations about patterns of leisure engagement.

The concept of *style* incorporates both what people do and how they do it. The evident diversity in environments, social contexts, activities, and mental states does not permit taking leisure as a simple or monothematic phenomenon. Further, the same environments and activities may be chosen for different reasons and with different outcomes anticipated. Styles of participation cannot be reduced to quantities of time or categories of activity. The existential element of leisure allows at least part of the meaning of an event or episode to be created in the action.

In some early research an assumption of "stereotypes" (Kelly, 1985) was based on correlational analysis of social position variables and whether or not activities were undertaken. In time, reanalysis of much of the same data disclosed that the similarities in patterns among different social strata were greater than differences. Rates of camping participation, for example, vary little except for the upper elites and those who are poverty-stricken. However, styles of camping can be distinguished by cultural background and social position.

A second approach proposed that most adults seek some sort of balance in their leisure. There may be a dimension of compensation that offers a contrast to work conditions (Wilensky, 1960) as well as choices that reflect the expectations and orientations of economic positions. Most adults balance social and solitary, active and restful, high and low intensity, engagement and escape dimensions in their leisure selections. Further, the balance changes through the life course as meanings related to developmental tasks and social roles rise and fall. Most people do not do just one kind of activity but do a variety of things, seeking different combinations of environments, investments, and outcomes. They seek relaxation at one time and excitement another, risk and also security, social involvement and also separation and quiet. As analyzed in Chapter 4, leisure reflects developmental preoccupations as well as the institutional resources of each period in the life span.

However, yet a third approach has also been found useful in dealing with the realities of empirical findings. National surveys have revealed a significant set of activities that are common to most adults and do not vary greatly through the life course (Kelly, 1983b). This "core" of activities consists for the most part of engagements that are relatively low-cost and accessible. Watching television, interacting informally with other household members, conversing in a variety of settings, and engaging in sexual activity are common to adults through most of the life span. Other such activity includes walking, residential enhancement, reading, and some regular events with kin and friends. This core occupies the greatest amounts of time, especially those periods that must be inserted between scheduled events. Further, core activities that express and develop primary relationships are highly valued by most adults.

The best-supported model of leisure would seem to be one that combines the core and balance approaches. The core tends to cross social lines due largely to relative availability. The core is almost resource-free for those living with others in a residence. The balance, however, tends to vary more through the life course and among those with different access to resources and different sociocultural backgrounds. The balance may include considerable entertainment involvement for late adolescents, family outings for parents, and cultural events for those with higher education levels. Some engagement is expected if one is to be an accepted group member, a "normal" teen, parent, or neighbor. Styles of balance activity are most likely to vary by socioeconomic level, with the wealthy traveling more to upscale locales and resorts. Leisure, then, can be said to have a *career* in which activities and styles change as both personal aims and social resources shift.

One basic question about such change is "Why?" Is it all just a matter of opportunities and socialization? If so, then the shifts and patterns should be quite predictable. Or, do social actors make decisions with direction? Are there some kinds of ends toward which leisure is directed? Do leisure careers have direction as well as change? The analysis of personal and social identities that follows is one answer to that question. The central theme is that of *becoming* in which there are some ideas and feelings about what we would like to be. However, this theme is expressed and developed in the social contexts of community and intimacy, among those who are important to us.

Existential Community

The concept of existential community uniting decision and relationships is not a contradiction in terms. Most simply, there is decision involved in inaugurating and developing a personal relationship. Further, as any existential decision involves risk, so the decision to engage in a relationship of sharing and trust—of intimacy—entails the risk of hurt, betrayal, manipulation, and loss. Community comes at a cost when the self is invested and vulnerability is exposed. While there may be no relationship wholly without residual or final defenses and self-protection, community with depth of commitment incorporates a lowering of protective mechanisms.

As introduced in Chapter 3, Martin Buber offered a disjunctive typology of relationships in his *I and Thou* (1937). He describes the common "I-it" relationship in which one person is used for the ends of another. The relationship is instrumental. Most secondary relationships are explicitly instrumental and often based on acknowledged terms of exchange. "I will do this for you, and in return you will do that for me." Economic exchange is only the most obvious of such relationships.

In many social situations the primary set of expectations is of reciprocal action with mutual benefits. Whatever sharing of expressivity may occur in the encounter is secondary to the aims of gratification, exchange, or task completion.

However, there is also the "I-thou" relationship in which personal sharing, communication, and acceptance of the other are primary. The end is the relationship itself. Common or reciprocal action is not manipulative but enriching for the relationship. First, there is acceptance of the other. Second, there is a commitment to build the relationship through the giving and receiving of knowledge, the disclosure of self that is at the center of real acceptance. Third, there is bonding that may develop in mutual activity but is not limited to contexts of either play or production. Fourth, there is a commitment to honesty and to the relationship itself. All of this involves great risk. The possibilities of betrayal by the other in the revelation of such knowledge, exploitation for the gain of the other, or some breaking of the trust are always present. To risk "I-thou" relationships is an existential decision in the fullest sense.

The "I-thou" relationship is the essence of intimacy. Intimacy is the most personal level of community. Both intimacy and community incorporate commitment, recognized terms of relationship, and accepted continuity. Community may involve several others in a group commitment to be together in some specific context or action. Intimacy is the most personal level of community, limited to the dyad or small group. Intimacy has the widest scope of action because the relationship is most pervasive. The dyadic intimacy of a marriage may range from the intensity of sexual intercourse and other communicative openness to the legal arrangements of property sharing and transmission. Intimacy that is not tied to such a central social institution as the family may nonetheless be quite deep in its sharing and commitment to the other as well as its openness of disclosure and vulnerability. In an "I-thou" relationship the essence is sharing with the other rather than use of the other. In such sharing a variety of actions may express the relationship. The wider the sharing, the greater the risk. Such human relationships are multidimensional, with sexuality as only one possible component.

We will return to the concepts of intimacy and community in addressing functional arguments for leisure in human society. From this perspective leisure is defined as social space for the expression and development of intimacy and community, as freedom *for* primary relationships. The "I-thou" approach to intimacy will underly that analysis. However, first we examine the larger context of social relationships. The premise is that we learn who we are in society and especially in community.

Leisure and Social Identity _____

Soon after we are born, we are assigned a name by the nurturing institution—in most cultures the family—that gives us our first place in the society. However, the specification of who we are and how others identify us is a lifelong process. Our social identities are learned and developed in a social dialectic rather than simply assigned. The terminology we will employ to examine this process distinguishes three kinds of identity (McCall and Simmons, 1978; Kelly, 1983a:92):

- *Personal identity* is one's self-definition in a role context.
- *Social identity* is the definition by others of our taking a role.
- *Role identity* is how a role is enacted, a style of behavior.

A role is the general set of expectations attached to a position in a social institution. "Classroom teacher" is a role. The role is taken and enacted in a particular style by each actor. The enactment, however unique to that actor, is carried out within the norms that are accepted for the role in that context. Therefore, I may define myself as a particular kind of teacher, assuming the role identity of my style of teaching. In the institution of the university my social identity as a teacher is reinforced by a set of identifying symbols, legal terms, rewards and sanctions, and expectations.

Some identities are assigned and others assumed. Assigned, or ascribed, identities are those into which we are born or those we are given through some institutional process. In a stratified social system there are ascribed statuses based on the family of birth, placement in the economy, or some other mechanism of placement. During younger years we are assigned by law to the identity of student. In some systems sets of formal examinations then assign further student identity to some and worker status to others. The social identities ascribed by others may be linked to the social system or be specific to a particular group or setting. However, even for assigned identities, there remains the question of how the identity is accepted, defined, and enacted. Acceptance and rebellion are both possible in response to assignment.

Assumed, or achieved, identities are those we reach out to take. We may strive to achieve identity as an athlete, political figure, scholar, shop-floor leader, or family provider. The process of assignment and assumption of social identities is lifelong. It combines the opportunity structures of the society with the initiative and action of the individual. In all cases the process begins with where we are. In a rigidly stratified, or caste, system the opportunities are limited to those possible for a birth caste. In a society with multiple paths for moving toward new identities, choices and resources may be more critical than birth placement. In any society an actor either accepts assigned placement or acts to initiate change.

Further, individuals claim and are assigned multiple identities. In a variety of contexts we have somewhat different identities. We may be scholar at school and nurturer at home, fiery leader on the playing field and docile factory hand at work. Social identities are more than social positions. They incorporate how others view and define us in those positions. As a consequence, social identities are learned. They involve our interpreting the responses of others as we assume identities and our defining the meaning of the social identity for us. There is, then, a kind of dialectic between the social identity and the personal identity, how others define us in social contexts and how we define ourselves. Personal identities are not built in a vacuum but in the give-and-take of social interaction. Further, the multiple identities of our lives include those that persist from one setting to another and those that are specific to one environment or even event. Such identities shift through the life course as age-related expectations change and we move from one institutional environment to another.

The structures of social and personal identities are found in the institutional role sequences of the life course. From dependent infant to dependent frail elder, we move through a prescribed series of roles that expand into a complex set of work, family, education, community, and leisure identities and then in later years contract in complexity and scope. The general roles are both assigned and assumed. Our social identities within those roles are based on how others define our role performance. Our personal identities are how we define ourselves as actors within the role context. The other pole of the dialectic from structure is the line of action by which the actor seeks to establish personal identity as social identity. We try to achieve agreement between our style of enacting a role and how others interpret our performance.

Note how the language of the theater has reoccurred in the foregoing description. One metaphor of social analysis is that of the social drama in which individuals "play" parts or roles in ways that are directed toward securing particular responses (Brissett and Edgeley, 1974; Goffman, 1957). The dialectic of social action is more than "taking" a role and meeting expectations. Interaction is more than conformity to norms. Rather, we assume a role in ways that attempt to make it ours. Our portrayals may be within the general dictates of the drama and script we are assigned, but we add our own interpretations to the role. We may imitate the style of another player, or we may strive to be unique. In either case, we are choosing something of how we will play the role—be it that of father, daughter, teacher, or teammate.

The intent of such role playing—whether overt or hidden—is to elicit certain kinds of responsive interpretations from others. We play to the critics, the significant others whom we believe to have power to determine rewards or alter the contexts of our performance. In doing this we employ a variety of methods and instruments. We take advantage of the screening of our stage to hide some action and display what we want seen by others (Goffman, 1957). We use all the symbols of appearance to announce to others who we are and how we would like to be defined (Stone, 1962). Clothing is only an initial symbol of our identities. All roles do not require uniforms, but there are general norms for apparel appropriate to most social positions. However, our choice within or on the margins of those norms announces something of how we want to enact the role. Apparel is reinforced by demeanor, posture, vocabulary and manner of speaking, and a series of other signs and symbols of identity. For example, it does not take experienced students long to evaluate how a new instructor defines the teacher role and what reciprocal student portrayals are expected. Such portrayals are differentiated by age, sex, and other ascriptions but are also open to a range of presentations. Further, we may wish to carry our salient identities to other settings. The trucker wears his company or rig-brand cap to a ball game. The business executive carries the "right" briefcase onto the plane. The skier wears the patch-emblazoned jacket to the grocery store. In so many ways social actors seek to present personal identities that will be established as social identities.

Learning Who We Are among Others

George Herbert Mead (1934) laid the basis for a sociological analysis of how we learn to be social actors. He described how the child develops the ability to act toward the self, to interpret his or her own behavior as intentioned. The "me" as the object of intentioned action by the "I" is playing the role of the self. In an expanding social universe the child comes to act toward specific others in ways that elicit desired responses. In a later period action may be directed toward "generalized others" who occupy certain positions and may be expected to produce predictable behaviors based on the roles they occupy. On the one hand, the child is learning about "social structure" in which roles determine behavior and permit a design of action. On the other hand, the child is learning that a role may be performed in ways that produce different responses and definitions of the actor in the role. For example, taking or being assigned the role of pitcher in a baseball game not only determines a complex set of reciprocal expectations but also is action that will be interpreted and evaluated by other players and observers.

However, such learning about social contexts is only part of the process. Charles Horton Cooley (1902) supplemented the perspective with the concept of the "looking-glass self" in which the actor is continually learning about the self from others. We develop self-images by interpreting the responses of others to our actions and presentations. According to Cooley (1902:153), this self-image consists of three elements: imagining how we appear to others, interpreting the judgment of others, and experiencing feelings such as pride or shame. In this spiral process the actor presents the self in some line of action intended to elicit certain interpretations by others. The others respond in ways that are then perceived and interpreted. That interpretation impacts the personal identity of the actor in that situation and may have lasting consequences for self-definitions and future presentations.

The point is that we are continually learning and relearning who we are. In one episode a presentation may be affirmed and a self-image strengthened. In another the response may be disconfirming and require us either to explain it away or to revise our personal identity. Especially in our younger years, the self that we imagine ourselves to be is likely to be assaulted by the responses of others who reject our portrayal through scorn, neglect, or derision. We discover in time who we are and some of the limits of what we may become in the process of social interaction.

As already described, leisure and play contexts may be quite central to this process. Not only for children and youth but for adults in any period leisure identities may be critical for affirming and developing our self-definitions as men and women. Games, contests, encounters, and interludes are often more problematic than the relatively fixed social settings of work or household. In leisure actors may be most able to try out identities and read the results. The contained nature of many leisure episodes and events allows for feedback that can be immediately perceived and interpreted.

Ralph Turner (1968) highlights the action-evaluation side of the dialectic by pointing to the concepts of self-esteem and self-estimation. Individuals form self-concepts in a selective process. All roles are not equally salient. Rather, on the basis of perceived adequacy in assuming roles and feedback on performance we evaluate ourselves in those "ego-involved" roles. Self-esteem is based on this evaluation of role adequacy. A more generalized self-estimate is combined out of the role-based evaluations. Through the life course some roles may be abandoned based on negative evaluation and others given greater salience in the general self-estimate. Therefore, how we define ourselves is learned in the socially based process of role enactment, performance evaluation, and the interpretation of the responses of significant others.

There is, then, an ongoing dialectic of self-definition and definition by others. This is made up of both particularities and generalities. Some occasions play an especially critical part in this process. Perhaps the exposure of performance and the composition of the perceived evaluating group make a single success or failure critical. In other cases the actor may predefine a series of situations as of low salience for self-esteem so that even marked and public failure has little consequence. We may "hedge our bets" in situations where we anticipate little likelihood of achieving a clearly strong role performance by announcing probable failure. We may play the role, employing symbols communicating that we do not engage in the action seriously.

Erving Goffman (1967) in one of his insightful excursions into face-to-face interaction used a gambling term to refer to "action" episodes. The "action" is where something is on the line, where there is some risk. His examples are chiefly those of leisure settings in which outcomes will be recognized. Gambling, games and sports, social enterprises seeking sexual response, and other social gatherings in which outcomes are problematic are the settings for "action." The action itself is fateful in the sense of having outcomes without being ultimately serious. Yet, it is in such encounters that self-estimates may be tried out, tested, evaluated, and revised. For example, Goffman (1967:210f) suggested that there are many locales for "making out" with other persons in sexual encounters. These encounters are processual in that signs of interest may be offered and exchanged in ways that permit safe withdrawal without serious loss of face. However, as the game progresses from interest signaling to flirtation to the risk of an action proposal, the possible loss escalates. Insofar as such encounters are central to self-esteem, to self-definitions of sexual competence and attractiveness as a man or woman, they entail greater and greater risk as they progress. Flirtation can always be redefined as a game without serious action intent. "Your place or mine" renders such redefinition difficult. Not only the action episode but also a critical dimension of self-definition is on the line. And the outcome may be a lesson learned and remembered all too well.

The Spectrum of Roles

One unfortunate sociological misconstruction has been the frequent pairing of work and leisure as the poles of life in society. The implicit model is that there is a fundamental choice between the domains of work and leisure, with work usually having priority. Leisure, then, is defined as a separate and secondary sphere in some undefined way opposed to work. Community and household studies offer a more complex and accurate model. Social actors—people—carry on their lives

with a multiplicity of role relationships. Rather than paired dichoto-
mies, these roles are enacted in ways that are sometimes complementary and sometimes in conflict, occasionally separate and often related,
seldom static and generally changing.

The role spectrum for any person consists of roles currently central,
roles that are in the process of being left behind, and roles that are on
the horizon but not yet entered. These roles are based in the major
institutions of the social system—work, family and intimate groups,
the polity, community, religion, and leisure. Further, in almost all such
roles there are both productive and expressive elements. At work there
may be play in episodes of action for its own sake. In the family there
is depth of both obligation and enjoyment of the other without condition.
In leisure there is both disciplined and sustained goal-oriented activity
and self-contained immersion in the moment. In religion there is boredom and self-transcendent experience. And most adults are in a continual process of juggling, balancing, integrating, separating, and re-
formulating those role engagements.

Not all roles are alike. There is some specialization in function and
orientation. Therefore, we tend to enter the various roles with different
expectations and intents. Religion is more likely to be a serious realm
rather than leisure. Intimate communities—family or other—are expected to be most accepting and profound in communication. Work settings generally have the most pervasive performance requirements and
evaluations. Leisure is most likely to be for its own sake, for the moment
and the experience itself. Yet, almost every dimension of any role context is to be found in some degree in all the others. More important,
the self that essays the variety of role enactments has some continuity.
What we learn about ourselves in one context has carry-over into the
others. Life is not either/or—in freedom or obligation, fun or drudgery,
community or alienation.

The Paradox of Leisure

Some are uncomfortable with the idea of leisure *roles*. Leisure according to some ideals is too rarified, free, and expressive to incorporate
the regular and shared expectations of roles. Even from the more open
perspective of role playing rather than role taking, roles seem too
structured to be leisure. Such a perspective ignores the obvious fact
that many of the activities assumed to be leisure—sports, games, and
parties as examples—have quite clear and explicit role designations
and expectations (Kelly, 1983a).

On the other hand, the reservation is correct in raising the issue of
openness and freedom. Is it not also the case that leisure is most likely
to have at least a relative openness in outcome or structure? Is it not

true that leisure settings tend to be most amenable to experimentation with portrayals and self-presentations? Leisure may not be free of role structure or evaluation, but it may still be the domain of life in which there is greatest latitude for experimentation and the least serious consequences for failure. The stakes may be limited by agreement and social definition. Leisure is not separate from the rest of life but may also incorporate some disengagement from the central and persistent commitments of the life course. The play of flirtation described earlier may have outcomes that alter self-evaluations but not the drastic consequences of failure in a central negotiation of a marriage.

The paradox of leisure, then, is that it is more often both/and than either/or. Even though weighted toward freedom, it has its disciplines. Even though focused on the experience, it may produce lasting results. Even though separate and playful, it has structures and roles. The freedom, flow experience, and self-containment are relative rather than absolute. And in it all, the self is learning something more about the crucial questions of "Who am I?" and "What may I become?"

Here I am offering a label for this perspective, one that contains some of the paradox of leisure and of all social action. The general perspective will be called *social existentialism*. It is a perspective that takes seriously both the social contexts of action and the reality of decision with consequences. At the center of the approach is this idea of *role identity* in which the actor plays even the most structured role with some individuality and personal style. And in this portrayal the actor is always "becoming" in the process of learning a little more about how the self is defined by others. Much of the subsequent analysis draws out the basis and implications of this perspective.

Bonding, Intimacy, and Selfhood

There have already been hints in this presentation that leisure may be considered as at least a quasi social institution. From a functional perspective this is possible only if leisure provides something the society requires for existence. In the sociological paradigm that posits the social system as an integrated set of institutions with complementary functions, each institution is said to have primary functions that make essential contributions to the survival of the system. In ordinary structure-functional analysis the school prepares one for adult participation, the church adds value consensus and reinforcement, the polity contributes control and defense, the family provides reproduction and sexual regulation, and the economy offers the production of goods. From this perspective leisure is defined only as secondary to the primary institutions. Moreover, leisure is most often viewed as an adjunct to the economy as the mode through which workers are rested and refreshed for their primary duties and as a context for learning the mechanisms of role taking.

More recently, evidence of the importance of leisure in the value schemes of individuals has led to some reassessment of the place of leisure in the social system. Further, research on leisure engagement has made it plain that it is much more than a time for recuperation to most people. Rather, leisure combines personal and social meanings in activity that receives priority in allocations of resources far beyond a residual resting up for what is really important. Is it adequate to assign leisure to a strictly secondary place in the society when institutions that are significant to far fewer adult lives, such as the church and school, are held as central?

In a presentation that incorporates analysis of animal behavior, historical and anthropological evidence, and current sociology of leisure, Neil Cheek and William Burch (1976) argue that leisure is a social institution. The argument is based on more than resource allocation and personal priorities. Given the biosocial nature of humankind, the bonding of individuals in lasting relationships is seen as necessary. Primary groups are the first contexts of reproduction, nurture, and learning for the young. In such groups persons learn and develop, receive protection and shelter, and find their base of operation for social participation. While the family is the first such primary group with special responsibilites for sexual access, reproduction, social identification, nurture and protection of infants, and often property holding and transmission, the family does not exhaust the range of primary groups. For the child that range expands into the play world of the neighborhood, the socializing world of the school, and in time all the contexts of close and persistent relationships.

Cheek and Burch's analysis is that leisure takes such an important place in values and priorities because it is the social space in which primary relationships are developed, expressed, and enhanced. Social bonding in the sense of intimacy is more than a functional operation based on mutual tasks. Bonding has its affective components of emotional sharing. It has components of the mutual experiences of personal histories, built-up communicative symbol systems, personal self-disclosure based on trust, and the expression of commitment. Intimate bonding is more than a function of the family. Significant relationships may be inaugurated and developed in any social context—work, school, church, or neighborhood. However, for relationships to grow and deepen, there must be more than propinquity and common tasks. The expressive elements of intimacy—affection, humor, self-disclosure, playfulness, and other enriching engagement—require some openness for mutual action. The relative freedom and noninstrumental character of leisure are a central context of the development and expression of intimacy. Relationships are built up and expressed in the spaces of play, of activity that is not bounded and focused by predetermined outcomes. Such play may occur in designated times and places for leisure. At least as often, expressive intimacy occurs in the interstitial moments of playful exchange that offer interludes in the midst of institutional enterprises. Nevertheless, from this perspective bonding requires an environment that permits and encourages affective sharing to come to the fore. Leisure, conceived of in terms of relative freedom and noninstrumental expression, is that environment.

The argument moves beyond primary bonding to suggest that social identification is also facilitated by leisure. The learned preferences that are called *tastes* serve as an instrument of identifying membership in some groups and separation from others. Such tastes, often learned and expressed in leisure, are bonding elements of identification. . The "we group" of primary others is one that shares more than activity. Primary groups of social identification display their agreement styles and modes of behavior in ways that symbolize inclusion and define exclusion. Some such groups are based on ethnic cultures into which members are born. Some are particular to generational cohorts and demonstrate both the independence and group solidarity of youth. Some are rooted in social stratification and give public evidence of inclusion in an elite social strata. All provide both a personal sense and public symbolism of belonging. Tastes in clothing, activities, environments, behavioral styles, consumer spending, language, and other factors are signs of bonding with a particular group.

Now the argument comes full circle. The primary groups described— whether familial, peer, ethnic, stratified, developmentally expressive, or based on some other shared dimension—are the first source of social identity. We define ourselves in our relationships to such groups. We are individuals, but always individuals who have learned and are learning who we are in such contexts of bonding. Further, such primary groups not only shape our life-styles and tastes but include the significant others with greatest influence over our choices and self-evaluations. Negative feedback from those outside our primary groups can be written off as irrelevant, misinformed, or otherwise in error. Negative or affirmative responses from those with whom we identify have to be taken seriously. When we define ourselves so fundamentally in relation to family, intimate dyad, ethnic association, or a play group such as a team, we are most vulnerable to responses from that source. Who we are and who we are not are both defined in and by those to whom we are most deeply bonded.

Neil Cheek (1982) has analyzed certain settings of leisure in terms of their contribution to such bonding. He asks why it is that some settings—nature-based outdoor resources in particular—are so highly valued even though most people can enter them infrequently. His answer is that focusing on natural beauty, freedom from space limitations, and change elements is not enough. Rather, most research has demonstrated that people enter such environments in groups, usually groups of intimates (Field and O'Leary, 1974). When people move out of ordinary environments with their routinized tasks, the natural setting becomes a context for expressive interaction. There is opportunity to engage in affective interaction that communicates and develops the relationships themselves. Cheek argues that our most important relationships, those that are central to who we are, require such expressive interaction as they meet the functional requirements of economic support and maintenance. We are beings who need intimacy, the multidimensional sharing of *being together* as well as doing things together. In a social ecology characterized by considerable fragmentation and dispersion, leisure is a necessary social space for the location, development, and enrichment of primary relationships.

In 120 depth interviews with adults age forty and over in Peoria, Illinois, leisure was seldom found to be a separate domain of life cut off from friends and family (Kelly, in press). Rather, the leisure that persisted as significant through the later life course tended to be integrated with such primary others. Some individuals had retained important investments in leisure that were central to self-definitions of competence and worth and separate from family. Some had identified with particular leisure groups that were an alternative to family, work, religious, or neighborhood associations. However, most often leisure was integrated with family and other intimates. Especially for those with fewer cultural resources and less educational background, leisure most often was primarily a setting for interaction with close friends or family.

From some perspectives this bonding dimension of leisure is a denial of its freedom (Dumazedier, 1967; de Grazia, 1964). Because such primary relationships are replete with role expectations and obligations, the very idea of *family leisure* seems a contradiction. Leisure, from this point of view, has to be separated from institutional roles rather than integrated with them. Whatever the validity of the concept, it runs counter to social reality. Human actors become and act out who they are in the company of those who matter to them, not in some special segregation. We are truly social beings in so many interrelated and profound ways. Leisure that is so special that it is unrelated to intimate bonding would then be truly secondary and residual.

As defined thus far, leisure is not freedom *from* all constraint and structure. Rather, leisure is freedom *for* real action in the midst of life. Leisure is constituted out of decisive action that creates what does not now exist. Leisure is doing something new, creating new reality, and becoming something more. That action may at some times be a withdrawal, a separation from other engagements. At other times it is a more intense concentration on engagement with another person, on communication, or on a challenge. The activity is a context for decisive action for the self. When the decision includes significant others—as it so often does—then the relationship itself is part of the becoming, the creation of something more than existed before. Leisure is freedom for the investment of self, in intimate bonding as well as in self-defining activity.

Is leisure secondary to other roles and meanings? Sometimes it is. Is leisure a fundamental space for the expression of our being as socially bonded and defined? Sometimes that is the case also. Leisure, then, is one theme of life found as a dimension of many times and spaces rather than set apart from all others.

Leisure and Identity

Of course, when leisure is seen as relative freedom in the midst of life rather than as residual, the potential for negative as well as positive outcomes is accentuated. When leisure becomes an important life space for the building, expressing, and evaluating of identities and intimacy, then losses are not trivial and limited to the moment. A number of examples will serve to illustrate the problem:

- When a young man's identity is concentrated on prowess in a particular sport, failure to make the team or to perform up to expectations can prompt withdrawal or a loss of confidence in other developmental contexts.
- Social acceptance is so crucial to the self-esteem of both male and female adolescents that integration or exclusion from critical events such as parties or excursions may evoke waves of negative self-evaluation with consequences for all possibilities of social initiative.
- Leisure settings are most common for the establishment, exploration, and development of intimate dyads. Success in preparation-period enterprises of dating and interaction-oriented events is likely to undergird a sense of competence in such settings and relationships. Failure or rejection will have carry-over into the process when it

becomes most serious, when longer-term relationships and commitments are being sought.

- In the establishment period expectations for marriage include satisfaction with companionship in a variety of settings. Leisure has been found to be an issue producing conflict as well as an opportunity to expand the affective components of a relationship. The expectation that couples will enjoy being together and sharing experiences is a significant part of marriage along with fulfillment of parental, economic support, maintenance, and nurturing tasks.

- In later life social networks that provide emotional support, shared and communicated caring, and specific help also have their leisure components. The family, friends, and neighbors who become the primary community of support are at the same time those with whom leisure is shared (Kelly, 1982). Especially as the circle of intimacy is reduced by death, illness, and mobility restrictions, the community of significant and helpful others tends to be those with whom all aspects of life are shared. In the Peoria study intimate friendships on which older persons rely emotionally as well as in other ways were developed and expressed in a variety of shared nonwork experiences. On the other hand, loss of intimate community can turn the last years into a lonely and bitter period.

The Dialectic of the Personal and the Social

There seem to be two avenues of significant loss in intimacy and community. The first is the reduction or blocking of the initiative toward relationships of depth due to past failure. When a person defines himself or herself as unwanted, unacceptable, or incapable of intimacy, then taking the risk of reaching out and offering is blocked by fear of failure. The risk of being hurt, rejected, or even humiliated again is just too much. A loss or failure to develop social self-esteem prevents some from trying. Such failure and fear may be expressed in a variety of defense mechanisms that transfer the explanations to others and produce personal alienation from love.

Richard Sennett (1974) has described a second kind of alienation that seeks intimacy at the cost of community. He refers to the "tyranny of intimacy" in which closeness is promulgated as a moral goal. All relationships of value are to become those with aims of intimacy and of self-expression. Such a concentration on intimacy at the cost of wider community is a product of the loss of effective action outside the immediate. Personal identity is developed when social identities are blocked, subverted, or spoiled. Lines of action are directed toward the self in a kind of narcissism that requires even the most immediate

others to contribute to the self. Lost is the distancing of wider community that allows for play, risk, and the freedom to create. All action
is serious because everything is directed toward the self. Public action
is not political in the sense of critical analysis and remediation but
economic in acting primarily as a consumer. The self with its accepted
social position and possessions is the center of life, with action oriented
in toward the center rather than out toward the social world. Sennett
(1974:266–67) argues that the larger community is a context of play
that makes possible creativity. When all is directed toward the self,
then play becomes too risky and too consequential.

Again there is a dialectic here. Leisure is a context of intimacy, and
intimate relations are central to the development and acceptance of
the self. From this perspective leisure is critical to discovering and
enhancing who we are—our personal identities. From the counter perspective leisure is separated enough that its outcomes are not always
critically consequential. Leisure may be a context of play in which we
experiment with ourselves, our environments, and the outcomes of novel
action. Further, a preoccupation with the self—narcissism—eliminates
the possibility of action directed outward toward the institutional contexts of our lives. Yet, without such public action, our actions become
circumscribed by the social forces that we have neglected. Effectual
action is limited to such a tiny sphere that we are cut off from the
larger society. We become social consumers rather than social actors.
Leisure, then, from the dialectical perspective is both intimate and
public. It involves both personal and social identities as we learn and
develop them in a multilayered social world.

Personal Identity in a Structured World

Erik Erikson (1950:89) developed the concept of "ego identity" to
combine sequential and persistent elements in identity formation. Even
a child is said to form a sense of ego identity, defined as the cumulative
confidence in "one's ability to maintain inner sameness and continuity."
However, this inner confidence is matched by outer confirmation. How
the self is defined by others also has continuity. *Ego identity* is the
integration of relatively consistent self-other definitions across a variety
of interaction contexts. It is a mutual reinforcement of personal and
social identities *within* the reflexive interpretation of the self by the
self. Through each developmental period, effectual action produces an
affirmative ego identity as a self who can complete lines of action. The
various domains of life are not separated, but all have some part in
the development of ego identity.

Leisure, then, has a place in this process—not cut off from other
contexts but related to them in the personal continuity of ego identity

and the social continuities of our multiple roles in which the same people have more than one reciprocal role. Nevertheless, leisure does have some special characteristics that stress certain aspects of the development of self-definitions. Most have been described earlier and will only be illustrated here.

1. Leisure events are often discrete, with a beginning and end. A game, social event, project, or adventure may be brief or prolonged. However, there is often a definition of event in time and space. As a result, there are outcomes that can be specified and measured. The climber makes it up and down the cliff face. The contest has a conclusion and a final score. The dyadic exploration leads to a decision or dwindles away. The framed episodes of much leisure can be assessed as to outcomes. Actors can evaluate their competence and effectuality according to results, not just the often-ambiguous responses of others. Such results may then become markers in self-evaluation.

2. Some leisure episodes and events are also relatively nonserious in the sense that the outcomes do not threaten central social roles and investments. The won or lost sports contest, the completed or incompleted pass, the graceful or ungainly coffee table or other project, and the cross-cultural exchange seldom determine economic positions or rewards, the survival of intimate relationships, or fundamental identities. They are arenas for risk in which success may enhance ego identity with the loss of failure relatively minor. Leisure may be a space for trying and testing with potential loss controlled.

3. In the same way, leisure offers the possibility of novelty and exploration. Central roles as worker, parent, lover, or leader may be too valued to risk in any experiment. However, in leisure—in such a segregated environment as that of a resort—it may be possible to try something quite new. Whether or not you fall off the sailboard ten times, forget your lines in the evening show, or have to admit exhaustion and quit does not bring about a collapse of your entire world. On the other hand, in a life that has become routinized and largely devoid of the excitement of the new, the chance to launch out can be a critical factor in revitalization.

4. In a bureaucracy or any occupational setting with set norms of behavior, any change in self-presentation may be quite upsetting to others and may provoke negative repercussions. However, a leisure setting for interaction may allow for more flexibility. Trying out a comic characterization, taking charge in a decision-making moment, or just cutting loose and being alone can express elements of our identities that we have repressed in other social environments. And in the less-constrained context we may learn something more about who we might become.

5. The indeterminacy of much leisure is also a provision for self-testing. At the beginning of the card game, tennis match, or regatta, no one has a score advantage. The conclusion is not known in advance, however uneven the past results. Right there in that event there are measures of skill development, learning, and concentration on the tasks. Whereas the aim of most business and bureaucratic organization is to minimize the indeterminate and problematic, leisure may be devised conversely. The problematic elements are measurable and uncertain without being ultimately fateful. They may be cumulative without being final.

Therefore, as previously proposed, leisure offers some special opportunities for the development of personal identities in social settings in which there is interpretable feedback. The relative freedom of leisure becomes an arena for *becoming*. Further, the reciprocities of interaction can often be delineated and interpreted with a greater clarity than in other institutions.

Social Identity in Mass Society

Working on who we are and what we may become does not necessarily require a narcissistic preoccupation with self. Rather, becoming is most likely in interchange with other actors. Our social nature makes solitary self-redefinition difficult. Yet, defining what we would like to become and establishing lines of action that move us directly toward those goals are not without problems. An existential approach to identity must be balanced by a realistic assessment of barriers as well as opportunities.

Because such becoming is a social as well as existential process, the nature of the social context is critical. In Chapter 8 we explore the relation of social division and differential power to leisure. However, whether one takes a conflict or consensus view of the social system, there is general agreement that modern society is a mass society. Industrialization, urbanization, mass media, and a routinization of social services have diminished the personal dimensions of interactions. Mass media, mass transit, eight-lane expressways, mass retailing, institutionalization of religion, and corporate health services are just examples of the factors affecting the loss of the personal quality of interchange among people who know each other. We are identified by numbers and plastic cards to the clerk, physician, and teacher. We often gain knowledge through impersonal TV and work for corporations where no officer knows our names. In such a mass society achieving a social identity outside a very small circle seems almost impossible. Once we step outside our residence or confront an economic world beyond our little work group, we are really no one at all.

It is such anonymity that turns so many adults to home and family as their primary investments. Here we are known, our presence recognized and absence noted, and what we do has some impact. It is no wonder that we may feel alone and inconsequential in a society in which adult children may live hundreds of miles away from their parents, marriages seem less and less secure, and intimate relationships are often serial rather than integrated into a stable community. We seek social identification, a recognition of who we are. We strive for some sense of effectuality, assurance that in some way our lives make a difference. Orrin Klapp (1969) has analyzed ways in which individuals seek some social identity in mass society. When intimacy is disappointing and work becomes a drag, conventional ways of seeking relatedness and meaning do not provide their promised fulfillment. Ethnicity may give some a sense of belonging and history. Religion can yield a sense of lasting meaning as well as a community of those who reinforce belief in such meaning. Voluntary organizations give some a context of recognition and community. For many, however, such conventional means of social identity are not intense enough. Some seek more gripping attachments and more vivid symbols of identification.

As a result, there are those who attach themselves to religious groups and cults that offer an exciting promise of being special and a new community filled with fervor and direction. Others join nonreligious cults that offer a promise of life-changing engagement with committed devotees, a distinguishing vocabulary and set of symbols, and an avenue for action. Such groups may center around meditative awareness, political rebellion, or an activity such as running. What they have in common is that they lift the committed out of mass anonymity in which nothing seems to make a difference into an emotion-filled community that knows and values its members and establishes lines of action considered effective.

Of course, most people do not join such cults or movements. They live out their lives in relatively conventional ways and make do with the meaning, satisfaction, and identification afforded in their ordinary roles. Some become so deeply involved in one role—whether family, work, or leisure—that they believe they know who they are. Their personal identities—as father, toolmaker, or softball coach—are validated in the social circles where they are recognized. They live in a world bounded by such recognition and view the larger worlds with an uneasy suspicion. They blame politicians, computers, and intellectuals—singly and collectively—for all that seems wrong with mass society.

However, there are some who have been found to seek and secure their social identities in another way. They are those whom Robert Stebbins (1979) calls "amateurs," people who engage in "serious leisure." He examines the extraordinary involvement in leisure of musicians, archaeologists, baseball players, and community theater participants. They are distinguished from more ordinary leisure participants by a number of factors:

1. Their involvement is quite intense. They not only play hard but also tend to give considerable thought and imaginative attention to the activity at other places and times.
2. Their standards of performance are essentially the same as professionals who make their livelihood at the activity. Therefore, they invest considerable time and disciplined effort in mastering the skills required.
3. They define themselves in terms of the leisure role. They are, first of all, actors or violists, pitchers or rock-hounds. The investment in the activity is rewarded, at least within a small circle of fellows, with a recognition of competence.
4. They tend to shape their goals and, when possible, their timetables around the investment. Even when remunerative employment has to claim priority in scheduling most of the year, they arrange special times and opportunities around the activity.
5. They define their significant others—those whose esteem they most value—from among their avocational peers. Their primary community, at least outside the family, is the immediate group of fellow participants.
6. They often seek a wider recognition for this social identity through the use of symbols that can be taken into a variety of contexts. Equipment and labeled apparel are especially popular as identifying level of accomplishment in the nonwork investment.

Such leisure is not viewed as relaxation from or recuperation for more central and demanding roles. Rather, such leisure may be a "central life investment" into which are poured resources and from which are expected considerable meaning and satisfaction. The meanings may be multiple: the investment yields a depth of involvement or excitement in the time of participation. It offers not only companionship during participation but also an ongoing community for interaction. In a world in which being special is difficult, the investment yields satisfying personal and social identities. The "amateur" receives positive feedback from important others that she or he is someone who counts in this context. And the disciplined effort usually returns the satisfaction of demonstrated and evaluated competence. All of this, of course, may be labeled satisfaction or even pleasure. But the dimensions are based on the central investment of self and resources, of intense time and disciplined learning.

Some kinds of activities lend themselves best to such investment. They are those that offer an essentially infinite field for improvement of skill, clear feedback of evaluation, a community of peers and exemplars, and some system of recognition and acceptance. Amateurs are not a majority in any society or social strata. However, they are more than an odd minority who have gone some deviant way. Amateurs exemplify the extent to which leisure can provide a primary context for the development of identity. Further, such devotees may be on the leading edge of adaptation to social change if traditional economic roles offer central investment meaning to a smaller and smaller proportion of adults in a postindustrial society.

Also, in a less encompassing mode, leisure engagement may become at least a secondary identity for many in mass society. Thousands wear insignia of their football team on the day of an important match. Bowling-team shirts from an industrial league are worn in other settings. Caps identify those who own a particular brand of motorized leisure vehicle. Shoes announce a devotion to running. Sports equipment is carried on the airplane instead of business-related luggage. The distinctive apparel of a sport is worn to the supermarket. All these are little ways of telling the world that a person is not just a computer-identified number or a nameless cog in the economic machine. More and more, these symbols and signs of "being someone" are leisure-related. There is developing a quasi ethnicity around leisure investments that is made up of participation style and identification with a community. Activity is more than doing something; it is also *being someone* in that activity engagement. In the next chapter some of the meaning of this for styles of self-presentation in interaction contexts is explored. The thrust of the analysis is that we may seek to develop and establish social identities in those social spaces that offer the greatest likelihood of recognition. Leisure is only one of those social spaces, but for many it is an important one.

An Analytical Transition

In Chapters 2 through 5 the unit of analysis has been the individual actor. We began with individual states of consciousness related to leisure and moved on to decision, development, and now to identities. All of this is in the framework of life as a process of becoming. In this chapter we began a transition from the individual to the social. Personal identities are more than definitions constructed in self-examination and analysis. They are formed in a dialectical process that involves the interpreted definitions that others communicate to us. Further, they take shape in the context of the social identities that we develop through the life course. We learn who we are by taking action in a world that also tells us who we are. The concept of *identity* brings together the existential line of action with the role context of expectations and learned meanings. Through the symbol systems of the society we interpret the responses of others and reformulate our self-definitions.

This dialectical process takes place in leisure as well as in the environments of the traditional social institutions. Further, as examined in the next chapter, it occurs in the processual episodes and events of social interaction. Leisure is existential in its decisions, orientations, and styles. However, it is also social in its learned forms, meanings, and consequences for selfhood. At this point in the overall analysis we move from a focus on the existential to the social, with the concepts of personal, social, and role identity as mediators. All of this remains in a life-course framework in which the sequence of roles provides a context for continual learning and relearning who we are and might become.

References

Brissett, Dennis, and C. Edgeley, eds. 1974. *Life as Theatre*. Chicago: Aldine Publishing Company.

Buber, Martin. 1937. *I and Thou*. Edinburgh: T. and T. Clark.

Cheek, Neil. 1982. "Social Cohesion and Outdoor Recreation." In *Social Benefits of Outdoor Recreation*, ed. J. Kelly. Champaign: Leisure Research Laboratory, University of Illinois.

———, and W. Burch. 1976. *The Social Organization of Leisure in Human Society*. New York: Harper & Row, Publishers.

Cooley, Charles H. 1902. *Human Nature and the Social Order*. New York: Charles Scribner's Sons.

de Grazia, Sebastian. 1964. *Of Time, Work, and Leisure*. New York: Doubleday & Co., Anchor Books.

Dumazedier, Joffre. 1967. *Toward a Society of Leisure*. Trans. by S. E. McClure. New York: The Free Press.

Erikson, Erik. 1968. "Identity, psychosocial." In *International Encyclopedia of the Social Sciences*, ed. D. Sills. New York: Macmillan Publishing Co., Inc.

Field, Donald, and J. O'Leary. 1973. "Social Groups as a Basis for Assessing Participation in Selected Water Activities." *Journal of Leisure Research* 5:16–25.

Goffman, Erving. 1957. *The Presentation of the Self in Everyday Life*. New York: Doubleday & Co., Anchor Books.

———. 1967. *Interaction Ritual*. New York: Doubleday & Co., Anchor Books.

Kelly, J. R. 1982. "Leisure in Later Life: Roles and Identities." In *Life after Work*, ed. N. Osgood. New York: Praeger Publishers, Inc.

———. 1983a. *Leisure Identities and Interactions*. London: George Allen & Unwin Ltd.

———. 1983b. "Leisure Styles: A Hidden Core." *Leisure Sciences* 5:321–38.

———. 1985. "Sources of Leisure Styles." In *Recreation and Leisure: Issues*. 2d ed. eds. T. Goodale and P. Witt. State College: Venture Publishing.

———. In press. *Peoria Winter: Later Life Styles and Resources*. Lexington: Lexington Books.

Klapp, Orrin. 1969. *Collective Search for Identity*. New York: Holt, Rinehart and Winston.

McCall, George, and J. Simmons. 1978. *Identities and Interactions*. rev. ed. New York: The Free Press.

Mead, George H. 1934. *Mind, Self, and Society*. Chicago: University of Chicago Press.

Sennett, Richard. 1974. *The Fall of Public Man: On the Social Psychology of Capitalism*. New York: Random House, Vintage Books.

Stebbins, Robert. 1979. *Amateurs: On the Margin Between Work and Leisure*. Beverly Hills: Sage Publications, Inc.

Stone, Gregory. 1962. "Appearance and the Self." In *Human Behavior and Social Process,* ed. A. Rose. New York: Houghton Mifflin Company.

Turner, Ralph. 1968. "Role: Sociological Aspects." In *International Encyclopedia of the Social Sciences,* ed. D. Sills. New York: Macmillan Publishing Co., Inc.

Wilensky, Harold. 1961. "The Uneven Distribution of Leisure: The Impact of Economic Growth on 'Free Time'." In *Work and Leisure,* ed. E. Smigel. New Haven: College and University Press.

CHAPTER 6

Interaction Theory

ISSUES

The processual character of leisure is demonstrated in social interaction.

In social interaction we learn both *who* we are (identity) and *where* we are in the social system.

Social interaction may itself be leisure when the primary action is the encounter. The problematic element of leisure interaction may be defined as nonserious when outcomes do not have negative social consequences that impact institutional roles.

Metalanguage is employed to signal that a play episode is being developed in the midst of an interaction setting. Such communication may itself be the main ingredient of play. Play episodes are often interstitial interludes in the midst of nonleisure settings. Leisure, then, may be created in the midst of almost any social interaction.

Face-to-face leisure interaction, or social play, involves shared definitions of openness in the situation that enable actors to try out different portrayals and presentations. Leisure events may be constructed with greater or lesser consequence and intensity.

The rules and rituals of social interaction may enable actors to negate openness through the manipulation of communication and action toward predetermined ends.

The metaphors examined thus far lead to a common dimension of *process*. Leisure is not an undifferentiated block of time or activity; it is not a single attitude, action, decision, or identity. Leisure may occur in a specially defined time and space or in a moment in the midst of highly task-oriented enterprises. However, in any case, leisure occurrences have some career—they may be anticipated, begin, develop, end, and be recollected. Whether complex events of long duration or momentary episodes, leisure occurrences are processual.

The process character of leisure is most evident when the occurrence is social. Leisure is in part individual experience, a state of consciousness. However, that state occurs in an environment of some kind of action, be it physical or totally imaginative. Leisure is also in part decision. But the decision inaugurates action that has a beginning, development, and end. That action, momentary or substantial in time, has dimensions connoted by *play* as openness and the existential possibility of creation. In the context of leisure personal development and identity definition are part of the outcome, even when the attention focus is fully on the experience itself. Leisure is more than action; leisure is meaning. For an individual leisure may have both immediate and persistent meaning as something is learned about the self in the environment. Embedded in any meaningful activity are the processes of becoming, learning, and creating who we are.

Further, leisure is a context for learning *where* we are. All that we do and are takes place in time and space environments and also in sociocultural contexts. As Mead (1934) described, games teach the nature of social roles and the "generalized other," just as any social engagement teaches something about the social system. Not only the consistent features of institutional organization and value orientations but also the nuances and subtleties of more specific situations are learned and revised in any social interaction. How do factors such as age, gender identification, defined relationships of kin and nonkin, and ethnicity shape what is expected of us? What are the crucial differences in behavior, vocabularies, and symbols of presentation from one setting to another? When are normal cultural restrictions on behavior set aside in a period of "carnival" or an event of separated privacy? In every processual occurrence we are both learning and applying what we believe we already know.

Process and Environments

While some leisure occurs entirely in the mind and imagination, most of the activity we designate as leisure literally takes *place*. The environments are one factor in the process. Some activities, such as sports, require a specially designed or prepared space. The meaning of sited outdoor activities, such as backpacking, is so closely tied to the environment as to be something quite different if moved from a mountain wilderness to an agricultural road. Further, environmental factors such as population density, perceived crowding, resource quality, and climate have been found to have profound influence on both choices and behavior.

However, these are only the most obvious aspects of environmental factors. Perhaps even more significant for most leisure are the characteristics of the *social environments*. Most leisure takes place in some social context. Other people are not only present but are part of some intentioned interaction. Even watching television seems to be less a solitary activity than once assumed (Robinson, 1977). The episodes of leisure are so frequently composed of social interaction that *play* generally suggests nonserious social activity. The institutional setting is not limited to recreation locales. Social interaction that is nonserious, for its own sake, intrinsic rather than extrinsic in aim, expressive rather than productive, or relatively bounded in explicit meaning can occur in family, community, work, political, and religious locales. Various studies of workplace behavior, including one of shipyard workers (Brown et al., 1973), demonstrate that the banter is more than relief from being on task. Social acceptance of "being one of the lads" requires an ability to enter into playful exchanges employing sets of symbols, vocabularies, and shared experiences. A study of an English secondary school found that a high proportion of the communicative interchange was spontaneous rather than role-determined and playful rather than task-related (Woods, 1979). In fact, the author suggests that such social play is necessary if the social fabric of the institution is not to become rigid and stultifying.

The social environments of leisure may be referred to in a number of ways. Here three terms are used almost, but not quite, interchangeably. *Social space* refers to the time and space parameters that give some structure to interaction. *Social world,* when referring to a leisure occurrence, connotes the agreed-on cultural values and symbols that give "meaning shape" to the interaction. *Social context* is the most inclusive term and encompasses all the elements of setting from spatial design to symbols, values, roles, and institutional resources. All three denote the parameters of time, space, composition of the interacting others, and institutional structures. The perspective here is that leisure can occur in any social context but not without being to some degree shaped by the specifics of the social environment.

Interaction as Leisure

In the previous chapters primary attention was given to the individual actors who engage in leisure behaviors. In this transition to a more social perspective the focus is on the nature of the interaction. Individuals *act,* but their interaction forms a process that can be identified and analyzed. The unit of analysis here will be the episode inserted in a larger context or event constructed through intentioned interaction. What happens in a leisure occurrence? What makes it leisure, and how does leisure or play emerge in social settings of face-to-face interaction? The contexts vary, but the object of analysis is always the bounded process of interaction in which the primary meaning is in the process itself.

Process, Structure, and Freedom _____

The *structures,* or continuities, of social interaction may be explicit or implicit, legislated or taken-for-granted. Erving Goffman (1967, 1974) made the implicit structures of face-to-face interaction the central theme of his analyses of a variety of social settings from peasant cottages to modern hospitals and from bureaucracies to games. He adopted a dramaturgical metaphor in which the actor constructs a line of action with responding viewers in mind. The social setting includes taken-for-granted sets of communication symbols and behavioral expectations that regulate how both actor and audience interpret that line. Goffman might stress the implicit defining rules in analyzing a mental hospital and the self-defining aims of the actor in describing gaming "action." However, there is always the dialectic between the covert and overt "rules" and the "action" that seeks a meaningful social outcome. And this action takes place in a social space that "frames" the activity with predefined schemes of interpretation (Goffman, 1974).

Social interaction is viewed as a process in which actors attempt to direct their action in ways that elicit preferred responses from interacting or viewing others. These responses are intended to validate, revise, or create social identities consistent with what the actor would like to be and become. The process, then, involves self-presentation designed to announce and establish the intended self through signs and symbolic action. In the interaction the actor is constantly "reading" the responses of others in the process and adjusting both the action and the aims to maintain some consistency of interpretation. In some episodes there is a specific testing of others' agreement on the success of the presentation when they are given a closing sign of acceptance or rejection of the identity. In a formal setting an audience may applaud or sit on their hands. In a dyadic encounter there may be an agreement or objection to a proposed joint action. In many episodes the symbolic responses are more subtle, yet interpretable.

Many leisure episodes are essentially such social interactions. In a variety of settings the real "action" is the meaningful encounter. The "frame" of the encounter may be quite informal, as around the coffee machine in an office. Or it may be extremely rigid, as in a sports contest with a book of formal rules overlaid with a complex set of "second-level" expectations of etiquette and behavioral norms. Goffman does not argue that implicit rules make all interaction essentially the same. Rather, different social environments contain quite different interactions. And these differences are central to understanding the variety of leisure settings, forms, and styles.

The varieties of social spaces are one dimension in differentiating leisure forms. Varieties in social worlds are part of the differences in styles of behavior. From this variety we can only offer illustrations of the dialectic between intentioned action and the overt and covert structures that frame the episodes.

The Problematic in Games. Some social leisure, of course, is just aimless "being together." The actors have no particular line of action other than letting the communication develop its own course—skipping from one peripheral comment to another or stopping to burrow deeply into a particular issue or action. However, many leisure episodes are characterized by a combination of structured context with open-ended yet measured outcomes. There is the dimension of the problematic woven through the event from beginning to end. The most obvious examples are games in which some bounded course of interaction results in an outcome that differentiates players. The game begins with a relatively equal baseline of resources, or an even score. The rules of playing are constructed to ensure that the outcome will be reached according to the variables within the game. Excitement and interest are produced when elements of chance mix with those of skill in determining the outcome. The most skilled player or team does not always win. From one perspective the game is an exercise in manipulation of its constituent rules and implements to attempt to determine the outcome. With its parameters of beginning and end, the game is a milieu for action in which the participants attempt to exercise superior skill, induce opponents to err, or otherwise manipulate the results. The meaning, then, is composed of both process and outcome made possible by the problematic structure of the game.

Games, however, are not the only leisure occurrences with a central problematic theme. In games we may attempt to develop strategies for establishing lines of action, demonstrating power or effectual action, or even determining the reciprocal action of others. A Monopoly board or backgammon set is not required for such strategies to be attempted. In all kinds of face-to-face encounters actors play games of relative power or dependence, seek to control the mode of communication to establish lines of action and control the options of others, and shape the consequent behaviors of those with whom they interact. Again, leisure settings may be defined as social spaces in which problematic outcomes are assumed. Who interacts with whom at a party and the style of communication are not predetermined. Who goes home with whom is sometimes open to negotiation. Who pays for drinks may be a game within a larger leisure context. Even recruiting and dismissing particular persons for an episode may be a problematic game employing skill, strategies, and implicit norms.

In *Interaction Ritual,* Goffman (1967) suggests several elements of the problematic in constructed leisure episodes. Action begins with an agreement on the "game" itself—its rules, procedures, and measures. The sequence of action moves from an initial "squaring off" to determination, disclosure, and settlement within a time frame brief enough to bound the action and hold attention. Whether applicable to a social encounter, sport, game, or other problematic exchange, the structure of the rules is the context for the problematic outcome. Further, the implicit norms may include procedures by which all players maintain "face," or identity, in a mutual scheme for avoiding embarrassment.

Leisure and the Nonconsequential. Another common element in face-to-face interaction in leisure episodes is that they are defined as "nonserious" (Huizenga, 1950). Even though the outcomes are problematic, they are contained within the social space of the event. The winner does not retain power over the loser in other social spaces or relationships. The settlement does not require a loss of resources or authority that cuts across all roles and determines other outcomes. As already suggested, this self-containment of much leisure offers an opportunity for riskful enterprise that minimizes the scope of loss. The penalties for losing a golf match are not on a par with losing a major account or contract in business. Failure to properly calculate a bid in bridge is not the same as failure to properly calculate the weight-bearing capacity of a bridge across a canyon.

In social interaction the bounded outcomes of leisure provide a context for concentrating on the interaction. It may not be that important who wins the game, scores highest in the contest, or receives the award. In fact, many leisure events are so constructed that the participation is the primary end, and differentiated measures are omitted entirely. Georg Simmel (1950) called interaction with the primary aim of interaction for mutual pleasure "sociability." In a social space defined as separate, actors "play" social games. Scores are not announced. Records are not kept. Celebrations incorporate all participants as equals rather than single out a few elite players. In such cases, whether the concentration on activity and interaction is part of the event design or implicit for some participants, there is greater freedom to concentrate on the relationships. The interaction process itself is primary. The spectacle, celebration, trip, game, or event becomes an environment for communication and a context for sharing. Not only "just hanging around" but also scheduled events may have their primary meaning in the process of social exchange that occurs.

The outcome of a leisure episode may not be the final score at all. Rather, the affective attachment of two persons or a group may be expressed or enhanced in the process. The point of backyard badminton is not to demonstrate superiority but to encourage joint participation for a father and daughter and to provide a chance for the father to *join* in the mutual activity. The dinner party is not primarily a provision of food, however carefully prepared, but a recognition and development of relationships. The trip to the pub is not really for drinking but for conversation in a social world where obligations and social ranking are left behind. The leisure event may be more a context than contest, more a social world than an arena for accomplishment.

Negative Social Consequences. This does not mean that all such leisure episodes and events have positive social results. Community is not always strengthened, communication enriched, or personal identities reinforced. There is always the possibility of inauthentic lines of action in which actors seek to manipulate others without regard for consequences for the others. Games may be used to seek advantage. Episodes may be staged to embarrass, trick, or otherwise put others at a disadvantage. Communication may be distorted in ways that obscure intents and manipulate others into responses that do them harm.

The fundamental aim of authentic social interaction is to develop bonding or community. Therefore, a prerequisite is honesty of presentation. Inauthentic interaction is aimed at putting others into a position in which their responses are determined. The game is played neither for the structured experience nor as an environment for communication. Rather, the intent is to coerce some redefinition of the relationship. The party conversation is not a mutual exploration of interests, an unfolding of selves in a process of sharing, but a contrived line of communication designed to gain some specific acquiescence from the other. The mode of interaction is not reciprocity but control. The very nature of leisure—activity for its own sake—is violated in such manipulation. Yet, considerable interaction that passes for leisure because it takes place in designated settings—bars, health spas, or dances—is just such behavior. The "action" is defined as gaining self-serving responses from others, no matter what devices are employed to gain the objectives. The basic structure of the game, fairness and equal access to resources, is violated by this inauthenticity.

Conventions of Communication. Any social world has its communicative conventions. Both language ge and metalanguage are understood as bearers of particular meaning in the situation. Examples of this process may be abstracted from almost any leisure setting. One of the most vivid illustrations is found in urban establishments in which eating and drinking is a context for meeting others to form temporary dyads or groups. There are not only first-level rules about seating, paying for drinks, tipping, courtesy, loudness or overt physical behavior, and other conduct, but there are second-level conventions that regulate behavior. For example, there are many bars—wine bars for youth or speciality bars for singles—that are orchestrated as settings where meeting and negotiating further relationships are fostered. Studies of such bars demonstrates that straightforward language is only the surface of communication. Gestures, body posture, direction of attention, eye contact, level of conversation that is loud enough to include fringe persons or quiet to exclude, and other behaviors are signs of distance or access.

Communication is carried out through a multitude of media. Prolonged eye contact may be an invitation, whereas a direct look followed by a firm turning away signals a lack of interest. Sitting square at the bar may indicate serious drinking, while turning at an angle open to others signifies a readiness to enter into conversation. Conventions of meeting vary from one setting to another. Direct self-introduction is acceptable at one, with a second-party introduction required at another. In some the bartender acts as go-between, while at others employed personnel keep a careful distance from the action. Even the way that clothing is adjusted and altered from the business setting to the bar suggests social intent (Cavan, 1967; Kelly, 1983:158). The point is that the *metacommunication* in which symbols and nonverbal signs are employed to signal the context of verbal exchange is integral to the interaction. Such metacommunication is constantly evaluated by others to test for consistency, congruities of signs and behaviors.

How does such interaction become leisure—expressive and bounded with its own meaning? One analysis uses the metacommunication concept to analyze a variety of interaction episodes (Lynch, 1979). The analyst defines episodes as play when they are redirected away from serious exchanges of information or opinion to the fantastic, imaginative, or bizarre. He describes conversations that take a sharp turn when a sign is given and acknowledged that from now on "This is play." Then the interchange can explore the humor of uniting the incongruous and out-of-context in the mutual construction of a "What if" word game. "What if" we flew to Acapulco tonight? What if we were to develop a sociological theory of Gilbert and Sullivan parody? What if the university were to become primarily an entertainment center in a society that decided it already knows too much? What if life were not a parody? A play episode requires a starting signal, a processual agreement on the terms of the play, a willingness to construct the episode, a signal of closing, and a transition back to normal.

The playfulness of an interchange is quite fragile and can be altered by a single moment of metacommunication. In an exchange of playful flirting a hand resting on an arm just a moment longer can signal that the game could become serious. An expression of hurt or surprise can turn a conversational fantasy into reality when actual feelings have to be dealt with. A number of signals that "This has gone too far" can bring the dream castle to earth in a hurry. The point is that metacommunication as well as direct exchange is involved in turning an interaction to play. Of course, there are social worlds in which such play is expected and others in which it may take several signals to communicate that even in this serious meeting it is time for a playful break. In gatherings with regular membership one or more actors may have accepted roles as jesters to break long stretches of on-task activity.

One function of metalanguage is to signal that the normal social rules and conventions are about to be suspended. In a committee meeting accepted rules of order are enriched by a set of taken-for-granted conventions about deference, appropriate vocabulary, and other behaviors. A deliberate violation of such conventions may signal that what is to follow is nonserious, a diversion from the task orientation inaugurated as an "interlude" in the proceedings (Kleiber, 1984). Inserted in the midst of business is a ludic moment—a break in direction or intensity from the normal process. In that moment,—if the group signals agreement—there will be a brief period of leisure, a play episode with its own self-contained meaning.

Interstitial Leisure. Leisure as social interaction may take place anywhere. Such leisure, or playful interludes, are more than silliness or diversion from manifest tasks. Why is it that adults usually list various forms of interaction with family and friends as the kind of leisure they would least want to give up? Why is it that teens spend so much time "hanging out" and "fooling around" rather than engaging in clearly constructive enterprises? Why is it that "Third Age" persons in their culmination period, especially the last surviving member of a nuclear family, value personal interaction with others so highly? Informal social interaction, moments and minutes of communication, are not breaks from what is important in life. They are the very fabric of life woven through all the patterns of our life material. They are expressive and yet bonding; they are essential to our being and becoming as social animals.

Such interstitial leisure in the workplace has already been introduced, whether in office, shipyard, or school. For households and families interaction is itself the common substance of leisure (Kelly, 1983:124f). In studies in four communities, three in the United States and one in the United Kingdom, family and marital interaction in some form dominated lists of kinds of leisure evaluated as most important. Affection and intimacy, visiting family and friends, couple activity, play with children, family outings, and conversations were at or near the top of the rankings. Enjoyment of companions and strengthening of primary relationships were central reasons for leisure decisions. And this does not include the special events related to vacations and trips. Even the time is significant. John Robinson (1977) reports that social interaction follows only watching television in the amount of time not devoted to sleep, employment, and household and personal care. Although such interaction is frequently a mixture of lines of action in which expression and task designation, play and planning, are intertwined, it is usually the affective and bonding elements that bring members together.

When leisure is reduced to designated activities and events, it is possible that much is lost. First, there is all the solitary leisure that is conducted in the mind and imagination. Daydreaming and inattention may lift the spirit and make tedium endurable. Although there has not been as much research on daydreaming as its frequency would warrant, indications suggest that mental construction of distant or nonexistent episodes contributes more to getting through the day than we acknowledge. Second, there is all the social interaction that lightens the grimness of considerable task attention and spices the sameness of life's routines. As the existential sociologists argue, ordinary day-to-day life is much more an affective schema than a rational construct. We commonly live in a world of feelings and playful behavior at least as much as of goal-directed action and serious attention.

In this process of interaction with its seemingly infinite variation in modes of communication and action, there is more structure than appears on the surface. The levels of conventions and the interpretive consistency of language produce a high degree of predictable regularity. Nevertheless, shot through the process are moments with self-contained meaning as well as events that are designed for expression and openness. The freedom of leisure, then, is found not only in decisions about lines of action and allocation of resources but also in the ability to lift a moment out of its institutional context and requirements. We do play in all sorts of settings and occasions. Although inaugurating such play in some contexts entails risk, it is done—more often than some task-oriented officials would like.

Leisure Episodes and Events

The distinction between structured events and less-defined episodes is useful in locating leisure in its social contexts. Events tend to be planned and defined and usually occupy a clear social space. Episodes are more ad hoc in their occurrence. An episode may seem to just happen in the midst of a social context with other manifest aims. From the previous analysis of how interstitial leisure occurs it is evident that an essential condition in a social setting is some agreement on playfulness. Leisure requires a shared definition of its conditions: that the episode is to have its own integrity and bounded meaning.

Pure play may be difficult to find in most social contexts. The sharing of the definition may not be complete. The carry-over of role obligations and authority may alloy the freedom in many exchanges. The power to reward or sanction in other contexts may intrude on leisure episodes and events in which participants have other domains of association. In such situations what appears to be play may actually, but subtly, be serious. The failure to offer proper deference in leisure may prove costly in work or family contexts. The metacommunication of freedom and playfulness may be quickly rescinded by an actor with institutional power.

For family interaction the boundaries between self-contained play and consequential interaction may be especially fragile. Parent-child role expectations are seldom completely abandoned in play. The complex web of communication symbols that develop between marriage partners may intrude at any moment of interaction. Further, the fact that such relationships have a career means that transitions in such intimate relationships may make some communication and interaction ambiguous or ambivalent in meaning. Remember that the dilemmas of development are reciprocal in their role contexts. The security versus challenge themes often create conflicting aims for participants in a leisure event. Or individual actors may be ambivalent about their own intentions. We enter leisure as whole persons who can seldom completely throw off the identities of the rest of life. As a consequence, leisure episodes may be brief when "real world" roles are asserted. Leisure events may be complex in interaction meanings when multiple identities are mixed into the process. Nevertheless, there are a number of elements that characterize face-to-face leisure episodes and events, and several are explored in the following discussion.

Shared Definitions of Play. The sharing of agreed-on contextual meaning for an interaction episode depends on the success of communication in direct speech and metalanguage. Especially in environments where leisure and play tend to be rare, the signal of "This is play" has to be received and in some way returned before the nonserious interaction can begin. Often there is some negotiation in the communication. Some acceptance of a suspension or even reversal of normal role expectations may be required. A child may want to play at being mother or father in order to scold the parent. A subordinate may want to suspend normal organizational hierarchies in order to pull off a particular game. Some form of "You be me and I'll be you" is a common play form. However, it can lead to conflict if all parties are not playing.

Gregory Bateson's concept of "metalanguage" is more than a reference to the possibility of nonverbal communication. Rather, the indirect modes of communication provide a context in which direct communication can be interpreted (Bateson, 1972). Especially in fragile episodes of play set in the midst of institutional goal-directed activity there has to be clairty of signals given and accepted that what is about to happen is not serious. The frequency with which an instigator does not wait for a return confirmation and has to say retroactively "I was just kidding" suggests that such negotiation is both necessary and often incomplete. "I didn't mean it" is a common expression in intimate relationships. It generally follows a failure of metalanguage to communicate a suspension in serious exchange.

For example, how do parents play with children? In some contexts the meaning is unambiguous. A father who regularly takes off his tie and sits on the floor with a young child when returning from work is unambiguous in setting the context of whatever mock struggle may ensue. At a picnic all the signs point toward play. In fact, a warning may be ignored so that a parent has to reverse the signals by saying, "I mean it; don't climb on that log." We are able to move in and out of play readily enough on most occasions. Yet, leisure contexts are special in that they set the premise that what occurs is for fun. Further, some leisure displays the premise that the interaction is central to the episode or event. There is an implicit permission given to focus on the relationship rather than the activity, to use the setting for social ends.

In social exchange there is also the possibility of the reverse signal of "I'm not playing." This may come in an expression of anger during a game or conversation. It may reorient what had been defined as a casual flirtation. It may be a refusal in response to a "Let's play" signal. The failure to interpret such a signal accurately can result in serious repercussions. The point is that the lightness or transcendence of reality that characterizes play is not automatic in any setting. A social world of leisure may begin with the premise of play and a social world of religion with seriousness. However, interaction can shift back and forth in moments between action and communication that are self-contained and for their own sake and those that express position and purpose. The success of such rapid transitions depends on shared vocabularies in which a single word or gesture is understood to alter the meaning of action.

Leisure Settings as Defined Openness. The ambiguity of so much interchange suggests that not only vocabularies but also environments provide certain agreed-on premises for interaction. One characteristic of most leisure settings is a certain openness to action and results. Much of life, on the job or in the home, has predefined objectives. Completing the report, balancing the accounts, closing the sale, getting the meal on the table, raking the leaves, and so on are not indefinite in their aims. Although play may occur during the line of action, the end does not change.

Leisure settings, on the other hand, remain relatively open. A picnic may involve a meal, but the details of timing and presentation may be adjusted to other factors. A game may be won or lost by anyone engaged. A dyadic conversation does not have an agenda that has to be completed. There is at least some possibility of letting the event take its own course, of responding to unanticipated contingencies, and of allowing the conversation to explore new areas of ideas and feelings. The event, game, or conversation—in the social context defined as expressive rather than task-determined—becomes the focus of the meaning. It is more than an interruption of the business of the occasion. Playing out the line is what the occurrence is all about.

This does not avoid all ambiguity. Again, a critical example is the negotiation of sexual identities in leisure settings. There is often the intent of gaining some kind of sexual compliance in interaction. Such compliance may range from a smile or momentary touch to intercourse. More often the aim is more bounded, a demonstration of "coquetry" (Simmel, 1950:50–51) in which erotic signs are exhibited in a game in which no real outcome of sexual action is expected. The half "yes" and half "no" are balanced in calculated incompleteness. The aim is less often some major "conquest" than an affirmation of the potency of sexual identity. Some sign that a significant other defines one as an acceptable man or woman—perhaps even attractive—is all that is sought. Some communication of placement on the "sexual hierarchy" of the social context is more than enough. An affirmation of placement or worth, as examined in the previous chapter on identities, is the real agenda for considerable leisure interaction (Zetterberg, 1966). Such affirmation is made possible by the defined openness in which every line of action is not predetermined. In the episode sexual identity is a renegotiated object of play rather than an established definition.

There are many possible examples of this special openness. In each, two orientations meld into strategies for action. In each, the leisure context facilitates both self-presentation designed to validate some identity and interaction that can establish the self in a particular way *among others*. The dialectic of the existential and the social is at the center of such interaction episodes. The swimming pool is such a context:

> What actually happens at a public swimming pool on a summer afternoon? There are various styles of behavior—from lounging near the fence and maintaining a convenient distance from the water to exhibitionist diving,

a boisterous ball game, or solitary swimming of fifty laps. The variety is more than preferences for different degrees of physical exertion. Rather, it reflects both sides of the dialectic. On the one hand, the actors are presenting different identities through the media of the action. They are playing to selected observers and seeking to be defined as "cool," competent, risk-taking, sexy, or friendly. On the other hand, the styles of action are signs of how interaction is desired and implemented. Frolicking children, cardplaying students, self-conscious and posing teens, caretaking young mothers dividing their attention between conversation and protection, and lap-counting fitness seekers are all doing more than pursuing individual aims. They are entering and responding to social groups with particular modes of interaction. The leisure environment, the pool, provides a physical setting for the varieties of self-presentations and social styles. Further, the social world of the pool with its agreed-on customs and values enables actors to play out the identities and engage in the social interactions that express something of who they want to be and become. The pool is a kind of stage on which a variety of parts may be played and social exchanges negotiated.

Relative Intensity of Engagement. Some believe leisure to be primarily disengagement, relaxation, and separation from all elements of discipline and sustained effort. As outlined in the discussion of "amateurs," this approach ignores leisure in which persons make major investments of the self and in which they hope to receive significant identity confirmations. The issue of relative intensity is also important for social kinds of leisure. When we examine social interaction as leisure, it is evident that much such activity is quite demanding and intense. Few would argue that a cocktail party is the most relaxing way to spend an evening or that negotiating a relationship in any setting is a good way to rest up for productive endeavors. It might seem that solitary leisure is more likely to be relaxing than social engagement. However, physical fitness exercise or poetry writing may be both solitary and demanding.

In the schema relating the interaction dimension to that of relative intensity developed by the author (Kelly, 1983:149; see Chap. 2, Fig. 1), the intensity dimension varies both in terms of engagement with the activity itself and with other people. Involvement in doing and in interaction may be quite casual or intense, or one dimension may be at a high level and the other low.

Socially intense leisure in which the interaction component is primary would be illustrated by a deep conversation at a party or even by considerable "fooling around" by teens. Such intensity may also vary according to the kind of social relationships being expressed. Further, the level of intensity may rise and fall during the course of an episode.

In the social games described by Simmel (1950:49–50), the dynamics and hazards of the action may become quite intense just because the "stakes" are contained within the episode.

Csikszentmihalyi (1975) argues that intense involvement may be highest when the structure of an activity is fixed and permits full attention to be given to exercising a skill. However, there are also times in which uncertain outcomes and problematic identities raise emotional involvement to critical levels. One central factor is the significance of the identity being presented and the centrality of the relationships to our self-definitions. I am likely to invest much more attention and effort to a presentation of my new work to my peers than to a pickup game of beach volleyball with my extended family. Also, whether or not the outcomes of the engagement have extended consequences will affect intensity. Intensity is more than environmental; it is also a matter of intentioned action by the actor. One rule is that social interaction is most likely to be intense when the others matter, the outcomes are problematic, and the presentations salient to who we want to be.

The Constructed Leisure Event. Many leisure events combine consensual elements of relative intensity, behavioral styles, salience of outcomes, communication modes, and reciprocal expectations. However, there is also a tacit acknowledgment that all this structure has been constructed for the event and can be revised when warranted. A break in the agreements can destroy the whole fabric of the event. For many institutions the social construction of their existence is obscured by a social consensus that their structures, value systems, and roles are the way they ought to be (Berger and Luckman, 1966). The government, family, church, and economic systems are sustained by well-learned sets of values that are mutually reinforcing. Ideologies are accepted as grounded in a givenness rather than as the products of particular cultures and interests.

Leisure events, however, are somewhat different. Their constructed nature and consequent fragility are more evident. In highly organized enterprises such as professional football, committees change the rules each year. In neighborhood games children often spend more time negotiating the rules and procedures than actually playing the game. Some have suggested that such negotiation is a critical element of socialization. Not only are debating skills practiced, but the constructed nature of social interaction is revealed. Life is not organized from above in an immutable scheme. What has been negotiated can be renegotiated. The social world is open to change and reorganization.

Examples are too numerous to list. Illustrating the ways in which a built-up set of rules and conventions can become almost too sacred to question are the norms and taboos surrounding proper dress and decorum at a tennis or golf club, behaviors indicating approval in a concert hall, rituals dictating the organization of a debutante ball, or the levels of rules governing a weekly poker group. The process of constructing the required framework of an event may have been completed so far in the past that the process is forgotten or even predates current participants. "This is the way it's always been" offers the sanction of tradition to the authoritative structure. In other cases the regulations are quite ad hoc and subject to amendment during the interaction process, as in a children's game of cops and robbers, a camping trip, or a skiing weekend.

There have been a number of analyses of regular poker groups that stress the taken-for-granted and multilayered nature of the social context (Crespi, 1961; Zurcher, 1970; Kelly, 1983:160). Such regulations tend to be revealed when a new member must be socialized into the proceedings. Both direct and indirect communication are employed to teach a neophyte what is expected. The first-level rules of poker are usually assumed with particular variations on betting, acceptable games, and pot limits added explicitly. However, the second-level conventions about such matters as bringing guests, eating and drinking, arriving and leaving, accepted conversation styles and subjects, and body control at the table are more often exemplified with corrections made indirectly or in a mode of humor. The alertness of a newcomer in picking up the implicit norms is a major factor in decisions about inviting a return. The rules and conventions are not arbitrary but usually reflect a present or historical assessment of such factors as group composition and size, amounts of money that can be lost without jeopardizing central commitments and responsibilities, group schedules, interrelated roles outside the poker setting, and the limits of the particular locales of the game. One of the appeals of poker is that the outcomes on any night are problematic. Seldom will any one player repeatedly win or lose. Last week's victim may be this week's champion. The comprehensive regulations are in place to permit concentration on the game itself and to allow its uncertain outcomes to happen with a minimum of external bias or interference. As Huizenga ((1950) suggests, the play is set apart not only in its results but also in the parameters of the drama played out each week around the table.

Leisure events are constructed to provide a context for certain kinds of involvement. Some are relatively unstructured because the central aim of the event is the development of the process itself. Some kinds of parties or business settings have a minimum of rules and conventions so that social relationships can be developed in the setting. What Goffman calls "fancy milling" (1967) may give the appearance of being wild

and free when in reality there are a number of conventions for interaction. In such milling both the interaction process and the outcomes
remain rather open.

In other events the structure is quite rigid. In such cases clear and
consistent rules are in place and accepted to enable participants to concentrate on the bounded interaction. In a racket sport encounter there
is to be no debating of rules or environmental considerations. Rather,
the exhibition of skill and the measured contest can be given full attention. The process develops within a strict framework prescribing
the limits of the action. The outcome may be open, but the procedures
are not.

One question raised about leisure interaction is, "Can there be an
event in which 'nothing happens'?" That is, there would be no action
except the construction of communicative interaction. There would be
no recognized outcome, no measure of gain or loss, and no line of action
requiring a later follow-up. Two or more people would simply meet,
inaugurate a completely self-contained episode, carry it through to its
termination, and close the encounter. Even though there might be some
identity agendas operative, the interaction would be completely for its
own sake with no external referent. The episode would be fully autotelic, intrinsic to the moment and spontaneous in its construction.
Even in Simmel's "sociability" there is some mutual knowledge of the
meaning context, however conditional. The difficulty in finding a clear
example suggests the complexity of most leisure interaction even
though the "ideal type" of total self-containment may be a useful concept.

Negation: Rules and Rituals. All this attention on the taken-for-
granted structure of most social interaction may lead to ignoring the
negative elements of such constructions. Although complete openness
may be rare or even impossible when two or more people with their
personal and social agendas meet and interact, rules and rituals should
not be accepted without further critical analysis. The fact that outcomes
are problematic may obscure the rigidity of event structure and possible
bias in how different actors are affected.

Well-socialized persons in a traditional social system may become
so enmeshed in the way things are that they fail to exercise options
for change. It is possible that even the constructed nature of leisure
events may become hidden by a preoccupation with rules, forms, eti-
quettes, conventions, and observable styles. Concern with being accepted in a leisure event or setting may prompt concern with exhibiting
proper behavior at all times. In the process the contingent character
of leisure may be lost. Play may be as hard to find on the playing field
as in the office. The experiential and experimental qualities that might

set leisure apart from task-directed contexts do not emerge. They are smothered by the built-up rituals that prescribe what is acceptable and proscribe what is deviant. The point is that situations called leisure are not automatically or unambiguously social spaces that produce play. The freedom of leisure may be abandoned in interaction totally shaped by the social norms and expectations—implicit and explicit—that develop in and around any repeated kind of event. The openness of leisure may be overcome when actors are unwilling or unready to play with the script and alter the portrayals that have been previously accepted or applauded.

Another kind of negation occurs when an interaction episode becomes a contrived manipulation of others. Then the interaction for its own sake is shaped by extrinsic ends. The self-contained experience becomes a game in which one party attempts to use the play definitions to gain some advantage through deception. The definition of play or leisure is employed to disarm alters in the episode and render them open to manipulation. Symbols and signs are used to mask the line of action rather than communicate its nature. A negation of play is possible in almost any leisure occurrence. Such a violation of the meaning context may spring from the fears or anxieties of one actor who is unable to allow interaction to take an undetermined course.

Just the label of *leisure* is no assurance that freedom will be found and exercised. The presumed characteristics of leisure interaction that facilitate both identity development and experimentation can be subverted. The social process is, after all, dependent on reciprocity in acceptance as well as initiative in novel lines of action. There may be no social world as limited as the leisure of a country club dinner, a symphony guild ball, or an afternoon bridge club. There may be no event less adventurous and flexible than an athletic contest or community celebration. The problematic dimensions of leisure episodes and events may require risk and struggle for realization. Their social construction may be buried under a history of authority and propriety.

Leisure as Social Occurrence _____

No limitations can completely close off the significance of social interaction as leisure. Woven through most kinds of events, settings, and activities commonly held to be leisure is the dimension of social interaction. Just as episodes of leisure may be found *in the midst of* almost any social context, so some element of social interaction is found in most leisure. Even a solitary action may be a rehearsal for an anticipated event. Further, the interaction may be the primary meaning of the activity. The activity or setting may be a vehicle for expressing and developing relationships. The primary orientation may be bonding. This is especially the case with primary or intimate relationships, which seem to require some leisure opportunities as well as common tasks.

Several issues have emerged in the foregoing discussion:

- Just how free is leisure when the interaction cannot be wholly separated from ongoing relationships and roles outside the event?
- Is the alleged openness of leisure seriously alloyed by all the processes of meeting the expectations of others and seeking to present ourselves in acceptable modes of behavior?
- Are the taken-for-granted social norms of ongoing interaction a fundamental denial of the freedom of leisure?
- Do the identity agendas of social actors overcome the elements of the problematic in leisure encounters? Is such interaction much more contrived than leisure ideologies allege?
- How can the processes of leisure interaction be interpreted in ways that incorporate both sides of the dialectic—individual lines of action and social contexts?
- Whatever the complexities of social interaction as leisure, are the interludes and episodes of nontask interchange what "get us through the day"?
- Just how far can we take the common definitional dimension of leisure as "an end in itself"? Is it more accurate to refer to elements of play—existential activity with bounded outcomes—as primary in the meanings of leisure episodes or events?

The significance of expressive action and interaction through the entire life course (Gordon, 1976) does not permit a denial of either the social elements of leisure or the complexity of recognizing its processual nature. Leisure is, among other things, social occurrence. As such, it is not segregated from the ongoing process of life together but is woven through the entire texture of life.

References _____

Bateson, Gregory. 1972. *Steps to an Ecology of Mind.* New York: Ballantine Books, Inc.

Berger, Peter, and T. Luckman. 1966. *The Social Construction of Reality.* New York: Penguin Books, Inc.

Brown, R., P. Brannen, J. Cousins, and M. Samphier. 1973. "Leisure in Work: The Occupational Culture of Shipbuilding Workers." in *Leisure and Society in Britain,* eds. M. Smith, S. Parker, and C. Smith. London: Allen Lane.

Cavan, Sherri. 1967. *Liquor License*. Chicago: Aldine Publishing Company.

Crespi, Leo. 1968. "The Social Significance of Cardplaying as a Leisure Time Activity." in *Sociology and Everyday Life,* ed. M. Truzzi. Englewood Cliffs: Prentice-Hall, Inc.

Csikszentmihalyi, Mihaly. 1975. *Beyond Boredom and Anxiety*. San Francisco: Jossey-Bass, Inc.

Goffman, Erving. 1967. *Interaction Ritual*. New York: Doubleday & Co., Anchor Books.

———. 1974. *Frame Analysis: An Essay on the Organization of Experience*. New York: Harper & Row, Publishers.

Gordon, Chad, and C. Gaitz. 1976. "Leisure and Lives: Personal Expressivity Across the Life Span." In *Handbook of Aging and the Social Sciences,* eds. R. Binstock and E. Shanas. New York: Van Nostrand Reinhold Company.

Huizenga, Johan. 1950. *Homo Ludens*. Boston: Beacon Press.

Kelly, J. R. 1983. *Leisure Identities and Interactions*. London: George Allen & Unwin Ltd.

Kleiber, Douglas. 1984. "Leisure as Interludes." Unpublished paper.

Lynch, Robert. 1979. "Social Play: An Interactional Analysis of Play in Face-to-face Interaction." Ph.D. diss., University of Illinois at Urbana-Champaign.

Mead, George H. 1934. *Mind, Self, and Society*. Chicago: University of Chicago Press.

Robinson, John. 1977. *Changes in Americans' Use of Time: 1965–1975*. Cleveland: Cleveland State University Communications Research Center.

Simmel, Georg. 1950. *The Sociology of Georg Simmel*. Trans. and ed. by Kurt H. Wolff. New York: The Free Press.

Zetterberg, Hans. 1966. "The Secret Ranking." *Journal of Marriage and the Family* 28:134–42.

Zurcher, Louis. 1970. "The Friendly Poker Game: A Study of an Ephemeral Role." *Social Forces* 49:173–86.

Woods, Peter. 1979. *The Divided School*. London: Routledge and Kegan Paul Ltd.

CHAPTER 7

Institutional Theory

ISSUES

Institutional theory is based on a functional analysis of the social system.

In traditional approaches leisure is seen as functional and secondary. Therefore, analysis has often been an attempt to measure determinants from other roles and related resources. The pervasiveness of major institutional roles is presumed to shape the derivative domain of leisure.

Economic roles have complex and variable relationships to leisure. Carryover from structural dimensions of role requirements, resource allocation, and timetables impact leisure aims and opportunities. Some reciprocity of learning and development in work and leisure has been discovered.

Alienation in economic roles may have both personal and social consequences in other life domains. Economic roles are the basis of social-class differentiation with both its manifest and hidden injuries.

Family interaction may be leisure, often part of the "core." Also, the family or household is a common social context of leisure. The role expectations and resource allocation of the household reflect changing aims through the life cycle as well as social change in family structures.

The intersecting careers of work, family, and leisure are reciprocally related through the life course.

In a secularized society religion can be defined as leisure—discretionary rather than an essential of social solidarity.

Leisure is ethnic in the sense of being in and of a particular culture. However, leisure may also be a context for the development and expression of a culture.

In the role sequences of an institutional social system, leisure styles are developed in a dialectic of role expectations and decision.

The existential dimensions of leisure confront the negations of resources limited by social stratification and the systemic support of leisure that is seen as functional.

In the previous transition from an individual to a social basis for the analysis of leisure, attention was focused on face-to-face social interaction and on the actor. Now the second part of the transition must be made; from the social actor to the social institution. In the dialectical spiral being developed here the existence of regularity with determinative power over action does not eliminate decision and interpretive lines of action. On the other hand, the reality of decision does not preclude the structural institutionalization of norms, roles, authority, and the like as *social forces* that shape behavior. Rather, in this and the succeeding chapter we examine social and political contexts of leisure in both functional and conflict modes. Implicit is a view of social analysis that encompasses both action and structural perspectives, that is both existential and social.

The context of experience, development, decision, and interaction is more than immediate and sequential. Rather, the life course is traveled in company with others who are interrelated in relatively clear and consistent ways. Behavior occurs in a system of social organization with a high degree of regularity and predictability. Further, the regularity is persistent over time to the extent that change is understood to require explanation and radical change to be quite rare. The metaphors employed are based on the persistence of social forms:

- Social organization is described as a *system* with regular patterns of prescribed behaviors based on agreement about what is right and what can be expected of others. The system consists of a number of institutions in which actors generally conform to the norms that are prescribed for those enacting designated roles. In short, in such social organizational settings we know what to expect of others and what they in turn expect of us.
- The basic institutions of the social system are related in a *functional* scheme in which each contributes in a special way to the survival requirements of the system. Therefore, the economy, polity, school, church, and family each contributes to continuation and development of the overall system. From this perspective, leisure must provide something essential to the social system in order to be considered a social institution.
- *Social solidarity,* or cohesiveness, requires that the institutions be functionally interrelated in ways that are consistent with an overall value system that is learned and accepted by those living in the society. Although such a society may evolve or change in response to external forces, the presumption of relative cohesiveness is supported by the fact that for the most part people know what is expected of them and adhere to those expectations. The very concept of deviance presupposes a normative system from which to deviate.

Leisure in a Functional System _____

The functional argument for leisure as a social institution has been made by Neil Cheek and William Burch (1976). They refer to the social need for contexts in which to develop and express primary relationships, especially family and friendships. The case for considering leisure a social institution would focus on functional necessity, not its equality with the economy, government, or family. If leisure is defined as activity chosen in relative freedom with openness adequate for expressive and creative experiences, then its functions depend on the social need for such action. The creation of play and the bonding of interaction without predetermined outcomes and goals are not peripheral to social survival. The central issue is the extent to which leisure is required in complex modern societies for their enactment. If learning requires the institutional specialization of the school and value reinforcement of the church, then does not creative action and intimate bonding call equally for the legitimization and opportunity structure of leisure as a social institution? Leisure may, however, be a major dimension of life management and priorities and a theme of increasing importance to individuals without being an independently functional necessity.

The counterargument would be that leisure has secondary rather than essential functions. For example, leisure may enhance family relationships, but it is the family that provides the social system with reproduction, infant nurturance, primary socialization, household protection and shelter, social identification, and the basic unit of economic consumption. Further, leisure may contribute to the recuperation and even health of those active in the economy, but again the outcome is secondary. It is the economy that provides the essential goods for maintaining the society.

The counterargument may be persuasive once the premises of the functional model are granted. Leisure may from a personal perspective be defined as essential to life as we know it. Leisure is, as already argued, central to expression, development, and community. It is woven through the social fabric in time and meaning. Nevertheless, from a social perspective the purposes of leisure are not fundamental in and of themselves. Family relationships do not require leisure, however much we have come to count on leisure as a context for their expression. Creative thinking and production can take place in many environments. In fact, some leisure romantics assert that a holistic view of leisure does not differentiate it in time, space, or meaning from the whole of personal and social life. If this is true, then those who have no difficulty identifying institutions such as the school and state are not likely to agree that leisure is a social institution, ancient or modern. Rather, leisure would be seen as a dimension or theme within the institutional system.

One significant implication of this is that leisure could still be approached as derivative and secondary. The common sociological approach to leisure has a two-step basis. First, leisure is secondary to the basic social institutional structure and functions. Second, leisure can be best analyzed as determined by its relationship to those institutions. Leisure has a place in the economy, primarily as recuperation for productive work. Leisure contributes to family solidarity, offers a time for contemplation and religious practice, gives play contexts for expression and development, offers symbolic expressions of basic social values, and may be an alternative setting for school-related learning. However, from this perspective leisure is defined by its relationships to the institutional structure. The first question of both theory and research would be, "How does the economy or the family or the polity determine leisure?" The analysis of leisure would begin with the primary institutions.

Early Research on Leisure Determinants

This focusing on primary institutions is essentially what has occurred. The twentieth-century history of leisure scholarship in North American and Europe has been dominated by sociological analysis of leisure's social determinants. The primary question was usually that of how work determines leisure. The agenda-setting books were *Work and Leisure* (Smigel, 1963) and *The Future of Work and Leisure* (Parker, 1971). The assumption in both was that leisure is derived from work, that economic relationships determine the forms and meanings of leisure.

In the 1930s community studies in North America dealt with leisure in the context of community institutions. However, leisure was not assumed to be peripheral and residual. In "Middletown" leisure was viewed as a major social space expressing the values and resources of the community (Lynd and Lynd, 1956). In "Elmtown" leisure was an environment for adolescent development as well as for a reinforcement of the social stratification of the community (Hollingshead, 1949). The study of suburban leisure by Lundberg and associates (1934) approached leisure as derived from the value scheme of this new upper-middle-class setting. Leisure was seen as a product of its community social context but not as strictly determined by a single set of institutional relationships.

There were significant efforts to be more inclusive. The Kansas City study of Robert Havighurst (1957) and colleagues attempted to delineate the multiple meanings of leisure for adults. In Europe, Joffre Dumazedier (1967), although thoroughly sociological in premises, studied the leisure of industrial workers in a relatively comprehensive way. In Annecy the family and expressive orientations and contexts of leisure were examined along with relationships to work patterns and constraints.

In North America however most leisure research took a standard form. Especially when government agencies supported the research, the aim was to predict participation in designated activities and use of public resources by survey methods. Samples of populations were asked what they did—sometimes with frequency and locale included— as well as who they were. Demographic descriptors of age, sex, socioeconomic position, and location were employed to form aggregates for analysis. Rates of participation of aggregates indexed by sex, income, and occupation level, for example, were measured. Particular attention was given to indices of economic placement, occupation type or prestige level. More often implicit than stated, the assumption was that what people did as leisure was determined by the socialization and resources associated with such social-position variables.

The expectation was that social aggregates—segments of the population that did not interact but that shared such demographic characteristics—would be found to have distinctive leisure patterns. Partly because of concentration on types of activity that are status-based, such as participation in community organizations, and partly because of statistical methods that did not distinguish strong from weak relationships, early research seemed to support the approach. Further, the common wisdom was that life-styles can be distinguished clearly by such indices. In time, however, the approach was found to be less than adequate. More discriminating statistical analyses, more inclusive research designs, and perhaps some social changes led to skepticism and, in time, a rejection of the approach. Although some participation— especially at the high end of the cost spectrum—remains differentiated by socioeconomic status, the simple determinative model was not demonstrated to be adequate. Such aggregate analysis was found to account for less than 10 percent of the variance in participation frequency for all but a very few activities (Kelly, 1980).

As will be examined further, the resulting disillusionment did not lead to a withdrawal of sociologists from leisure research but to application of more complex and sophisticated designs. First, social groups that do interact were found to be more significant than aggregates in shaping leisure choices (Field and O'Leary, 1976). Second, socialization factors such as education were added to family histories as important elements in leisure patterns. Third, choices were found to be responsive to situational factors at least as much as to more consistent determinants (Kelly, 1978a,b). Fourth, families were found to be more powerful contexts of leisure learning than economic positions (Kelly, 1974, 1977). And, fifth, among social status levels styles of leisure engagement seemed to vary more than the activities themselves. The level of analysis began to shift from macrosocial aggregation to microsocial interaction contexts in which leisure interests are learned and expressed. At the same time, the dependent variable was also being questioned. Common activities such as reading, walking, and swimming were seen to have considerable diversity in styles, meanings, and locales.

Role Changes in the Life Course

One approach to refocusing the analysis was through adoption of a life-course perspective. This approach remained sociological in that the framework is that of the sequence of institutional roles characterizing the span of years. As introduced in Chapter 4, the central roles of individuals change through the life course. Family roles shift from dependent child to more independent adolescent to launched and reestablishing young adult to spouse and parent and in time to widow. Work roles change from the preparation of being a student to job seeker, trainee, settled worker, advancing and plateauing worker, preretirement worker, and retiree. Further, both sequences of roles may be disrupted by traumas such as health loss, divorce, unemployment, or business failure, and society-wide events such as wars and economic recessions.

It is not necessary to accept a strict determinist model in order to incorporate the role context of the life course in an explanation of leisure. Leisure is not separate from the central roles of work and family or from those related to the other institutions of school, church, and government. Rather, even a nondeterministic institutional approach would incorporate ways in which role contexts impact leisure resources and orientations. Further, major role transitions mark major changes in leisure as well.

For example, the contexts and orientations of leisure were found to shift in the transition from being a full-time student to postuniversity early-establishment roles (Kelly and Masar, 1981). Further, the more comprehensive the role shifts, the more leisure contexts and meanings were altered. Those who had entered establishment roles as workers, marriage partners, and parents had their leisure transformed more than persons who had made only one role change.

Also, many of the changes in leisure patterns associated with age disappear when role-transition variables are entered first into regression equations. There is little question that no single role change has as great an impact on leisure as becoming a parent (Rapoport and Rapoport, 1975; Kelly, 1983a:37). Especially when the mother relinquishes an employment role in the process, resources, locales, aims, and associations of leisure become oriented toward the family as well as constrained by caretaking tasks. A young father, who may give up his softball or soccer league participation, is responding to parenting role expectations more than to some age-related loss of skill or physical aptitude. In the same way, a widow who ceases to go to the theater when her husband dies has not magically lost interest at age seventy-five but now has no companion for the event. Age is an index of life-course role sequences more than a determinative factor itself.

Further, the role contexts are not independent of each other. Among Tyneside shipbuilders (Brown et al., 1973), leisure was found to be dominated by family and home rather than workplace associations. Even in this craft context, most associations of informal interaction on the job were left behind at the gate. When workmates were met at a pub, wives were included about half the time. Leisure was most often familial in companionship or located in the home setting. No clearly identified work-based culture of leisure was evident despite the common friendships developed *on the job*. Rather, the leisure of those craft workers was similar in overall form and content to the American skilled workers studied by MacKenzie (1973), British blue-collar workers (Bacon, 1975; Kelly, 1982b), and American blue-collar workers in the Midwest (Kelly, 1976).

Dramatic variations are dampened by the fact that leisure contexts are quite similar for a variety of people. The separation of the workplace from the residence, nuclear-family makeup, availability of mass media such as television and of private transportation with the car, levels of income permitting some leisure budgeting, and a variety of perceived opportunities in accessible environments are common for 80 percent or more of North American households. Further, expectations related to childrearing, marital companionship, home care, and the commodity context of the household are more similar than different for those with some discretionary income and at least high-school educations. As a result, similarities seem to outweigh differences across income and occupation levels.

The really dramatic differences can be summarized quickly:

- Young males are significantly most likely to engage in sports and to drink in bars.
- Males are much more likely than females to go hunting.
- Persons with higher levels of education are most involved in the fine arts as both producers and consumers.
- Persons with high incomes engage in more leisure in distant locales, especially those requiring expensive travel, housing, and access.

The less dramatic differences are more in style than the choice of activities. Income and social-status levels differentiate where people go out to eat and drink more than how often they do so. The privacy and convenience that can be purchased or leased by those with high incomes distinguish jetting to Europe for a family vacation from driving a six-year-old car to a public park. However, taking a vacation trip as well as the role expectations shaping the interaction may be similar for the corporate officer and factory worker.

Institutional Functionalism and Leisure

Does the inadequacy of deterministic models mean that the institutional role contexts of life have little to do with leisure? Is leisure, as some have suggested, a rarified experience that transcends its social contexts and is separate from the roles of the life course?

Rejection of one oversimplified metaphor does not require acceptance of another. Rather, in multiple ways, the institutional social system is a significant element in choices, opportunities, meanings, and styles of leisure.

First, as already indicated, institutional roles are carried over into leisure episodes. One does not stop being a father or daughter in a leisure setting. Rather, the setting or event becomes a context permitting somewhat different expressions of the relationships.

Second, institutional roles give a general shape to the structures of leisure. Work timetables have a primacy that determines the amount, frequency, and duration of periods available for nonwork activity. Economic position is a major factor in providing the income and assets that can be employed for leisure. Family-life-cycle period shapes both social companionship and constraints for leisure. A high level of "career orientation" generally produces priorities for the allocation of time and other resources toward work-related investments (Goldman, 1973).

Third, the social system is not static. Changes in institutional organization and norms may increase or limit the time available for nonwork. Greater flexibility in employment schedules may yield longer blocks of time for leisure requiring travel. Value shifts toward personal development—physical or mental—may increase the proportion of young parents taking time away from both the job and the home for themselves. Age norms may be altered so that older persons are encouraged to undertake activities formerly defined as "too young" for them. Income distribution shifts will have considerable impact on the shape of the market for many kinds of leisure resources (Kelly, 1985a).

Fourth, social roles tend to be reciprocal. Changes in the expectations for women will have effects on those for men. A greater economic component in women's role expectations and opportunities will impact both the employment market and family task expectations for men. Roles are often defined in relation to other roles. If norms for retirement are shifted toward a higher value placed on productive activity, then the availability of grandparents for nurturing and caretaking may be reduced.

Fifth, the usual premise of economic primacy in a social system need not produce a neglect of the power of other institutions to effect social change. Rather, changes in any institution will have impacts on the others, and any such change will impact leisure. For example, structural unemployment may transform entire communities and leave no facet of any institution unscathed. On the other hand, a family shift toward fewer children has already had impacts on the shape of the labor market as well as on leisure markets and religious institutional progress.

Sixth, a denial of the total determination of leisure by socioeconomic factors does not imply that leisure is independent. Leisure and family are closely intertwined for most adults in Western cultures. However, that does not call for replacing one single-dimension determinism with another. Even though both family and leisure tend to coexist in the nonpublic social spaces and have mutual influences, each has its own integrity as well. Even though leisure seems more related to consumption than production, it is not simply a product of market forces in the economy. Even though styles vary widely, leisure is not cut off from the dominant world views and value systems of the culture.

The pervasiveness of many roles suggests that leisure theory must incorporate the complex institutional structure of a society. However, the results are not static and all-encompassing. Rather, there is a dialectic in role negotiation as well as between two or more roles that are relevant to a social situation. There is, then, no *one* work-leisure relationship and no single family-leisure model. In the following discussion we identify some issues and propositions in the overall institutional context of leisure. Although there is considerable discussion of organization and structural variables, the previous attention to experience, orientations, and interaction processes should not be forgotten.

Leisure and Social Institutions ————————————

The two primary institutional relationships or contexts for leisure are the economy and the family. For convenience, the following discussion will refer to the economic institutional structure as *work* and to central and stable sets of relationships as *family,* though it would be more precise to refer to roles in the economy and to intimate roles and relationships. Many economic roles do not include the dimension of production that characterizes true work. Much employment gives no sense of engagement in enterprise valued and needed by the society. In the same way, many central intimate relationships are not strictly those of kinship. All couples are not married and all households not familial. However, the custom of referring to "work and leisure" and now "family and leisure" is well established. Then, more briefly, we also examine religion and culture as institutional contexts of leisure.

Work and Leisure

It should be evident that the theory being developed does not permit either leisure or work to be defined simply as the absence of the other. Leisure includes self-contained experience, personal development, existential decision, and interaction process; but none of these elements distinguish it from work. If leisure can occur anywhere, then it is not a matter of time and place. If leisure can include disciplined and intense investment in activity, the difference is not a matter of effort or skill. Rather, the dimension of activity primarily for its own sake, for the experience and outcomes based on the experience, characterizes leisure. Work, on the other hand, incorporates the dimension of production. Work is extrinsic in the positive sense of having the goal of producing something of value to the society. Work has a product, tangible or intangible, that contributes to the life of the society. In this sense work is economic in producing a good, or commodity.

There are problems with this definition. Some employment might be critically evaluated as not being work, as being without social benefit. Further, in its contribution to personal growth and health, to the development of creativity, and support of intimate relationships, leisure can be said to have social benefits. The fine distinctions are in the actor's intent and social definition. The social benefits of leisure are secondary to the experience itself, whereas work is aimed and organized to yield a product of social value. Further, there is agreement in the value system of society that work has to be done—wheat raised and bread baked—for the society to exist. Work is organized, in the economic system, to the end of production. Leisure, organized recreation or spontaneous activity, is oriented more toward the immediate. Works of art, personal growth, or skill development may result partly because they are not the primary aim. Play may be creative just because there is no required and predefined product.

Contexts and forms of work and leisure may overlap from this perspective. However, there usually is greater agreement on identifying the social organizations that make up the economy than those of leisure. Further, engagement in that institution is recognized as *work*. Such engagement may have continuity over the adult life course, referred to as a *career* in which today's performance is expected to lead to later reward. Some engagement is *employment* in which time and effort are rented for a predetermined rate of pay. And much economic engagement over time is really a series of *jobs* with no clear career orientation or reward system. In fact, considerable employment offers little or no sense of work, of contributing to the society through sustained effort. Such employment may separate the worker from a sense of product as well as from any control over the conditions of the engagement. Such employment is alienated from work, from a sense of contributing and meaningful labor.

In examining the relationship between work and leisure we use the word *work* to refer to the economic institution. The roles of this institution include careers and jobs, work and alienation, production and waste, creation and routine. Since leisure has already been found equally complex and multidimensional, no simple model or metaphor is likely to capture the full relationship between work and leisure.

Work-Leisure Metaphors. A number of models have been proposed to describe the work-leisure relationship. All share the fault of presuming that there are clearly defined entities on both sides of the schema. They generally focus on the mode of relationship rather than what is meant by either work or leisure.

For example, there is an economic model that assumes that both work and leisure are essentially measurable quantities of time. The relationship is usually described as a trade-off in which remunerated time on the job is chosen or rejected in favor of nonremunerative time called leisure (Kreps, 1968; Linder, 1970). The worker is said to choose more of one, to a point of saturation (Kelly, 1982a:129–30). At some point income is rejected because there is not enough time to use it. Up to that point most workers have been found to select work over leisure to gain the income. Recently, there is some indication that leisure is gaining value in the trade-offs of many workers (Best and Stern, 1978).

More sociological models focus on the nature of the economic relationship and the kinds of activities chosen as leisure. Such analyses are based on self-evident dimensions of the relationships. Without question, the reduction of the hours of the workweek in the period from the early days of industrialization to the 1950s released time and energy for leisure. Further, employment schedules give a basic structure to the social timetables for family, school, and leisure. The increasing geographical separation of workplace and residence has both produced new time costs for employment and given shape to the ecology of leisure. However, it is another matter to assert that the conditions and constraints of employment determine leisure choices and styles.

A framework of possibilities was outlined by Stanley Parker in *The Future of Work and Leisure* (1971) in a way that persisted in the literature. Parker presents three types of relationship:

1. *Identity* in which there is an extension or spillover from work to leisure.
2. *Contrast* in which there is an opposition or polarity between the two that may take the form of leisure that is an escape or compensation for work conditions.
3. *Separation* or segmentation in which there is no consistent relationship and each is largely contained in its own social sphere.

Parker (1983:88) also uses the terms *extension, opposition,* and *neutrality* to refer to the three possibilities. In his later work he also suggests the possibility that the causal arrow may not be unidirectional, that leisure in some cases may influence work. Further, the separation, or neutrality, model is consistent with the notion that leisure is more related to family and community institutions than to the economy, at least in locale and association.

Recently a number of studies have provided evidence of the complexity and variability of the relationship. Among the newer elements are

- The salience of work: Robert Dubin (1956) raised the question of whether work was the "central life interest" of workers. In a Midwest factory, the answer was work only for a minority. Leisure is more likely to be considered secondary or instrumental when the worker has a strong career orientation (Goldman, 1973). When employment is defined as instrumental, then even work schedules and relationships may be adapted to leisure ends (Levitan and Johnston, 1973). The central meaning of economic engagement becomes the enabling income to be used for greater ends, household support and nonwork activity.
- Work satisfaction: Disillusionment with the personal outcomes and opportunities of employment, which may increase over the years (Cohn, 1979) and even reach a crisis stage with some managers and professionals (Kanter, 1977), turns some to greater investment in home, family, community, and leisure.
- Situational analysis: Whatever the general relation between work and leisure, there are specific ways in which employment does impact leisure, and these should be studied through case studies as well as statistical analyses of data. Those who engage in physically exhausting labor or commute long distances to the workplace are likely to choose relaxing or recuperative leisure on weekday evenings. Those

whose employment is irregular or "off hours" have to make extraordinary arrangements for leisure companionship. Some work situations, such as being on a small college faculty, do afford considerable nonwork association with colleagues.

• Resource factors: Employment is a major factor in income levels and amount of descretionary income for most adults. Some economic activity offers considerable discretion over schedules as well. Both income and time resources vary according to employment conditions and together produce complex effects on leisure.

Such analysis has led to the identification of a number of related issues in the relationship of work and leisure.

Identification of Issues. Jiri Zuzanek, a sociologist, and Roger Mannell, a psychologist, have identified seven themes in the research literature (1983):

1. Changing allocations of time between work and leisure based on analysis of government workweek statistics have been examined. In both North America (Kreps, 1968) and Europe (Zuzanek, 1979) time-diary and labor studies have been compared to measure the effects of workweek changes on nonwork time uses.
2. Socioeconomic studies of productivity gains and choices between free time and income have been extremely common, with the work of Gary Becker (1965) leading to more recent analysis of trends and the possibility of greater weight being given to discretionary time in workers' decisions.
3. Possibilities of organization and scheduling changes such as the four-day workweek and flexible daily schedules have been explored. Impacts on productivity, leisure, family life, and satisfaction are still not conclusively measured.
4. Value placed on the various spheres of life began with a work-nonwork dichotomy (Dubin, 1956) but has become more complex as the influence of employment conditions, income, marriage, leisure, housing, neighborhood and community, and other factors in life satisfaction have been measured in multivariate designs. Most often, primary relationships or some combination of home and family have been found to be the central values for most adults (Campbell, 1981).
5. Studies of the relationship of occupational position to work commitment and a work ethic have been less than conclusive. In general, it appears that work conditions combined with some career orientation are factors in instrumental attitudes or commitment to economic roles.

6. The direct effects of work, especially structural and organizational factors, on leisure have usually focused on spillover or compensatory possibilities. A segmentalist separation of work and leisure suggested by research that identifies no effects may be the result of inadequate measurement and reliance on global rather than more specific relationships (Miller and Kohn, 1982).

7. Social psychological studies tend to concentrate on attitudes and perceptions about work and leisure. Satisfactions, subjective alienation, self-concepts, and relative commitment are among the dimensions investigated (Kornhauser, 1965; Kabanoff and O'-Brien, 1980).

In general, they agree with previous analysts that no single model—spillover, compensation, or segmentation—has enough support to be proclaimed dominant. More often, quite different research approaches have found weak elements of spillover (Pennings, 1976), compensation as a secondary element in decisions (Kelly, 1976), or a multivariate set of relationships, both structural and attitudinal, that cannot be captured by any single model (Zuzanek and Mannell, 1983).

It may be the failure of any research design to yield dramatic results that has led to a scattering of approaches rather than a cumulative building of research designed to develop and refine theory. Further, possible cultural differences confound already-inconsistent findings. For example, in the United Kingdom, Bacon (1975) found little evidence of either workplace satisfaction or alienation carried over into leisure. However, methodological limitations and cultural specificities have discouraged replication in North America. Currently, two approaches are being employed. One attempts to measure dimensions of attitude and behavior such as intellectuality and complexity while controlling for possible intervening variables in a sophisticated linear regression analysis (Miller and Kohn, 1982). A second approach employs the computer to sort and weigh as many variables as can be thrown into one data-gathering basket in the hope that something significant will fall out. The likelihood of theory advancement from such a design is rather low.

However, examination of a variety of dimensions of the work-leisure relationship may be expanded to identify new possibilities. Parker (1983:75f) suggests areas of such investigation. For example, intensity of involvement and effort or, conversely, disengagement and alienation may covary over the life course. Or, an expansion of the scope of the institutional model might find that factors of commitment, satisfaction, participation style, or other attitudes or behavioral modes may be similar in home, family, community voluntary activity, school, or church as well as in the economic sphere. Further, work may not be monolithic but include a variety of environments, associations, orientations, roles, and styles of engagement that spill over or call for compensation in a variety of leisure contexts. Simply relating two global domains of work and leisure seems a gross oversimplification of a multidimensional set of realities.

Recognizing some of the complexity and multidimensionality of the problem, we must not overlook such elements as the following:

1. Whether in the economic or leisure domains, individuals have been socialized in the same culture and carry learned value orientations, cognitive processes, interaction styles, and self-concepts in both spheres. On the action level, there is spillover that is based on cultural and institutional learning.
2. Certain structural factors clearly carry over. At present the time-tables for leisure are dependent on economic schedules. Further, locations and the physical and mental requirements of the job affect situational predispositions for leisure. After eight hours of heavy lifting, few steelworkers are interested in three sets of tennis.
3. Economic resources for leisure are largely determined by economic position. Further, there are a number of economic roles that have reciprocal leisure expectations—whether located at a factory-gate bar, prestige country club, or community Rotary organization.
4. Further reciprocity is possible as skills, self-definitions of competence or incompetence, and modes of communication and interaction are developed in one sphere and employed in the other. Such cognitive variables as rigidity, locus of control, affiliation/independence, and information processing may be developed in either domain and exercised in the other (Iso-ahola, 1980).

Advances in understanding would appear to begin by turning the one-way arrow of determination into a two-way dialectic. Further, the presumption that only work and leisure roles are involved in the dialectic is naive from the premises of institutional/functional sociology. For example, trade-offs in intensity of involvement and commitment are not limited to work and leisure (Noe, 1971) but encompass other institutional roles as well. Family and community roles enter into the reciprocity, complementarity, and trade-offs as well as work and leisure. Further, patterns change through the life course, with different domains in ascendancy in different periods.

One issue, however, merits particular attention. Structural and subjective alienation have often been confused in the literature. Robert Blauner (1964) distinguished four types of alienation: powerlessness, meaninglessness, isolation, and self-estrangement. Powerlessness in relation to the work process is a structural factor based on control of the means of production. Meaninglessness may be based in structural conditions but includes attitudinal elements of a sense of purpose in production. Isolation may be on immediate as well as organizational levels. Self-estrangement is a subjective consequence of the lack of both control and engagement in which the self finds productive expression. From a functional perspective such alienation may be ameliorated by alterations in work conditions, organization, and socialization. From conflict perspectives, which are explored in the next chapter, the power arrangements of the society are based in economic control and can be altered only by fundamental change. In either case, however, there is the presumption that a person cut off from productive engagement at work will in some ways be further alienated in nonwork.

Research on such alienation in North American has not been consistent. However, a common theme has been that workers in regimented economic roles who are denied contexts of expression and control are less able to exercise freedom and spontaneity in the family-community-leisure spheres of their lives (Torbert, 1973). At the present time, research on the converse problem of unemployment is indicating that being cut off from productive participation not only adversely impacts economic resources but also attacks self-esteem, a sense of social solidarity and participation, social identities, and self-definitions of competence and worth (Jahoda, 1979; Raymon, 1983; Raymond, 1985). The point is that economic roles are integrally related both to other social roles and to the developmental dimensions examined in Chapter 3.

The argument being developed thus far stresses the entire institutional role set through the life course rather than a dichotomy involving the domains of work and leisure. Further, the structural dimensions of institutional organization and role definitions are an essential context for understanding the definitions and development of the actor who plays a number of intersecting roles in any day or period of life.

Social Class and Leisure. Theory that views a society as divided rather than as an organic functional system is examined in the next chapter. However, even the most systemic approach recognizes that in modern societies there are disparities in both rewards and power based on economic position. In the United States economic reward differentials between white and black citizens have increased in the 1980s, and the purchasing power of upper-middle income levels has become further distanced from those whose income is based on unskilled labor, whether white- or blue-collar.

One of the striking findings in the author's study of life transitions of persons age forty and above in Peoria, Illinois (Kelly et al., 1986), has been cohort differences in economic and educational resources.

Further, the proportion of those now in their seventies and eighties with marginal resources who have had to adapt to traumatic changes with acceptance and retreat rather than utilize personal and community resources to rebuild was found to be quite high. When economic roles are tenuous and easily lost and opportunities to develop reserves are blocked by low incomes and periods of unemployment, traumas of illness and economic reversal devastate the socioeconomic resource structure of life. Personal resiliance in remarkable measure is required to cope with diminished living conditions and lack of protection against further setbacks.

The interrelated dimensions of such deprivation were analyzed in a study of *The Hidden Injuries of Class* (Sennett and Cobb, 1972). Such an analysis is similar to the Peoria study in documenting the cumulative and interactive burdens placed on those who have little leverage in the labor market. When low education levels, outmoded skills, easy replacement, and failing health are combined with racial, age, and gender factors of labor-market discrimination, then viability in a market economy is radically truncated.

Another view on social class and leisure is based on the critical writings of Thorsten Veblen (1953). In *The Theory of the Leisure Class* he argued that leisure has become a symbol differentiating upper-class life-styles from those of the masses who were required to work. Although the details of the analysis first published in 1899 are now dated, the concept of leisure being employed to distinguish social classes through adoption of tastes and styles demonstrating relative affluence remains significant. When residence and work are separated and consumer goods available on credit, leisure styles may be a primary index of social position.

Insofar as leisure opportunities are supplied by the market, economically marginal persons tend to be left out by those who segment their markets in an assessment of discretionary income (Kelly, 1985a). Insofar as leisure requires access to private transportation, entry fees, special equipment and apparel, and costs for acquiring skills, those in the deprived classes are cut off from opportunities that most take for granted. Among the "hidden injuries of class" is an inability even to consider activities and environments that are common to 70 percent of the population. Rather, day-to-day life is a struggle to keep things going and to maintain a viable context for food, shelter, and nurture (Howell, 1973). As leisure sociologists have written so prolifically on gains in average nonwork time and other resources, they have tended to ignore the significant proportion in a social system who are far below the mean in resources. As more and more attention is given to market provisions for leisure in Western economies, those without the discretionary income to provide economic demand may be neglected even more.

In a system in which economic and social factors are interrelated, there may also be a compounding of limitations. For example, the increasing number of employed single-parent women not only have to cope with multiple role expectations and extreme time pressures but also the common limits of income and economic opportunity defined for women who have been out of the labor market during childbearing periods. In a society that differentiates economic opportunities according to standards other than productivity, such as gender and race, limitations snowball through the life course. Leisure differences are more than matters of taste and cultural preference.

Leisure and the Family

An institutional approach to the relationship of leisure and family includes at least three components. First, family activity is itself a major form of leisure. Second, family roles are so pervasive that their expectations become a central dimension in most decisions for those living in a nuclear-family context. Allocation of resources—time, income, transportation, residential space, and energy—usually takes other family members into account. Further, the role expectations associated with being a spouse, parent, or child so influence familial leisure that some deny that minimum requirements of freedom can be met. Family-related leisure has elements of obligation as well as expression. And, third, intimate relationships are not only a context but also an end of leisure. The expression and development of primary relationships—familial and other—are major outcomes sought in leisure.

Family Interaction as Leisure. Despite the emphasis on the work-leisure pairing, as early as 1970 Kenneth Roberts devoted a chapter of his small book on *Leisure* to the family. He asserted what is almost common sense: that leisure and the family are closely related. He referred to community studies in North America and the United Kingdom that demonstrated that considerable nonwork time is devoted to various forms of familial interaction, both formal activity and informal interchange.

A recent three-community sequence of research (Kelly, 1978c) provided further evidence for the centrality of family interaction to adult leisure. Four kinds of interaction were ranked in the highest ten in importance to adults: marital affection and intimacy ranked first, family conversation third, couple interaction fourth, and play with children seventh. Outings with family, such as picnics, were given fifth place in importance. Along with visiting family and friends, a similar ranking was later found in a British New Town (Kelly, 1982b). More recently, these findings were supported in studies in a Parisian suburb (Hantrais, 1983) and among Chicago steelworkers (Raymond, 1985).

This research seems to run counter to studies from the 1950s and earlier, such as Mirra Komarovsky's (1964), that describe a sex-segregated leisure style for blue-collar families. One possibility is that there has been some social change. More recently, Gavin MacKenzie (1973) reported that the majority of the skilled workers he studied most enjoy their leisure as couples, with only three of the 194 studied omitting their wives from the discussion of leisure. Outings with other males were not abandoned but seemed to be occasions amid the common pattern of familial interaction. Joint parenting activities, especially with school-age children, occupy both fathers and mothers in nonwork engagement.

This does not mean that such activity always consumes the most time. John Robinson's (1977) time-diary research in North America reports that media use, primarily TV, takes about 40 percent of the time not devoted to employment, sleep, and family and personal care. About 30 percent of nonwork time goes to social interaction, most often with other family members. Further, the time labeled "family care" includes elements of communication and interaction that may express and develop satisfying relationships. And time is not a measure of intensity or value.

Leisure interaction also has consequences for the institution. Dennis Orthner (1975) found that marital satisfaction was associated with the proportion of time spent by couples in joint activity. Such interaction patterns change through the family life cycle (Rapoport and Rapoport, 1975). The intense care and nurturing by parents of preschool children turns more to companionship and institutional support when children enter school. Adolescence and the back-and-forth patterns of launching involve a dialectic of support and independence-seeking that may in time turn to adult companionship and sharing between parents and children. Not only does the household expand and contract in size, but the intensity of interaction waxes and wanes according to the developmental periods of the children.

There is still much to learn about family activity as leisure. The extent to which such association mixes obligation and choice has only been given preliminary attention (Kelly, 1978c). The choice of joint activity with relatively intense interaction or parallel activity in which other family members are only present needs to be examined further in relation to the quality of communication and sharing. The extent to which family companionship is a convenience or expectation more than a preference remains to be measured.

Nevertheless, family interaction as leisure is central to the "core" of adult leisure (Kelly, 1983b). This theme has been verified across cultures and social strata. Further, positive relational satisfactions of enjoying companions and strengthening relationships rank with relaxation as the highest three substantive reasons for selecting important leisure (Kelly, 1978a,b). Many activities serve primarily as a context for such interaction. For vacation trips the enhancement of family communication is often a central intent. Most important, building intimate relationships is a central life concern and goal. Some leisure is chosen to contribute to that end as well as provide an immediate experience of pleasure. Finally, most persons prefer to have times when they can be relatively at ease with familiar and trusted companions. Identity testing and competence building often give way to being with others who know and accept personal identities. For many, family contexts are just that—the social contexts where we can be least calculating in our self-presentations.

Family Role Expectations and Resource Allocation. Any individual takes many roles. Some of these roles are quite discrete and segmented. For example, a regular pool or snooker group may have no carry-over in personnel to work, family, or neighborhood so that leadership in that social world is separated from other roles. On the other hand, other roles are pervasive in expectations or even legal requirements. A police officer is expected to act to enforce the law even when off duty. A physician is expected to take the expert role in conversations about health at parties or basketball games.

Family roles tend to be both persistent and pervasive. They influence decisions through the life course and across social contexts even when no other family member is present. For most adults family role expectations are even more far-reaching than those of work. Coordination of family timetables and transportation, use of residential space, and allocation of financial resources require that few decisions are made without some consideration of those in one's immediate living group. This is especially true for leisure. Entertaining at home, planning vacations, supporting the activities of children, meeting their school schedule constraints, juggling voluntary organization schedules, managing home space for everything from TV to privacy, and maintaining equity in allocating funds are all family-management tasks related to leisure. The role structure of the family with differential assignment of decision-making authority and task responsibility impact on how leisure decisions are made as well as their outcomes.

This intertwining of obligation and role structure with all family-based activity has led some to question whether family activity can be really leisure at all. Dumazedier (1967) at one time called it "semi-leisure," although his more recent work incorporates family contexts. Yet, the ecology of leisure alone makes such a separation unwieldy. The household base of so much leisure connects leisure and family. In the same way, the accessibility of family and household intimates as companions makes those relationships the most mobile when venues of forest, beach, or concert hall are sought. Coordination with those in the same household is so much easier than with those who live across town.

Although freedom and choice have been stressed as dimensions of leisure, leisure that complements major social roles has been found central to leisure patterns. Using a value scale in the university town study, only 38 percent of the high-value activities were "unconditional," or essentially free from a sense of role-related obligation (Kelly, 1978a). On the other hand, 56 percent of activities somewhat less valued were unconditional. The reason is not because people prefer constraint and shun freedom but because they value primary relationships and find such companionship satisfying. In general, people are more important in leisure than the form of the activity.

In the same line of research respondents ranked reasons for selecting the types of activity they would least want to give up. Some referred to satisfactions intrinsic to the experience, some to recuperation and relaxation, some to compensation for role constraints, some to satisfaction with relationships, and some to role obligations and expectations (Kelly, 1983a:130). The social-meaning statements ranged from relational "I enjoy the companions" through "It strengthens relationships" to "It's a duty." The two reasons ranked highest overall were those referring to enjoying companions and strengthening significant relationships. In leisure interaction with family and friends positive satisfactions of expressing and developing the relationships usually outweighed the obligation component. Further, items indexing satisfactions of expression and self-development along with excitement and involvement in the experience itself preceded reference to role expectations in assessing why such activities were chosen.

This does not mean that such roles are peripheral to leisure. Rather, life-course role sequences provide a changing institutional context. We expand our environments outward from home to neighborhood to school, community, region, and further. Intimates may relocate in distant places that become important to our personal "world map." At the same time, our central roles come to incorporate school, work, and community. Yet, always—whether we live in a family residence, a nonfamilial barracks or dormitory, or alone—there is some community of intimates with whom we develop intersecting schedules of association. If there is not, then forming one usually becomes a primary agenda.

One dramatic shift should be highlighted. As indicated earlier, no role inauguration so impacts leisure as becoming a parent. Especially if one parent is the primary caretaker, role requirements dominate the allocation of every resource—imagination as well as money and energy as well as time. In both the university and mill-town studies (Kelly, 1978c) there was a shift of over 30 percent by young parents from activities chosen primarily for the experience to those with central family-role meanings. At the same time, leisure tends to take on a nurturing or child-development orientation for parents invested in the new role. There is a positive satisfaction element as well as a set of limitations that seem inescapable.

An issue that will receive more attention in the future is that of *leisure roles*. Increasingly, a high quality of interaction—as well as companionship and support—is a major expectation in marriage. Members of a nuclear family are expected to listen, give attention to the relating of leisure events and outcomes, and offer affective support to such engagement. Further, family members are expected to recognize and affirm the priorities of others. One element of courting and early marriage is the learning of interests and skills that complement the leisure investments of the partner. Whether the interest is in modern art or the skill is waterskiing, some reciprocity of investment is part of developing the relationship. The quality of interaction and communication related to leisure may be as significant in marital satisfaction as the traditional breadwinning and caretaking tasks that have received so much research attention. Lillian Rubin (1976) and others have documented the failure of many husbands to meet the affective and communicative needs of their wives. Now changes in gender roles may make such issues more reciprocal than when relatively few women took on work roles outside the home. Leisure is not exempt from role expectations just because it is defined by some measure of discretion. Leisure worlds and relationships have their attendant regularities and complementarities of expected behaviors as do other social worlds.

Familial Aims in Leisure. We have already introduced the third theme in this family-leisure analysis. The other side of the constraint-obligation theme is the value placed on family outcomes in leisure. Here it will suffice to list some of the more significant:

- Leisure is a central context for the expression and development of intimacy in marriage and friendship.
- Leisure activities are developmental for others as well as for the self. Leisure events, such as those on a vacation itinerary, are often selected with the education or growth of children in mind.
- When ongoing lives are segmented and opportunities for familial integration limited, a leisure event may enable us to demonstrate and

symbolize solidarity and mutual cooperation in a special way. For example, camping has been described as an environment in which family roles of provision, nurture, and support become visible on the open stage of the campsite.

• Leisure may also provide protection from common interference and an opportunity for prolonged communication among family members. Some parents of adolescents report that getting the entire family in the car for a vacation trip is a unique time for sharing in depth.

From this perspective leisure is an interaction environment more than a set of activities. Some of the activity in this environment is explicitly instrumental—directed toward the development of intimate communities. Leisure is a social space in which the relative freedom allows us to concentrate on relationships as well as experiences. Leisure, then, is not *the* environment for anything. Rather, it has characteristics and dimensions that facilitate a variety of outcomes including the building and expression of intimacy.

The Family and Social Change. There are a number of institutional trends in family structure and role definitions that will have effects on leisure. Among the most firmly established are the following:

• A major increase in the proportion of households composed of single persons or single heads with children is occurring, and families headed by single women are especially increasing dramatically.
• A shorter childbearing period resulting in more households without children living at home and in the lengthening of the postparental period of the family life cycle is evident.
• Lower birth rates are being established through a reduction in the number of children desired and the number choosing not to bear children.
• An increase in the labor market of married women, including women with children living at home, is resulting in more two-worker families.

The implications for leisure are manifold. First, the assumption of a complete and normative family life cycle for most adults is no longer valid. The nuclear child-rearing family will be the central social context for leisure for fewer adults at any given time. More will undergo transitions and even sequences of familial contexts. The "reconstituted family" resulting from divorce and remarriage is increasingly common.

Second, the longer periods of adult life relatively free from child rearing offer greater opportunities for leisure that is oriented toward self-expression and development. When this role release is combined with greater discretionary income and time, leisure may occupy a more central place in priorities and life investments.

Third, two-worker families will have to develop new modes of time-income trade-offs as synchronized time becomes the most scarce resource and discretionary incomes increase. When such resource shifts are combined with new role definitions in which household tasks are less gender-defined and segregated, new styles of both joint and independent leisure may emerge.

Fourth, a negative side of such change involves the increase in child-rearing households headed by single women, whose typically lower incomes and heavier responsibilities for parenting and household tasks severely limit their freedom and resources for leisure. The institutional support for such families may increase but is more likely to be related to work than leisure.

Fifth, transition will mark more adult lives at any given time. This suggests that leisure will increasingly be employed to manage change and to open avenues for new life engagements and investments. Rather than existing in a stable social context, leisure will be one element of reconstituting both personal and social aspects of life.

Underlying these changes are two more fundamental themes:

1. People may come to expect more from life. Just getting through the life course in conventional ways seems to satisfy fewer people. They want experiences and relationships that are personally satisfying and enriching. They want more of marriage, more from work, and more in their leisure. Such a critical stance cannot help but reorient all aspects of life in a society.
2. It may be more accurate to refer to intimacy than to family as a central dimension of life (Kelly, 1983:145). Intimacy in the sense of consistent sharing, trust, and communication is sought and may be found in a number of contexts other than the nuclear family. There may be more diversity in those contexts. Insofar as this is the case, leisure may become even more an environment for exploring, establishing, and expressing intimacy than ever before.

Intersecting Careers: Work, Family, and Leisure

Institutional approaches have been placed in a context of the life course in the preceding analysis of work, family, and leisure. The framework of the life course includes a sequence of roles in which there are cumulative careers. In these careers the resources, relationships, skill gains, and losses have impacts on the next period. Life is not all upward and onward. There are failures and losses as well as accumulated rewards and resources. Both gains and losses in any domain of life make a difference in other domains. The careers of work, family, and leisure are intersecting rather than independent (Rapoport and Rapoport, 1975).

A simple diagram would look something like this:

Work career: Preparation → inauguration → consolidation →
               plateau → decline → retirement

Family career: Child roles → being launched → courting →
               marriage → childbearing → child rearing →
               launching → parental caretaking → grandparenting
               → widowhood

Leisure career: Childhood socialization in play → neighborhood →
               school and community → family of nurture →
               midlife establishment and investment → maturity
               and reorientation → evaluation → constriction

Elements of negation have been laced through this entire analysis. In one sense, the negation is the institutional context of leisure itself. The complex set of roles tied closely to opportunities is a pervasive limitation on the freedom of leisure. The cumulative interweaving of socialization and resources places parameters on what is perceived as possible. Further, the intersection of work, family, and leisure careers blocks as well as opens lines of action.

The intersecting career scheme illustrates the contextual negation of freedom in social structure. However, it also offers a basis for identifying limits that are missing from the scheme: The first is that it does not account for the disruptions and traumas that characterize the majority of lives (Kelly et al., 1986). Work careers are interrupted by unemployment, change of goals, economic setbacks, conflict at the workplace, health problems, and recessions. Family careers are beset with untimely death, traumatic illnesses, interpersonal conflict, divorce, and failure to move to the next normative set of relationships. Leisure careers are diverted by changes in resources, interest shifts due to new primary relationships, and declines in abilities or opportunities. Further, traumas and disruptions in any one career path will have impacts on the others. For example, loss of employment has been found to affect family relations, self-esteem, resources for leisure, and reserves for the future. The careers are intersecting throughout the life course.

Everything makes a difference for everything else. Work changes alter the time and income resources for family and leisure. Family changes impact the social contexts and often the goals for leisure. Leisure investments may reduce or enhance the time and energy available for family and work. Also, the expectations that are associated with new roles—in any life domain—may alter the orientations for other roles. An employment-based community position may well add a new set of associations for the family and contexts for leisure. The TV ad in which a young executive is given a vice-president's nameplate for his desk and the keys to an expensive company car and is driven to his new country club is not entirely fantasy. The next steps would have been trips to the shopping center for appropriate wardrobes and appointments with a realtor to find a new house in the right neighborhood. Resources, role definitions, opportunities, and social identities are all bound up with the intersecting roles of the life course.

Conversely, an economic setback requiring a student to leave school and seek income, early pregnancy and parental responsibilities, labor-market leverage limited by low-level entry, and a series of other related events and conditions create a career as well. It may be a career of instability and marginal resources for every aspect of life, but it is a career with cumulative consequences nonetheless. And who we *become* in the journey goes with us everywhere.

Religion and Leisure

According to traditional functional theory, the institution of religion provides essential glue that holds a society together. From the work of Emile Durkheim, concern for social solidarity prompted attention to the factors that build social consensus. If a social system is to be based on something more than the possession of superior force by the rulers, then there has to be agreement as to the rightness of the basis of authority. Religion as a social institution is seen from this perspective to be essentially conservative in the sense of reinforcing common values and views. What *is* is accepted as the way things ought to be, even ordained by divine fiat. Religion, then, helps cement the system by instilling the undergirding value system in the consciousness of citizens.

This perspective is quite a different matter from examining the relationship of religion as a form of social behavior to leisure. It may be argued that religious participation *is* leisure, one possible use of discretionary time and resources. It might even be maintained that churchgoing is re-creation in the sense of preparing the participant for more effective role taking as worker, parent, and citizen. Religion may reduce stress and renew dedication to the basic values and institutions of the social system. There are a number of possible approaches to seeing religion as one form of social behavior among others.

- Religion may be understood as leisure, chosen from among other possible uses of time and energy with certain positive outcomes anticipated. This approach presupposes a secularized society in which religion is a choice rather than a normative obligation. Religion, then, can be analyzed as the most common voluntary organizational affiliation with its particular set of psychological and social outcomes. This approach incorporates sociological analysis that finds that churches for the most part bring together people who are already much alike in culture, values, and social status—people who are comfortable with each other.

- Religion may be viewed as in confict with leisure. The history of the church-recreation battle in many communities has been one of blue laws, which protect sacred times (especially Sunday) from conflicting activity, and compromise and retreat by the churches into a posture of cooperation and acceptance (Kelly, 1982:84). Some churches have attempted to offer alternative leisure to segregate their own members from contaminating influences. Some compete openly for weekend and vacation time with their own offerings. Such competition is concentrated on institutional schedules and priorities rather than meanings and purposes.
- Religion may be accepted as essentially private rather than social in nature. As such, it may be a form of leisure—contemplation and other engagement intended to enhance the lives of devotees who wish to invest in this spiritual enterprise.

What is missing from these approaches is the prophetic theme in much religion that stands over against "the way things are." This critical stance, despite being a minority position, seldom is abandoned entirely by established churches. Religion does usually celebrate the way things are or offer an otherworldly alternative that dampens the likelihood of revolutionary activity and commitment. Nevertheless, as is explored in Chapter 9, religion also may be a basis for reevaluation and a vision of unrealized possibilities. It may celebrate the potential of humankind rather than what has been realized.

From an institutional perspective religion has lost much of its determinative power in modern society. Only in communities with a particular ethnic-religious majority can the church shape the social schedule. Although there are regional differences in the United States, with church affiliation varying from 20 to 50 percent, in few locales is regular religious participation required for those defined as good people. Further, it can be argued that in a pluralistic religious climate, churches are more devisive than cohesive. Not only do Protestant-Catholic-Jewish-Orthodox-Eastern institutions pull neighbors in different geographical and ideological directions, but emotion-laden issues often find churches on opposite sides.

It remains the case that if an American is active in one community organization, it is most likely to be the church. It is also true that many who seldom "darken the door" still have profoundly religious world views. They often interpret their lives in religious terms and find comfort in religious concepts, whether or not they go to church regularly. Nevertheless, the traditional functional premises do not appear valid. It is now difficult to argue that religion is an essential integrative factor without which a modern social system will disintegrate. In view of the thorough secularization of many contemporary nation-states—Socialist and Capitalist, totalitarian and democratic—it is evident that substitutes for religion have emerged or been fabricated.

Leisure and Culture

When culture is defined as what is learned in a society—the values, language, thought forms, role definitions, world views, art, organization, and all that is taught in its institutions—then leisure and culture are obviously inseparable. In fact, culture is the context of leisure—and of everything else. Leisure is, after all, learned behavior. It is thoroughly ethnic, with its forms and orientations varying from culture to culture and among subcultures. Culture is also the material of leisure, the stuff out of which leisure experiences are made.

This is not the place to develop a thoroughgoing anthropology of leisure. However, three themes will be briefly introduced with the caveat that all three are much more important than the space allocated indicates.

First, as already suggested, leisure is thoroughly ethnic. That is, leisure always takes on the particular forms *and* meanings of its cultural setting. Economic conditions, role definitions, religious orientations, cultural histories, and other such factors shape leisure (Kelly, 1982:38–43). Gender-role norms and preparation for adult work roles have a pervasive influence on childhood games (Sutton-Smith and Roberts, 1981). Within a culture, subcultural groups have distinctly different leisure patterns based on family interaction patterns as well as ethnic forms of entertaining, celebrational inclusion, food and drink, games, and styles of communication (Gans, 1962). Values related to expression, age and sex grouping, locales, appropriate exchange of gifts and goods, and other styles of interaction shape leisure events and episodes (Kelly, 1982:245–46).

Second, the culture is the basis of leisure, as of all action and interaction. As introduced in the earlier analyses of leisure experiences and contexts, leisure is separate from nothing else in life. Rather, even the cognitive processes and forms by which we apprehend leisure possibilities and interpret the meaning of possible lines of action employ the learned linguistic forms of the culture. We create the culture by our actions and communication-based consensus. However, we also use the culture in the dialectic of social action. All this means that whatever we mean by leisure, intend by our actions, anticipate as outcomes, select as settings and action contexts, communicate to others, and understand ourselves to be doing and meaning is made up of the tangible and intangible materials of our culture *and nothing more*. We do not know ourselves or our environment apart from the forms we have assimilated in our lifelong socialization. The profound nature of the cultural basis of leisure is only partly revealed by cross-cultural differences, because even these are apprehended and communicated through our cultural forms and symbol systems. One obvious implication of this cursory analysis is that we need to utilize the tools of cultural anthropology much more extensively in understanding leisure.

Third, leisure provides a central—and perhaps essential—context for developing a culture. This perspective has been offered from a number of sources including the philosopher Josef Pieper (1963). The argument is developed further in Chapter 9. However, here it is necessary to introduce the concept as part of the institutional approach. The old question arises again: What does leisure contribute to the society? One recurrent answer has been that it affords a social space for thought—the creative and critical thinking that any social system requires. After all, no system is static. Therefore, it is necessary to examine where a changing system has been and is headed. Values and structures that were once appropriate may now impede necessary change. Visions of what might be, however communicated, are essential to long-term survival. The visual as well as language-based arts seek to offer and create such visions. Symbols may elicit understanding deeper than any language can denote or connote. The creation of a culture that does more than reproduce itself may be the most profound contribution of leisure that affords disengagement from necessity and engagement with the realm of creative ideas and symbols.

Whatever else one may see or prefer, leisure is thoroughly embedded in the institutional structures of a society. While this does not mean that some determination model of analysis is inevitable, it does mean that any free-floating concept of leisure is absurd. The cultural basis of leisure is a powerful negation of any concept that is abstracted out of its full contexts of realization and limitation. In the brief discussion of leisure styles that follows, the dialectic of decision and structural context will be illustrated further.

Sources of Leisure Styles ⎯⎯⎯⎯⎯⎯⎯⎯⎯⎯⎯⎯⎯⎯

Leisure takes place in an institutional social system. The sequences of institutional roles are central to leisure contexts, opportunities, resources, and orientations. Further, relative positioning in that institutional system affects the kinds of leisure that are accessible and considered appropriate. In a highly stratified system styles of leisure vary widely according to the distribution of rewards, resources, opportunities, and expectations.

That is one side of the argument. The other side stresses the variety of leisure styles within social categories and the similarities across strata. The similarities are based for the most part on factors already discussed. Developmental theory proposes that many life-course tasks are based on fundamental dilemmas that characterize a developmental stage. Adolescence, early establishment, midlife transition, later-life reassessment, and other periods have issues and requirements that cut across many social divisions. Also, the "core model" of leisure is supported by considerable evidence that at the center of both time use and orientations is a common set of available and informal activities that are engaged in through most of the life course. Added to the developmental and core elements of leisure are similarities in mass media exposure, public education programs, popular culture, and other homogenizing factors in the culture.

Further, analysis of the role-related aspects of leisure does not preclude considerable variation in the ways that roles are assumed. As suggested earlier, from the perspective of one theoretical metaphor, we play roles. That is, there is more to our assumption of roles than reading prescriptions for behavior and striving for conformity. Rather, there is a certain role distance in our performances. We see ourselves playing the role, interpret the responses of others, and orient our performances toward selected outcomes. We are not totally absorbed in our roles, even those most central to our identities. More often we have some concept of *how* we play the role.

This suggests that there is at least relative freedom in our social action. We are more than puppets in the hands of institutional determinants. Although the institutional role definitions are a context for our action, there is always something different about how we see ourselves in the roles. Further, leisure has some degree of social separation from other roles. No matter how pervasive work and family roles may be, we assume at least slightly different identities on the softball field or in the ceramics class.

A social dialectic (Kelly, 1981) takes into account both the contextual structures and the existential becoming of social action and interaction. Leisure, in such a dialectical perspective, is probably never asocial in being totally segregated from the socialization processes associated with a system of social institutions. We never transcend our cultures and what we have learned, even in the freest leisure environment. On the other hand, for our action to be leisure, there is never a complete absence of the existential dimension. We are never *just* role occupants.

In this dialectical metaphor leisure styles have sources rather than determinants (Kelly, 1985b). The "core-plus-balance" model provides a framework for analyzing both the similarities and varieties of leisure. A useful focus is more on style—how leisure is done—than on which activities are selected. The life-course model offers one part of the framework but is not exhaustive. Rather, ethnic variations in the overall culture, mass-media influences, cohort differences related to historic events and socialization processes, social status aspects of access and expectations, interests developed in education and other enriching contexts, and opportunity contexts as simple as climate and terrain are factors in stylistic diversity. There is no simple model that explains over 50 percent of the variance in what people do, much less how they do it. Rather, we are learning and deciding actors who move through our life-course role sequences amid a complex combination of influences and opportunities.

From this dialectic perspective, then, it might be useful to try to reconstruct some of the pattern of sources of leisure styles taking into account institutional social theory:

1. The social spaces of leisure are neither fully separated from nor integrated with institutional contexts. Not only do actors carry all their previous learning and development into leisure, but their current commitments and values carry over into leisure decisions and behaviors. There is "relative freedom" (Roberts, 1978) but not total autonomy. Leisure is not "open space" without roles or structure; it is "social space" with particular kinds of openness.

2. As many social roles are pervasive, so is leisure. Leisure enters the social spaces of work and family—in brief interstitial interludes, planned events, and ongoing orientations and purposes. There are opportunities for leisure almost everywhere. In many institutional contexts—work, family, school, and even church—leisure agendas and aims dominate interaction. School corridors are more than passageways, coffee pots more than caffeine dispensers, and kitchens more than food-supply depots. They are locales in which significant interaction takes place, primarily off-task and for its own sake.

3. In any social system opportunities for leisure vary. The institutional contexts of preparation, establishment, and later life form cumulative sets of resources for leisure. There are the personal resources of learned interests and skills. There are enabling resources such as space, mobility, language competence, and discretion over time. There are direct economic resources such as income and property and indirect ones such as job descriptions permitting leisure or offering special opportunities. There are social resources such as family, household, neighborhood, and community networks of companions. And all these resources together form a set of perceived possibilities, a personal self-definition including or excluding options, and a social environment that is relatively free or constrained. In this opportunity context actors have learned who they are, what doors are open and closed, and something of what is possible beyond those doors. In a stratified social system, these opportunity contexts vary widely and produce a differential negation of leisure's developmental potential.

An Alternative Model. To attempt to bring together some of the themes explored in this chapter, a revised institutional model is offered:

1. Leisure is based in the culture of the time and place. The world views, value systems, conceptual processes, language and thought forms, and age-related learning contexts are all parts of the leisure we consider, do, and develop.

2. Within a social system, leisure that is seen as maintaining the system will be fostered and supported. This is the *implicit negation* of leisure's freedom in a functioning social system. Leisure, especially that which is based on public and market provisions, will be oriented toward enhancing the institutional system. The relative freedom of leisure may offer dimensions and engagements that are counter to the normative social structure, but they will not be as central to the opportunity structure and socialization contexts as those that are system maintaining. Both consensus and institutionalized power will be brought to bear on supporting such leisure and sanctioning leisure seen as eroding or attacking the normative development and organization.

3. Nevertheless, leisure still has its other side. From the other pole of the dialectic, the elements of openness in leisure offer chances for actors coming to comprehend the constructed nature of the social system (Berger and Luckman, 1966). In real play, there is always the potential of glimpsing the "not yet," creating the novel, and comprehending the fragility of the given. The existential theme of leisure, even in a repressive social system, has the potential of undermining any socialization process designed to close the future and prevent critical analysis.

4. Leisure is expressive activity. However, it occurs in and through social institutions and employs institutional resources. The reciprocal roles, interlocking expectations, structured and controlled opportunities, and distributed resources are tied to all leisure—even daydreaming. Life-course changes are a processual context of what we do and seek in our leisure. Leisure is never *just* expression apart from its contexts.

Therefore, the institutional dimension of the dialectic is inescapable. The earlier endeavors of leisure sociologists may have been incomplete, but they were not irrelevant. There is always more, but there is no less than they were beginning to investigate. In fact, the institutional and cultural contexts of leisure are far more comprehensive and pervasive than their research designs could accommodate.

References

Bacon, William. 1975. "Leisure and the Alienated Worker." *Journal of Leisure Research* 7:179–90.

Becker, Gary. 1965. "A Theory of the Allocation of Time." *Journal of Economics* 75:493–517.

Berger, Peter, and T. Luckmann. 1966. *The Social Construction of Reality.* New York: Penguin Books, Inc.

Best, Fred, and B. Stern. 1978. "Lifetime Distribution of Education, Work, and Leisure." *Review of Sport and Leisure* 3:1–46.

Blauner, Robert. 1964. *Alienation and Freedom.* Chicago: University of Chicago Press.

Brown, Robert, et al. 1973. "Leisure in Work: The Occupational Culture of Shipbuilding Workers." in *Leisure and Society in Britain,* eds. M. Smith et al. London: Allen Lane.

Campbell, Angus. 1981. *The Sense of Well-being in America: Recent Patterns and Trends.* New York: McGraw-Hill Book Company.

Cheek, Neil, and W. Burch. 1976. *The Social Organization of Leisure in Human Society.* New York: Harper & Row, Publishers.

Cohn, Robert. 1979. "Age and Satisfaction from Work." *Journal of Gerontology* 34:264–72.

Dubin, Robert. 1956. "Industrial Workers' Worlds." *Social Problems* 3:131–43.

Dumazedier, Joffre. 1967. *Toward a Society of Leisure.* Trans. by S. E. McClure. New York: The Free Press.

Field, Donald, and J. O'Leary. 1973. "Social Groups as a Basis for Assessing Participation in Selected Water-based Recreation." *Journal of Leisure Research* 5:16–25.

Gans, Herbert. 1962. *The Urban Villagers.* New York: The Free Press.

Goldman, Daniel. 1973. "Managerial Mobility and Central Life Interests." *American Sociological Review* 79:119–25.

Hantrais, Linda. 1982. "Leisure and the Family in Contemporary France." *Leisure Studies* 1:81–94.

Havighurst, Robert. 1957. "The Leisure Activities of the Middle-aged." *American Journal of Sociology* 63:152–62.

Hollinghead, August. 1949. *Elmtown's Youth.* New York: Wiley & Sons, Inc.

Howell, Joseph. 1973. *Hard Living on Clay Street.* Garden City: Doubleday & Company, Inc.

Iso-ahola, Seppo. 1980. *Social Psychology of Leisure and Recreation*. Dubuque: William C. Brown Company, Publishers.

Jahoda, Marie. 1979. "The Psychological Meanings of Unemployment." *New Society* 6:492–95.

Kabanoff, Boris, and G. O'Brien. 1980. "Work and Leisure: A Task Attributes Analysis." *Journal of Applied Psychology* 65:596–609.

Kanter, R. M. 1977. *Men and Women of the Corporation*. New York:Basic Books, Inc., Publishers.

Kelly, J. R. 1974. "Socialization into Leisure: A Developmental Approach." *Journal of Leisure Research* 6:181–93.

———. 1976. "Leisure as Compensation for Work Constraint." *Society and Leisure* 3:73–82.

———. 1977. "Leisure Socialization: Replication and Extension." *Journal of Leisure Research* 9:121–32.

———. 1978a. "Leisure Styles and Choices in Three Environments." *Pacific Sociological Review* 21:187–207.

———. 1978b. "Situational and Social Factors in Leisure Choices." *Pacific Sociological Review* 21:313–30.

———. 1978c. "Family Leisure in Three Communities." *Journal of Leisure Research* 10:47–60.

———. 1980. "Outdoor Recreation Participation: A Comparative Analysis." *Leisure Sciences* 3:129–54.

———. 1981. "Leisure Interaction and the Social Dialectic." *Social Forces* 60:304–322.

———. 1982a. *Leisure*. Englewood Cliffs: Prentice-Hall, Inc.

———. 1982b. "New Town Leisure: A British-U.S. Comparison." *Leisure Studies* 1:211–24.

———. 1983a. *Leisure Identities and Interactions*. London: George Allen & Unwin Ltd.

———. 1983b. "Leisure Styles: A Hidden Core." *Leisure Sciences* 5:321–38.

———. 1985a. *Recreation Business*. New York: Macmillan Publishing Co., Inc.

———. 1985b. "Sources of Leisure Styles." in *Recreation and Leisure*. 2d ed., eds. T. Goodale and P. Witt. College Park: Venture Press.

———, and S. Masar. 1981. "Leisure Identities through a Life Course Transition." Champaign: Leisure Research Laboratory, University of Illinois.

———, M. Steinkamp, and J. Kelly. 1986. "Later Life Leisure: How They Play in Peoria." *The Gerontologist* (in press).

Komarovsky, Mirra. 1964. *Blue-collar Marriage*. New York:Random House, Inc.

Kornhauser, A. 1965. *Mental Health of the Industrial Worker*. New York: John Wiley & Sons, Inc.

Kreps, J. M. 1968. *Lifetime Allocation of Work and Leisure*. U.S. Department of Health, Education, and Welfare Research Report No. 22. Washington, D.C.

Levitan, Sar, and W. Johnston. 1973. *Work Is Here to Stay, Alas*. Salt Lake City: Olympus Publishing Co.

Linder, Steffan. 1970. *The Harried Leisure Class*. New York: Columbia University Press.

Lundberg, George, et al. 1934. *Leisure: A Suburban Study.* New York: Columbia University Press.

Lynd, Helen, and R. Lynd, 1956. *Middletown.* New York: Harcourt Brace Jovanovich, Inc.

MacKenzie, Gavin. 1973. *The Aristocrary of Labor: Skilled Craftsmen in the American Class Structure.* Cambridge: Cambridge University Press.

Miller, Karen, and M. Kohn. 1982. "The Reciprocal Effects of Job Conditions and Leisure-time Activities." Paper presented at the 10th World Congress of Sociology, Mexico City.

Noe, F. P. 1971. "Autonomous Spheres of Leisure Activity for the Industrial Executive and the Blue-collarite." *Journal of Leisure Research* 3:220–49.

Orthner, Dennis. 1975. "Leisure Activity Patterns and Marital Satisfaction over the Marriage Career." *Journal of Marriage and the Family* 37:91–102.

Raymon, Paula. 1983. "The Human and Social Costs of Unemployment." Paper of the Consortium of Social Science Associations. Washington, D.C.

Raymond, Lisa. 1985. *Leisure and Unemployment.* Ph.D. diss. University of Illinois at Urbana-Champaign.

Roberts, Kenneth. 1970. *Leisure.* London: Longman Group Limited.

———. 1978. *Contemporary Society and the Growth of Leisure.* London: Longman Group Limited.

Robinson, John. 1977. *Changes in Americans' Use of Time: 1965–1977.* Cleveland: Cleveland State University Communication Center.

Rubin, Lillian. 1976. *Worlds of Pain: Life in the Working Class Family.* New York: Basic Books Inc., Publishers.

Parker, Stanley. 1971. *The Future of Work and Leisure.* New York: Praeger Publishers, Inc.

———. 1983. *Leisure and Work.* London: George Allen & Unwin Ltd.

Pennings, Johan. 1976. "Leisure Correlates of Working Conditions." Paper presented at the American Sociological Association, San Francisco.

Pieper, Josef. 1963. *Leisure: The Basis of Culture.* Trans. by Alexander Dru. New York: Random House, Inc.

Sennett, Richard, and J. Cobb. 1972. *The Hidden Injuries of Class.* New York: Alfred A. Knopf, Inc.

Smigel, Erwin. 1963. *Work and Leisure.* New Haven: College and University Press.

Sutton-Smith, Brian, and J. Roberts. 1981. "Play, Games, and Sport." in *Handbook of Developmental Psychology,* eds. H. Triandis and A. Heron. Boston: Allyn & Bacon, Inc.

Torbert, William. 1973. *Being for the Most Part Puppets.* Cambridge: Schenkman Books, Inc.

Veblen, Thorsten. 1953. *The Theory of the Leisure Class.* New York: New American Library Mentor Books.

Zuzanek, Jiri. 1979. "Time Budget Trends in the USSR: 1922–1970." *Soviet Studies* 31:188–213.

———, and R. Mannell. 1983. "Work-Leisure Relationships from a Sociological and Social Psychological Perspective." *Leisure Studies* 2:327–44.

CHAPTER 8

Political Theory

ISSUES

In critical political theory society is seen to be divided among segments with conflicting interests rather than operating as a functional whole.

There are many historical examples of the use of leisure as an instrument of social control.

In a stratified social system leisure may be a reward for economic contribution and cooperation.

From a critical or conflict perspective those caught in the "iron cage" of economic roles may come to accept leisure as adequate justification for persisting in alienating activity. They may be persuaded that their interests coincide with those receiving investment rewards.

Leisure, too, may become alienated when defined as a commodity-intensive participation in marketed provisions and resources. Wage workers come to accept a false consciousness in which leisure is defined as earned consumption rather than authentic acts of becoming. This reduction of leisure to possessing things is a "one-dimensionality" that fails to grasp the fullness of free and creative activity. Leisure becomes a commodity rather than existential activity.

Alienation, the loss of self-creation, is fostered by mass media, fashion, and market-induced commodity fetishism. Freedom is seen as ability to participate in consumer markets.

Nevertheless, even in such truncated leisure there may be glimpses of freedom that impact other life domains. Marx's view of leisure as liberating activity implies that its realization may require struggle.

Empirical evidence for such critical theory is incomplete and inconsistent. Philosophical arguments rather than research provide a coherent base for the approach.

In Chapter 1, three types of sociological theory were introduced. Chapters 2, 3, 4, and 5 are related to the Weberian interpretive metaphor that takes account of the definitions of social actors. Chapters 6 and 7 reflect the institutional or structural model that treats society as a functional system. Chapter 8 presents conflict theory that is based on the social analysis of Karl Marx and those who find his thought essential.

Institutional theory presupposes that a society is a more-or-less organic system composed of functionally interrelated and complementary institutions. Whereas the polity has a monopoly of force and can coerce compliance with laws and dictates, in a nontotalitarian state a general consensus is developed on the rightness of the system. The state employs its force internally for protection rather than coercion. Those who do not conform to the norms of the system may be coerced only if they are deemed a danger to the system, to others, or perhaps to themselves. The degree of force that must be exercised internally varies according to the homogeneity of the population and the degree of consensus.

However, there is another metaphor of the social system that does not presuppose such a consensus. Societies are seen as divided rather than as an organic system. Two or more segments of the population with different interests are in open or covert conflict within the system. Therefore, if one segment or class is to dominate the society, it will have to exercise some degree of force to gain the compliance of other classes. The ruling class has to find a way or ways to ensure that subordinate classes will act against their own interests.

Such *conflict theory* is profoundly political in that the fundamental presupposition is that there is differential power within the system. From this perspective the themes of social analysis are conflict and control rather than consensus and cooperation. Further, such conflict theory inevitably has a sociological component. Such a system is found to have negative consequences for those who are controlled. In order to gain their compliance, the system in some way forces those subject to it to act contrary to their own interests or even contrary to their human nature. Such a consequence is usually termed *alienation*—a social condition—or *estrangement*—a psychological state.

Political theory based on a conflict metaphor has a number of dimensions that are found in almost all versions. Before introducing sources of those themes that are especially pertinent to leisure, a brief outline should aid in the transition from approaches that assume a high degree of unity within a social system:

- The society is seen as a system bound together by the power of one segment or class to shape the institutions of the system to serve their interests.
- This power is usually found to be based on control of the fundamental economic organization of the society.
- The aim of the elite with such power is to maintain both their own position of control and the system that enables them to reap the rewards of such power.

- The institutional system is not independent of such control, but rather serves the power elite through a system of rewards and penalties that ensure compliance with the system-maintaining requirements identified by the elite.
- As a consequence, the maintenance of the power differential becomes the first criterion of political and social action. This distorts the lives of both rulers and ruled. The basic denial of freedom to the subordinate classes makes it impossible for them to develop their lives according to their natures. They are cut off from the means to determine their own action. Their social condition denies them the full possibility of existential becoming.

It is, of course, possible to find elements of such control in any social system. Certainly any system that is politically totalitarian cannot permit the freedom of action, expression, and thought essential to human development. Any political system in which a self-established elite controls the institutions of a society with the primary aim of perpetuating the system cannot provide a full social context for existential action. The label "democracy" or "republic" offers no assurance of fundamental freedom.

Analysis of systems that have democratic political structures and relative openness in their social institutions is both difficult and subtle. However, some conflict theorists argue democratic forms are no guarantee of social freedom. Rather, those forms may be manipulated by a class with a basis of power that enables them to exercise control. The system, then, covertly consists of different classes with differential access to power. A ruling class is able to use the system to maintain control and gain a disproportionate set of rewards at the costs of distorted conditions for the remainder of the population. Further, when such a metaphor is applied to a society such as the United States or a Western European democracy, leisure is said to be one element in the system of control. In fact, leisure is seen as a trap offering pseudo freedom to those who falsely believe that they are acting in their own interests. Leisure is said to offer the illusion of freedom as a compensation for more fundamental alienation.

This metaphor raises again the issue of consciousness. If leisure can be defined purely as a state of mind or consciousness, then there is no possibility of false consciousness. One either feels free or does not. On the other hand, if there is a possibility of deception in which a perception of freedom is illusory, then there must be some essential social conditions for leisure. Leisure might give the illusion of real choice when the actor has been seduced into a predetermined behavior or attitude.

A Historical Instance. The commonplace historical example of the political use of leisure is that of the city-state of Rome. In the later periods "bread and circuses" were given to nonproductive citizens to distract them from the actual conditions of their lives (Kelly, 1982). The ruling elites offered an escalating program of violent spectacles along with an economic maintenance system to divert the populace from organized opposition. Fundamental alienation from political power, economic productivity, and social integration might be ignored by citizens sufficiently entertained and believing that such diversion was a reward sufficient to purchase their compliance. With selective repression of initial efforts at organized revolt, a society that did not afford opportunity for full human development might endure for several generations.

One problem with the introduction of the political use of leisure through this example is that the conditions seem so different from contemporary societies. How can an American president or British prime minister be a mirror image of a Nero or Caligula? How can a modern Western economic system tied to public education be compared to the strict limits of a caste system and slave economy of Rome? How can today's constitutional guarantees against tyranny be parallel to the imperial cults and senatorial conspiracies of that ancient republic? Beginning with Rome makes it all too easy to dismiss the issue (Brantlinger, 1983).

However, such an easy response does not seem to make the issues disappear. Rather, at least some aspects of the manipulation of individuals through leisure appear from quite a variety of sources. All are not based on critical, or conflict, theory. For example, the manipulation of choices through various mass-media marketing devices is an accepted economic practice. The impacts of media visions of leisure that are oriented toward costly environments, expensive equipment or clothing, or even sexual conquest have been questioned even by those who engage in the practices. Is it not possible that a market system engenders manipulation through precisely the same processes by which it offers choices? Is it not likely that there is some distortion in the values and images of life that we *learn* through our institutions? One can support the system and still take a critical stance toward many of its practices. Therefore, the analysis that follows compares functional arguments for socially adaptive leisure with conflict arguments that such leisure is alienating. The same phenomena are examined from both systemic and conflict perspectives.

Social Stratification: A Divided Society _____

By definition, modern, or complex, societies are divided among population segments with greater or lesser power, economic rewards, opportunities, or even freedom. However, some argue that this division is functional in accomplishing the different tasks that have to be carried out for the system to survive. Others argue that such divisions involve exploitation by elites in a system allocating resources by criteria other than contribution to the common welfare. Further, whether leisure is defined as a fundamental resource for human development or a reward for acquiescence to the system is based on frequently unexamined premises.

Leisure as a System Reward: The Functional Approach

Social stratification has been a fundamental theme of sociology from its founding. Modern postindustrial societies are characterized by divisions. The indices of differences may vary among different systems. In traditional preindustrial systems rigid castes were often determined almost wholly by heredity. In capitalist industrial societies wealth has been the primary criterion. Both the level and source of income and financial assets distinguish elites from those who have in some way benefited in lesser ways from the system. Therefore, some element of power—the ability to shape institutional actions—is usually entered into the stratification equation. Max Weber (1958) offered an enduring distinction that will be followed in this discussion. He defined *social class* as "life chances"—placement in the socioeconomic system determining access to resources and opportunities. *Social status* is defined as "life-style"—the characteristic modes of life of those in identifiable classes or strata. Further, the stratification metaphor denotes a higher–lower set of segments that are layered rather than continuous. There are distinctly different opportunity structures for defined classes and different styles for status groups.

The class-status distinction is critical for the analysis of leisure. Leisure styles are understood as a central dimension of status-based behavior. In fact, leisure may be *the* critical element distinguishing strata that symbolize their level of transcendence of economic necessity (Veblen, 1953). From a functional perspective leisure is a status-differentiated part of a system that rewards those economic and social behaviors making greater contributions to the society. Greater rewards are said to accrue to those who take the greatest risks, endure the most arduous preparation, or perform the most important tasks. The reward system draws individuals into such actions and keeps them motivated to behave in a productive manner. From a conflict perspective, leisure has class-differentiated chances and access to resources.

In a modern capitalist economy a primary requirement for the system is that capital be invested in the economy rather than hoarded or expended on immediate consumption. Therefore, investment is rewarded in a measure that encourages such behavior. If investment is seen as the *prime* requisite of the system, then it will be rewarded beyond other contributions. Further, since monetary return is only more of the same and for the wealthy not immediately usable, other kinds of reward accompany the economic. Among these rewards are prestige and power. Prestige is recognition of superiority, as when universities grant degrees and trustee authority to the wealthy with the tacit assumption that wealth is a sign of wisdom. Power is more important. To maintain a system that will reward investment over the long term, those who make significant investments are also granted access to political power.

The premise is that such differences in rewards, prestige, and power are required to elicit necessary behaviors of financial risk, personal preparation, and responsible citizenship. That life chances are to some extent perpetuated by the differential opportunities is seen as a cost of the system, but one that is mitigated by the relative openness fostered by public education and other mobility avenues. Also, the control over the labor force that is endemic to the system is held to be necessary in order to ensure the consequences of investment. Economic power must accompany investment, from this perspective, in order to attract risk capital.

Few would deny that the lower and relatively powerless classes have less opportunity than those born into upper levels. That those at the very bottom may not only be denied equal opportunity but injured by their deprivations is admitted. Some, of course, justify such injury by "blaming the victim" and pointing to alleged moral or motivational deficiences of the poor. Others justify the costs of class by emphasizing the means of ascension available to those who strive to rise.

One critical response to stratification is a simple recognition of serious differences in opportunity that are built into the system. Such *opportunity structures* are more than reward differences. For example, women in the economy are not only consistently paid less for equivalent jobs but are given different entry and advancement opportunities in many economic settings. Functionally, this may produce an adequate work force for many dead-end and low-reward jobs. The explanation given is not one of discrimination but of the "market." In this case, the labor market sorts out workers according to a number of criteria and offers the rewards and incentives required to fill needed positions. That is, the system operates to allocate workers to required tasks and positions.

The concept of the *market* is crucial to this metaphor purporting to explain the system. The exchange of goods and resources is said to be governed by a "law" of demand and supply and the "invisible hand" of price (Smith, 1902). Prices fall as supply exceeds demand until production is adjusted to a viable return level. Conversely, supply will be increased when prices rise due to scarcity. Economic limits and problems with this self-adjustment model have become both evident and

critical (Kelly, 1985:Chap. 2). However, the functional model of stratification is partly a market model. The reward system operates to attract individuals into economic positions and behaviors as the labor
and capital markets require. Leisure is defined as *reward* for functional
behaviors that are supported out of economic surplus. Leisure, then,
is earned rather than being a human condition or right.

The functional argument continues with the concept of *welfare* in
which lower strata may need access to opportunities for health, education, and recreation beyond those they can purchase on the market.
The first argument for public services such as recreation programs is
equity. Even those with the least economic resources require some opportunity for health-supporting activity. Public recreation, it is argued,
is functional for the society in undergirding the health of low-level
workers and providing outlets for energy that might otherwise take
destructive directions. The liberal concept of state welfare programs is
that the entire society benefits when those with little purchasing power
in the market receive basic supplements that support their present or
potential contributions to the system.

Leisure, then, may be understood from the reward perspective as
earned by useful behavior. Since the most valuable behavior is investment, extraordinary leisure rewards may accrue to those who have
the economic resources to make significant contributions. The elites
may own what others can only rent, exhibit distinctive styles, and
maintain private access to rare resources. For those who contribute through their labor, the market system allocates leisure resources
in proportion to the value and scarcity of their product. For those in
the lowest strata some minimal set of leisure resources may be provided by the state in recognition of their potential value to the system.

Equity may be the basis of public opportunities, but efficiency is the
criterion of allocation. From a welfare perspective and in a condition
of scarce resources, how can priorities be determined? The basic rule
is that of economic efficiency. What provisions yield the greatest return
on the public investment? Which resources produce the most use, the
fullest return in functioning, and the greatest sense of reward? Further,
such return may be long-term as well as immediate. Setting aside
parkland may produce more for the dollar over several decades, although a carnival provides more pleasure-yielding enjoyment in one
weekend.

The point is that leisure has economic value as reward and welfare.
It has a political dimension in that a stratified social system may have
to make decisions about the allocation of opportunities beyond those
determined by economic markets. One does not have to be a Marxist
to accept that leisure has political dimensions in contemporary society.

Leisure as an Instrument of Control: A Conflict Argument

Thorsten Veblen (1953) saw leisure as a symbol of social differentiation, a matter of style and status. Contemporary social critics have gone farther to see in leisure one facet of the control of working classes by economic elites. Leisure as consumption is one part of the overall market structure. With rising income levels, leisure markets may become increasingly important to economic growth. At the same time, insofar as leisure is defined in consumption terms by workers, they may become more and more dedicated to cooperative performance on the job in order to secure the income that makes such leisure possible. The main criticism of marketed leisure from a functional perspective might be that a balance of re-creative leisure should include a full measure of physical activity and stress reduction.

A critical perspective begins with an analysis of leisure as consumption and market response rather than existential decision and becoming. However, that is only the beginning. The critical dimension that is usually overlooked in popular analysis is political. The root issue is not a matter of personal awareness but of social organization. Narrow definitions and lack of active and creative initiative in leisure are the result of more than a failure in education or outmoded life-styles.

There are several forms for such critical analysis. However, the most influential form is based on the work of Karl Marx and the variety of social critics who have revised Marxian themes. Nevertheless, a pervasive theme, the image of modern workers trapped in an "iron cage" of economic technique, is derived from the thought of that thoroughly anti-Marxist sociologist, Max Weber (1958). Weber focused on rational organization and the emphasis on productive technique in his analysis of a socioeconomic system that exercises more and more control over the lives of workers. Weber opposed Marx's materialist basis of historical analysis with his proposition that even a religious doctrine, Calvinism, had been a factor in the rise of capitalism. Later Marxist critics have adopted Weber's analysis of how the capitalist stress on market-driven production has led to a reduction of freedom and self-determination in the workplace. In recent years, concern over worker disenchantment and alienation has led to considerable convergence on the problems of negative and alienating work conditions from those with widely differing assumptions and aims.

Critical Political Theory. No brief presentation can incorporate all the themes, evidence, and subtleties of such analysis. For our purposes, a general outline is required before going on to concentrate on the place of leisure in the argument. The main themes of such critical political theory follow:

1. The social system is divided into two main segments: those who control the economy and those required to labor for wages. Control of the means and mode of production—of the instruments, locales, and organizational processes of the economy—is vested in those who provide investment capital. As a result, the prime aim of the system is to yield an adequate return on such investment over a period of time. Workers, then, are one instrument of production that are rented when needed and nurtured in whatever ways support the production process.

2. The social system is composed of many institutional structures, all of which are subordinate to the economy-based elite with the power to shape the system to its ends. The polity, or state, may have a democratic, or representative, selection system, but that system is determined by those who finance election campaigns and provide technical knowledge to governmental instrumentalities. The polity serves many interests and is responsive to many needs, but all within the framework of system maintenance. The fundamental aim is to conserve the economic system and to meet its requirements. The school system, on all levels, is to prepare students for later productive contributions. A multitiered education system evaluates as well as educates. It sorts students and sends them into the labor market with differing credentials that determine the levels on which they may seek employment. It thus serves the economy.

3. However, this process is seldom overtly coercive. Rather, the integrated institutions generally produce individuals who "believe in the system." They engage in education for the purpose of preparing for economic roles. They learn almost from birth a set of values and world views that are consistent with the system. And on those occasions when dissatisfaction becomes acute, there are sanctions that bring most recalcitrants back into line. Among the most profound sanctions is a withdrawal of purchasing power in a market economy.

4. This analysis is profoundly political. The dimension of power is fundamental. One group with certain economic resources has the power to shape the system to their ends. The remainder of the population, far and away the numerical majority, must cooperate with the system in order to gain the rewards that provide a viable context for life. Not only "extras" such as music and mountain lakes, but the necessities of household nourishment, residence, health care, transportation, and clothing require market purchasing power. Anything more than survival-level minimums of market purchase requires some value participation in the economic system (or a violation of the system entailing the risk of punishment). The market, then, becomes an instrument en-suring economic cooperation. People work in order to live in the sense of having access to the most basic and life-enhancing resources. Workers are controlled, then, not simply by the direct or indirect coercive power of the state, but by the resource-allocation system of the economy.

To this point, the so-called critical argument is little different from the functional one. Vocabularies of both arguments have their positive and negative connotations, but both describe an interrelated system in which the market functions to distribute resources in a way that ensures general cooperation with economic requirements. There may be a subtle difference in the insistence of critical analysts that political power is concentrated among those with economic leverage rather than being dispersed, or pluralistic. But the real difference rests on what are seen as the outcomes of the system. From a functional perspective all this works reasonably well to meet the needs of the populace. From a critical perspective the consequences for most people are far less than optimal.

A significant concept is that of *interests*. Are the interests of those with little economic power coincident with the interests of the elites? Does the system allocate resources in a way that supports its contin-uation *and* the life conditions of the greatest number of its people? Or, as critical theorists would have us believe, are the interests of the elite so different that their control of the system results in a truncated and distorted set of life chances for the majority? In the Marxist vocabulary, does the ruling class exploit the working class?

The "Iron Cage". To examine this issue, it is necessary to review the arguments of critical theorists who are sure that the fundamental consequences of this system are the estrangement and alienation of individuals from the life-sustaining and -developing contexts of human existence. Again, an enumeration of relevant parts of the analysis may serve to introduce the point of view:

1. What is this "iron cage" of life in an industrial society? The met-aphor was offered by Max Weber (1958) to refer to a rationally organized production system that controlled work conditions in a dehumanizing way. The end was seen as efficient production rather than some sense of contribution and workmanship. The metaphor has been adopted by a variety of theorists including Michael Foucault, Jurgen Habermas, Herbert Marcuse, and others concerned about the debasement of work as productive human engagement into controlled and segmented tasks. *Closing the Iron Cage* (Andrew, 1981), an analysis of Taylorism and the "scientific management" of production, argues that technological rationality threatens to comprehend leisure as well as work. Despite a dated and incomplete grasp of current leisure research and theory, the author presents a political approach to leisure that exemplifies the control theme. Control in the service of production is found to be pervasive rather than limited to the factory and the office.

The "iron cage" is the subordination of the processes and contexts of economic life to production efficiency. Human "scale," meaning, community, or anything else is sacrificed to lowering the labor cost of production. Although enlightened management may develop programs designed to raise the levels of workers' sense of meaning, community, and environmental control, the goal is productive engagement. Concern with worker health through recreation, programs of continuing education, and enhancement of company identification and loyalty rest on the foundation of increased productivity. Labor, then, is a "factor of production" rather than a central element of human existence.

2. For workers economic engagement is primarily instrumental. It offers more than income. A job is also a social identity, a definition of being valued, a fulfillment of powerful expectations, a central life role, and a context of some expression of community. But first it is instrumental, a means to the end of supporting the contexts of life for self and those for whom we are responsible.

3. Instrumental definitions and management for efficiency lead to "alienation" both on and off the job. Alienation as a life condition is a loss of essential selfhood. The concept is based on a philosophical image of what human life can become. For Marx human beings are to be existential in the sense of deciding and creating what they may become and social in the sense of needing to develop free and expressive relationships in community with others (Walicki, 1983:52). When human beings become enslaved by political or economic forces that block such becoming and community, then they are alienated from their own essential natures. For Marx such alienation has been forced on workers in a system in which relationships are "reified" and meaning is expressed in terms of "things." When the exchange of commodities becomes the central meaning of work or family or leisure, then lives are cut off from their own potential. Social conditions are dehumanizing rather than developmental.

Such alienation is a social condition, not simply an attitude or state of mind. It is enforced by coercive political power when necessary and fostered by an institutional consensus where possible. However, there is the subjective side of alienation. A sense of *estrangement* accompanies alienation as at least an undefined awareness that we are caught in nets not of our own making. Blauner (1964:15) identified the elements of alienation as the negation of "autonomy, responsibility, social connection, and self-actualization." These dimensions are fundamental to being human and are more than *feeling* anything, however deep or profound. To abolish such a condition requires social change, not just awareness or adjustment.

4. How does such a condition occur? Partly it is the result of mass production and specialization in the organization of production. Partly it stems from a separation of management from the actual conditions of production in a complex organization. But according to neo-Marxist theories, it also rests on the ways in which social organization has become segmented and dis-integrated. Work, family, community, leisure, and everything else have become instrumental. And the end is a false one! It is the possession of commodities. Work is turned from productive engagement into time and a paycheck. The family becomes primarily an institution for property holding, and even children are defined as possessions. Community is turned into a competition for positions and prestige. And leisure is defined as *spending* income and time in a "discretionary" mode. The most basic relationships become perverted into a possession-oriented means rather than ends in themselves. Leisure is at best a reward that must be earned and at worst just one more instrument to demonstrate status. Nothing is intrinsic; all is for the sake of something else. And, in the end, the something else is an illusion—another means to an unattainable end.

Alienated Leisure.   What are the consequences for leisure? Is leisure as alienated as work? This critical analysis finds that leisure has become distorted by such "commodification" so that it is not a domain of freedom and becoming but an instrument of economic and political control.

The Marxist concept is that of "commodity fetishism." At the least, leisure should be a haven from the "dull compulsion of economic relations" (Marx, 1970:737). However, because of the fetishism that has been inculcated through the learned value system of capitalism, even this space of relative freeom has been invaded. It may be for some a time of "recreation," for returning to production with renewed strength and vigor. However, it is not a space of real freedom for becoming. Rather, it is defined in terms of the things that can be possessed and utilized, consumed and displayed. "Time for education, for intellectual development, for the fulfillment of social functions and for social intercourse, for the free play of bodily and mental activity . . . are sheer moonshine!" (Marx, 1973:265). The reach of capitalism turns even leisure into a response to production in which freedom is lost to the desire for ownership, control, and status.

When life is defined in terms of the ownership and control of things, then real freedom has been surrendered to the system. However, the problem is social in the sense that its root causes are systemic. When the fundamental conditions of life are beyond the influence of all but an elite few, then the remainder are likely to seek some domain in which they can exercise decisive influence. For many the family appears to provide such a social microcosm. However, the family domain has been so invaded by external forces that it may seem even more resistant to decisive action than other institutions.

Leisure, defined as "what you don't have to do," ought to be most free. However, in that domain, too, matters do not seem that simple. Acting in creative and expressive ways that yield results of growth and development requires not only risk but also swimming against the river of conformity. Leisure, too, has its norms and expectations. Leisure, too, is depicted in the mass media in ways designed to engender certain kinds of behavior. Leisure, too, becomes a product of the economic system.

What is a good time from a conflict perspective? For many, it has become associated with spending and consumption. The great vacation is going to the place where opportunities to spend money and watch others perform dominate the time—to a Disney World or Las Vegas. The family vacation is designed around the use of travel and activity-related paraphernalia. Weekends are spent in projects to use tools and other equipment around the residence. And far and away the greatest amount of time is spent in front of the television, a medium for the direct and indirect promotion of the purchase of material goods. At best, leisure may seem to be a kind of safety valve—a little sphere of pseudo sovereignty in which discretionary spending gives the appearance of freedom and choice. In reality, leisure has become a significant part of the iron cage in which compliance in the economic sphere is enforced by the economic necessity of making the payments on leisure toys purchased on credit. Lack of meaning and satisfaction on the job are compensated in the domain of leisure in which earned income and time are employed in consumption. The meaning of work is to be found in those things that are to signify personal choice and freedom.

Such "commodity fetishism," or dominating attachment to things, is proposed by Marx in *Capital* (1967:71–83) as a central element in worker alienation. Humans become enslaved by their own products to the extent that even the openness of leisure and the sharing of intimacy become reified into a mind-set of owning and consuming. Pleasure may be defined by expenditure so that the ultimate leisure activity becomes shopping. Relationships are gauged by domination and control rather than the quality of communication and caring. Even marriage for the alienated male is a choice of someone who will appear to support desired social status, and for the alienated female marriage becomes a decision based on economic exchange. An inability to determine central contexts of life drives men and women to try to make effectual decisions elsewhere. Because the outcomes of creative effort or relational risk are difficult to measure, market choices with concrete outcomes become a surrogate for real freedom.

Such alienation from the conditions necessary for human development—existential freedom and real community—is a social condition. However, one inseparable consequence is estrangement, a feeling of being cut off and powerless in a world that is not amenable to our lines of action. Such estrangement is more than a mood; it is the subjective side of a fundamental condition but with concrete results. We tend to try to secure some measure of control—over the circumstances of our living and even the associates in our interaction. Feeling powerless in a comprehensive sense, we try to achieve a localized sense of control. We may try to control other people, especially those for whom we can allocate rewards. We may seek some social space that is private, cut off from the social forces that surround us. Or, we may engage in activity that demonstrates some effectuality, some result of our action or decision. One explanation of the seriousness of so much leisure—especially activities incorporating competition or another measured outcome—is that they offer an opportunity to *do something* concrete. We have at least this little chance to *be somebody* in a world that is mostly out of control.

What, if anything, is wrong with this? Why not recognize that in a complex mass society we have to find such proximate environments for doing something that provides the satisfaction of a concrete outcome? If leisure can afford such an event, then it should be valued for what it is, not degraded for what it can seldom be. We return to this issue at the end of the chapter. Here let it suffice to draw the contrast between alienation and authenticity. Underlying the critique is the conviction that there is at least the potential of an authentic human nature in each being. The next chapter will explore some variations of this philosophical perspective. From a Marxist view being human means to be productive as a free member of a community in which growth is fostered (Fromm, 1961:28). Anything less means being separated from one's true self and from the reality of others.

Later Critical Theory. The "Frankfort School" of critical theory was made up of a number of critical theorists who applied Marxist and other tools to the analysis of modern society (Antonio, 1983). They attempted to reconstitute the dream of human liberation in relation to the totalitarian developments of Europe, both Fascist and Communist, and to a revised Marxist critique of Western capitalism. Their program has incorporated political, economic, social, and psychological elements. Among the most influential members have been Herbert Marcuse and Jurgen Habermas. Each has addressed leisure as one problematic factor in the repression found in modern industrial societies.

Marcuse (1964) is most famous for his analysis of the "one-dimensionality" of alienated humans who have surrendered their freedom and sensuality to commodification. His addition of Freudian dimensions to the Marxist argument elicited wide response in the counter-culture movements of the 1960s. His analysis of alienation incorporated the sensual as well as the social nature of humankind. Alienation is more than external control that cut individuals off from contexts of creative production and community. The alienation of commodity fetishism turns persons away from their own sensual and expressive natures to the single theme of possession. Control and ownership of *things* as symbols of real existence replaces a unified action with and toward others that includes the full dimensions of communication—bodily, emotional, and intellectual. Others become objects of our action, to be used and manipulated like things, rather than free and responsive actors with whom our free actions may be articulated. Leisure, then, becomes a domain of possession rather than sharing, of separation rather than community.

Habermas's complex and often opaque writings contain several references to the lack of real freedom in leisure. Two themes seem especially pertinent. The first is the power of mass media to shape consciousness and distort the ways in which life is interpreted (Thompson and Held, 1982:Chap. 3). Habermas has focused on problems of communication throughout his work. Without pursuing the complexities of his analysis, here we refer to a critical implication for leisure. It is that the thought-forms that we employ to think and speak about leisure are so distorted that we are trapped in inauthenticity. Leisure, socially defined as freedom, is too much the product of a socially inculcated value system to embody real freedom. Rather, it becomes a kind of slavery that we have learned to call free. The first theme is that of socialization that disguises control as freedom. The second is that of legitimation. In the *Legitimation Crisis* (1975) Habermas argues that the instrumentalities of society's institutions combine to create a consensus on the rightness of current values and structures. The media communicate a view of the life afforded by market participation. Leisure, as a reflection of the dominant values, reinforces the overall program of legitimation.

If all this seems difficult to penetrate, it is partly because of the interrelationship of themes. Again, Weber argued that the cage of modern industrial society is based on the devised techniques of efficient production. Techniques have their own logic and power (Ellul, 1965). Marxists, however, insist that there is a political dimension to the resulting control. The interests of a ruling elite are served by a social system in which opportunities are channeled into a production-consumption scheme that binds workers to the system. Neo-Marxists and the Frankfort School add that the system has so shaped the consciousness of the dominated classes that they have come to believe that their interests are served best when they are given the market power to purchase their own little set of commodities, falsely signifying freedom. In this system leisure as existential and social freedom becomes redefined as the ability to purchase those things that entertain. In fact, those leisure possessions may become fetishes that dominate decisions and the allocation of resources, thus producing both markets and a labor force that cannot take the risk of dissent. Underlying this argument is the Marxist assertion that social conditions create consciousness, that we are socialized to believe in the way things are.

Leisure as an Instrument of Political Interests ⎯⎯⎯⎯⎯

Again, the same evidence may be interpreted in two ways: supporting the viability of the social system and signaling its divisions and conflicts of interest. Further, the place of leisure in the social system has often been defined without a recognition that political dimensions are implicit in the analysis. The aim of the following section is to attempt to delineate the political premises of the two main metaphors. To accomplish this task requires some return to the premises of each perspective.

Useful Leisure: Style as Choice

From both systemic and conflict perspectives, modern leisure is a product of industrialization. This is not to argue that there has been no relatively free, expressive, or self-contained activity in less complex social systems. Rather, leisure as a set-apart, residual reward earned by participation in a separate production process is a phenomenon that has developed only with industrialization. Joffre Dumazedier (1967) has argued that leisure in this sense did not exist in preindustrial societies because the idleness of former elites was not leisure, religious obligations permeated holidays, time away from work was given to communal celebrations, and work and play were fused into a rhythm rather than separated. He has made his case by defining leisure as a separate and residual domain of life in which individual choice is exercised. Despite his sociological orientation, he posits an individualistic view of leisure in which personal freedom is exercised in action directed toward individual expression and development. The possibility that leisure may be—at least in part—more profoundly social is seldom explored in contemporary theory.

In any case, from these premises leisure can be defined as useful to the maintenance of the social system. Leisure is the time *given* to workers for their recuperation. Its primary function is to make them better workers. It should provide rest, reduce stress, strengthen supportive relationships, enhance physical and mental health, and generally serve the ends of productivity. Conversely, the "problem of leisure" is defined as the inability of workers to employ their nonwork time beneficially (Andrew, 1981:14). Dulled by routine or seeking escape, nonwork time is lost to activity that either stultifies or debilitates. Mindless television watching and release through alcohol or drugs may be the result of alienation, but such activities are also a functional problem. Leisure is not used properly. It is not managed in such a way as to yield the desired result, enhanced productivity. Intellectuals decry the waste and lack of creative investment. Recreation managers mourn the passive absorption rather than active participation. And corporate managers and owners seek ways to divert the waste of time to renewal and the development of healthy recreation.

Those who have promoted public recreation in the twentieth century have had to make a case for its value. In general, the case has been built on a functional model. The society will benefit from engagement in well-conceived recreation. In one classic text it was maintained that "Organized recreation, if properly directed, has a tendency to prevent the occurrence of social disorganization and personal demoralization. Recreation affords opportunities for the achievement of fair play, respect for law and order, and the inculcation of cooperative participation" (Neumeyer and Neumeyer, 1958:24). *Organized* recreation channels participants into activity that is physically healthful, socially consolidating, and politically integrative.

The relationship between industry and recreation is seen as reciprocal. On the one hand, economic participation buys leisure. It is part of the reward package. On the other hand, leisure is to be used for re-creation, to support effective economic participation. It is such re-creation that legitimates leisure. It is not seen as an essential element of human life but as an instrumental good valued in proportion to its contribution to economic efficiency. It supports the productive capacities of workers. Further, leisure—especially if it requires financial expenditure—is a positive part of the reward system that motivates workers. If workers were to live at a subsistence level with all resources allocated to survival necessities, there might well be a reduced incentive to do more than meet minimum requirements. However, leisure offers a realm of pleasure in which discretionary income may produce a direct and motivating reward that can be seen and felt.

From this perspective Marxist critics of capitalism are refuted in terms of the ability of the system to reward workers in terms they find satisfying. Marx predicted a bare subsistence level of wages that would not only enslave but also discourage most workers. Defenders of capitalism point to the standard of living of Western workers—their housing, education levels, health benefits, and especially leisure. Workers have vacation trips, recreation vehicles, access to special environments, and even second homes. They are rewarded far beyond the dreams of any defender or critic of capitalism a half century ago.

Leisure, however, is more than just opportunity for pleasure-producing spending. It is a domain of relative freedom that balances the relative constraint of economic roles. People are, after all, not just automatons or puppets. They have to have some compensating environments in which they may make choices, determine outcomes, and select companions. Leisure affords just this opportunity, compensating for the necessary limits of work and separated enough that its choices do not negate economic structures. On the highway the released worker controls power, determines direction, and escapes the supervision required on the job. And he drives *his own* car! At the stadium the same worker identifies with an exhibition of skill and with the outcome as *his* team wins or loses. And, in the best of all possible industrial worlds, he or she even plays on the company softball team, yielding health benefits and a feeling of solidarity with the corporate employer.

There are other functional benefits as well. In leisure the family institution is supported in ways that consolidate relationships. The family, then, reproduces itself and is the source of the next generation's labor force. The family even nurtures and protects children until they are ready for more specific economic engagement. Leisure is a context for the development and consolidation of this essential social institution. The same argument can be made for support of community organizations, political activity, religious affiliation, and other social functions. Leisure is defined as opportunity for engagement that builds the various interrelated facets of the social system. It has a place in reproducing the·society, in supporting its institutional and ideological structure.

From a critical stance Thorstein Veblen (1953) pointed to an element of leisure that may also be taken in a positive way. That is that the "right" leisure, recreation that is well directed, not only restores workers for productive engagement but also socializes them into a value system that enhances social solidarity. The linking of leisure goods and styles to social status reinforces the commodity-intensive character of leisure. As such, it supports markets for leisure-related production and places a premium on the financial rewards of employment. Further, leisure styles that accurately signify social status reinforce behavior that is expected in related social roles. The manual worker may be "rough-and-ready" in his physical pursuits. The professional may engage in social organizations on the appropriate level and in self-development activity. The homemaker/mother/caretaker may have leisure oriented toward the care and nurture of children. The general norms associated with central roles strongly influence how people define themselves and choose the modes of leisure that fit those social identities (Kelly, 1983).

And, when all else fails in the public spheres of life, leisure is a realm of the private that remains at least partly under control (Sennett, 1978). In leisure there is a separation from public roles that may engender a retreat into a protected area of life. When public roles—economic or political—offer little in the way of opportunity for personal development and effectual action, then the nonwork domains may become the focus of life. It is in those more proximate areas of family, home, clubs, church, hobbies, arts, and sports that the massive immobility of the larger society may be left behind. The individual may feel like *someone* who is actually doing something.

Note that this outline of how leisure may be personally meaningful and socially functional can be interpreted in either a positive or critical way. From the first perspective leisure does contribute to a system that merits support. From the alternative view leisure is a domain in which the constraints of economic life can be forgotten and preparation for production supported. The central issue is that of *interests*. Are the interests of all in a society basically the same, or is the society divided between those with power and those exploited by that power? Is leisure a social space offering opportunity for valued activity contributing to self-expression and valued primary groups? Or is leisure one more deceptive substitute for real freedom that is shaped by a system in which only a few are free? In either case leisure is political—one element of a system that requires voluntary compliance in its institutional functions.

Leisure and Alienation

Is the relative freedom of leisure a real social possibility or a manufactured illusion? If the former, leisure can be actualized—if only in limited times and places. If the latter, leisure is just one dimension of false consciousness and acquiescence to domination. The central theme is freedom. The critical metaphor presents a picture of life in a modern industrial society in which freedom is a chimera and alienation a social fact. This is directly counter to the functional metaphor in which alienation is a psychological attitude subject to remedy and freedom fundamental, if only partially realized.

There are a number of themes in the critical analysis of alienation. Here we introduce only a few that are especially tied to leisure. This is not in any way a full critique of the massive and complex literature on alienation and its manifestations.

Media, Fashion, and Fetishism. One central issue is how individuals become enmeshed in false consciousness, in self-definitions that are contrary to their own natures and interests. How can human beings come to define their own fulfillment in terms of possessions and their actions oriented toward things? How can they become ready and willing to be used as instruments of production rather than to *be* producers? How can they allow freedom to be defined as an ability to participate in the retail market?

The fullest answer is that the socializing institutions of the social system are indeed integrated. When there is a pervasive consensus on the values and world views that support the system, then basic socialization in the family is reinforced by the school, church, voluntary organizations, and even leisure. We come to believe in differential rewards, motivation by competition, and the rights of investors. We also come to believe a set of political tenets fundamental to democratic government. Therefore, there has to be some way of reconciling anomalies and inconsistencies in the system with what we believe it ought to be. The general way in which this is accomplished is through the development and inculcation of a *social myth*. We see what is through the prism of what we have been taught ought to be.

In modern society there is a new factor augmenting the institutional socializing institutions. Mass media, and especially television, receive the largest part of our discretionary time. They bring immediate, available, and inexpensive signifiers of meaning on demand directly before the viewer. Although convincing evidence of specific consequences for the consciousness of regular viewers remains scattered and inconclusive, the likelihood is that we come to see the world in ways that are at least partly shaped by the medium. Douglas Kellner has developed a critical theory of television that measures its contradictory images, messages, and effects (Kellner, 1981:40–46). He suggests that TV contributes to social solidarity without being monothematic or direct propaganda. He criticizes the Frankfort School for its lack of attention to the inconsistencies in "the culture industry." Television does portray more than system-supporting material, as in news coverage of the Vietnam war. Problems may not dominate programming, but the medium is hardly monolithic in portrayals of conflict and disintegrating elements in the society.

On the other hand, the combined entertainment and advertising impact of television is commodity intensive. The "good life" appears to presuppose a nearly unlimited supply of private space, leisure goods and opportunities, fancy cars, jet flights, expensive wardrobes, and continual sexual entree to attractive others. People alone are usually depicted as unhappy or emotionally disturbed. Those with life-styles that deviate from a possession-laden existence are usually secretly envious, afraid to compete, somehow misoriented, or eventually converted to more conventional contexts of happiness. Temporary relationships with a high measure of use or exploitation of others, demonstrations of power over others, and market measures of success run through daytime and nighttime drama, comedies, and made-for-TV movies as well as in the advertising. Leisure contexts are employed to lend glamour to episodes of interaction as well as to associate products with evident pleasure and symbols of success. Leisure is seen as a reward that can be purchased, as a stylistic symbol of power and approval, and as an environment for self-enhancing and immediately gratifying behaviors. Further, leisure is best for those with lots of money to spend on it.

Another element of the media approach to life and leisure is found in the marriage between advertising and fashion (Ewen and Ewen, 1982). An analysis of historical trends in fashion suggests that fashion change is more than a marketing device promoting the obsolescence and replacement of clothing, cars, and other consumer products that are still functional. Rather, the design–introduction–promotion–planned obsolescence–replacement design cycle has been employed to deflect social change. Clothing that was first adopted as a symbol of protest as well as antifashion functionality is picked up by the industry marketers and transformed into a style. Consumer culture is so responsive to every nuance and source of fashion that no symbol can exist for long without being co-opted by fashion markets. Thus an illusion of change is fostered by market mechanisms. The fashion industry has adopted the culture as well as clothing first taken as a protest by counter culture youth. Historical analysis reveals a cycle of introduction, negative response to the protest symbols, adopting and marketing, and a final negation or blunting of the point of the protest.

In general, such a media analysis simply points to many ways in which industry, marketing, and the media form a mutually reinforcing system for socialization. Further, elements of leisure are central to the process. For "mainstreamers" and those who seek such status, the media depict life in which leisure commodities yield happiness, prestige, and power over others. And even for those who would stand apart from the normative culture, market mechanisms can respond to co-opt symbols of protest and make them standard cohort-identifying goods with clearly segmented markets and widened appeal. In the process this season's rebellion becomes next season's fashion. However, perhaps even more significant in the long term is the deep and thoroughgoing portrayal of life in the society as "right" or at least "ok." Criticism is absorbed into world views that admit no radical change and gently suggest that individual adjustment is preferable to social reorientation.

The Theft of Freedom. In such an integrated system what is the meaning of *freedom?* This is a central issue for leisure when it is defined with an essential dimension of self-determination. Is freedom a little decision-set or a condition of life?

Herbert Marcuse (1961) argued that freedom is relative and varies in the different domains of life. In fact, as freedom is diminished by technology in the workplace, it may be enhanced outside. If automation were total, then "the sphere outside labour" would define freedom and fulfillment (1961:142). The problem is that a social system may be so integrated that such separation is impossible. If life is defined in a rigid and narrow way in economic roles, can it be widened and relaxed in nonwork roles? Is it possible to be an automaton at work and a creator in leisure? Is there a "leisure solution to the problem of work"?

Most critical theorists would answer "No!" The argument is twofold. First, social institutions are overlapping rather than segmented. For example, the school prepares students for economic roles. This preparation then impacts orientations toward leisure as well. Second, individuals cannot transform themselves and their characters in deliberate transitions from one environment to another. How we define ourselves and interact with others is not totally role bound, to be changed like a jacket or pair of gloves. Although capitalism has a vested interest in separating the realms of work and leisure, of production and consumption, in the end the effort fails. It fails just because the same actor with the same basic needs and abilities to decide and act moves from one domain to another. No matter how thorough the attempt to redefine action and intentions, we cannot draw impermeable barriers. An exercise of creativity in leisure will reveal alienation in work just as control in work affects the exercise of relative discretion in leisure.

Simone Weil (1972:157) wrote that there is no natural equilibrium between "man and the surrounding forces of nature." Rather, human activity is a *self-creating* force. Alienation is a cutting off of such activity and the conditions that make it possible. Alienated work denies the worker the right to produce, to contribute to the society in ways that return a sense of meaning. Alienated leisure denies the possibility of self-actualizing action in that realm of relative openness. Leisure becomes a social instrument rather than authentic human activity. It is reduced to being a useful adjunct to the economic system.

For Marx human beings who are not active in making their own lives, who are essentially passive, are dead (Fromm, 1961:30). Human passion is the essential striving to accomplish an end. When that striving is without an effectual result, human becoming is denied. If we love without response, we cannot become *loving persons*. If we seek to create but are denied connection with a product, we cannot become creative persons. If we seek to express our community with others and cannot communicate, then we are deeply alone. *Becoming* human requires an opportunity context in which freedom is real. Any system that treats persons as purely instruments for a greater end denies them the opportunity to become human. An active relationship with the world, what Marx called "productive life," is fundamental to the species-character of humanity. This productive life is felt by the individual "as a necessity, as a need, without which my essence cannot be fulfilled, satisfied, completed" (Marx, 1932:184). Marx was convinced that any system that produced men and women who defined their lives in terms of possessions rather than action that would actualize life was alienating throughout, in leisure as well as work.

Alienation, from this viewpoint, is more than feeling unrelated or nonproductive. It is being denied the essential conditions of selfhood. It is the "negation of productivity" (Fromm, 1961:43) and separation from the right of self-realization. There are, of course, non-Marxist approaches to the same theme. One that has attracted considerable interest is the self-actualization model of Abraham Maslow (1976). Maslow argued that persons are motivated by more than the drive to meet "needs." Rather, there is a hierarchy of elements in life beginning with survival requirements and rising to "self-actualization." This highest motive is the desire to *be*. Models of action that are based on causation are seen as only partial. A full psychological model of human action requires an existential dimension of being and becoming. Freedom is more than possibility; it is the exercise of human possibilities. Freedom is action toward "being," decision with a human end. That end is not just discrete accomplishment or response, it is—to return to the Marxian view—realization of one's essential nature. Discrete decisions and specific lines of action are understood in the larger context of becoming. Freedom is not a specific decision among identified alternatives but a condition of existential self-realization.

The issue, then, is whether or not this condition is denied by the alienation endemic to any social system. Can a society be so totalitarian that the political requisites of freedom are completely smothered? Can a society be so dominated by one dimension, the possession of market commodities, that real freedom is lost to the pseudo freedom of the market? Or, as an alternative, is it necessary to struggle for real freedom in any social system? In any case, the political metaphor offered here insists that alienation is more than an attitude and freedom more than a definition of the situation.

Hints of Alienation. Is there at least partial freedom in leisure *as we know it?* There is no definitive answer to the question, but there are some hints. For example, we may speculate about the competitive nature of so much organized leisure activity. Is this a carry-over from the economic domain or something built into the human species? Or we may question the ways in which leisure styles seem to correlate with social status. Is this just a question of economic resources or a persistence of role expectations into the domain said to be free and expressive?

There is now a line of inquiry that argues that the "need for achievement" is learned rather than inherent in human nature. Such achievement motivation has been found to vary among cultures, between occupational groups, and across the life span (Wigmore and Braskamp, 1985). Further, the various domains of life—work, family, leisure, and community—take on different salience in different periods of the life course (Maehr and Kleiber, 1985). Although individuals may have characteristics of greater or lesser competitiveness internalized and resilient to context shifts, this does not mean that this motivation is equally salient in every situation or social role. The point here is that many aspects of personality that have been assumed to be inherent now appear to be both learned and variable.

Persistence can be learned and developed, as one delightful anecdote about the "father of scientific management," Frederick Taylor, illustrates (Andrew, 1981:63). Taylor's approach to sports in college had been both competitive and technology oriented. He developed the overhand pitch in baseball because it got results and designed a new tennis racket to compensate for his weak backhand. He was successful in winning a men's doubles title in 1881 as a result. When advised to take up golf by his doctor years later, he altered the traditional apparel, lengthened his woods for distance, refiled his irons for backspin, and built a "putting machine" that was so accurate it was banned from use. Not surprisingly, he is reported to have said he would rather go to the dentist than play golf. He carried over his work orientation to the final degree. His story is unique, but the shaping of leisure by work is not. Technique rules many activities. All is measured by results, often in comparison or competition with others. And activities are selected because they contribute to economic roles and productivity rather than intrinsic satisfaction.

Karl Mannheim (1951:269–274) argued that the work-leisure carryover is reciprocal. Leisure may well be the "natural balance to man's work, the place for personality development and self-expression." However, the reverse is also true. Such activity may also be a criterion by which to measure the satisfaction received in work. Is it possible to appreciate and even create grace and beauty in leisure and tolerate drabness and ugliness without complaint in the workplace? Can we accept being robots on the job when we have been expressive during the previous evening? Can we comfortably use people at work when we have loved others at home? If we are truly productive in our leisure, can we settle for being segmented and functional in the workplace?

There are many attempts to introduce elements of leisure into the work environment. Decorations, music, coffee breaks, management-worker councils, extramural recreation, and even some task redefinition have been promoted as ways to decrease worker disaffection and increase productivity. From a political theory perspective these efforts can have only temporary results because they are superficial. The real issue is ontological—a matter of being—rather than epistemological—a matter of perception (Baxter, 1982:164). Cosmetic changes may alter perceptions for a time. However, in the long run powerlessness will be recognized. The conditions for fulfillment cannot be denied and then obscured by devices of any kind. Life is too much a whole to allow for that kind of segmentation, however useful to those who determine conditions and the basis for rewards.

Review and Implications _____

To review, there are a number of elements that functional and conflict theorists view similarly.

Leisure as Functional. First, the institutions of a society tend to reinforce a consensus on the rightness of the system. They form a functionally interrelated system in which participation in institutional roles is a socialization experience. The attitudes, modes of behavior, values, and styles of presentation that are accepted and rewarded are similar throughout the society. In all social engagement the social actor is learning, and learning how to get along is a mutually reinforcing process in which there is a sequence of appropriate institutional roles through the life course.

Second, functional and conflict theories assign a similar place to the market system of distribution in a capitalist economy. Not only does the market provide opportunity for choice, but it is a social space in which rewards for economic participation are exchanged for goods and services. Further, there is agreement that the aims and outcomes of market exchange tend to symbolize the life-styles and value systems associated with social position. The market is more than a neutral exchange process. As producers engage in marketing, they influence tastes and limit the choices available. Leisure expenditures are one aspect of the overall system, but a critical element in the reward system because of the self-directed and discretionary character of leisure choices.

Third, leisure is most closely related to family, household, and community in participation environments. That is, leisure is separated from economic roles in associations, location, and social aims. However, leisure is derived from work in resources and in meaning. Economic position and resources tend to determine the resources available for leisure, at least those that are supplied by the market. Further, those with the greatest economic power also are most able to determine the time and space contexts of their own lives. At least as important, leisure is defined as relative freedom that is *earned* through economic contribution. In a modern industrial society leisure is part of the reward system that serves to bond workers to productive roles and to encourage investment. Leisure, then, is secondary to economic roles. Although particular choices may not be determined or even predicted by economic position, general orientations toward leisure are based on the requirements, schedules, and measured productivity of economic roles.

In brief, the two metaphors are in agreement that leisure is tied into a system in which economic relationships are fundamental. There is also agreement that leisure orientations and values are usually consistent with the overall institutionalized socialization processes. This means that leisure is political in the sense of being developed in ways that serve the social system. However, there is also fundamental disagreement between functional and conflict approaches. That disagreement is based on whether the society is viewed as an integrated system or as divided among groups with opposing interests.

Leisure and Conflict. As a consequence of the differing views of society there is disagreement on several issues. First, from a conflict perspective, the human consequence of the system is alienation. With the essential contexts of their lives controlled by economic and political elites to further their own interests, workers and their families are denied integrated life chances to grow and develop. They are cut off from real productivity in work, where they are used as instruments rather than creators. Their leisure is defined as a compensating reward, but even this relative freedom is alienated by socialization that binds leisure to market-supplied things. Leisure is a reward for accepting alienation in work—a reward that becomes commodity intensive rather than creative and developmental engagement.

Second, underlying this conflict analysis is conviction that modern Western industrial societies are more closed than open. That is, there is far more determination of lives and far less real and self-determining choice than the dominant ideology would have members believe. This does not mean that the society is totally monolithic and determined. It does suggest that much of what passes for freedom is actually "false consciousness," an illusion that serves to bind those whose lives are severely limited to the system. When leisure is defined as relative freedom, it may also be defined as relative determination. The options are limited, not only by differential resources and scarcity but also by the learned dispositions of the non-elites who have come to define leisure in terms most amenable to granting prior reward and primary power to those with investment capital rather than to workers. Leisure serves the system first rather than offering the openness necessary for existential freedom and becoming.

Third, the problem, then, is more structural than psychological. Awareness of the real conditions of life is necessary to inaugurate change. However, that change must be in the system, not just in the minds of individuals. Learning to maximize becoming and push back constraints until leisure offers a little space of relative freedom may be crucial for developing an individual life or nurturing the young into some measure of autonomy. But to free the masses requires real social change, a revolution in the sense of a redistribution of political power. The elites will have to give up or share their power so that the system can offer some equity in response to the interests of all people. Such a revolution may come about in a variety of ways and at different speeds, but from a conflict view nothing less than revolution can bring an end to alienation. There is no substitute for the power of self-determination.

Fourth, conflict metaphors also question the whole matter of motivation. The premise is that human beings *want* to be productive. That is, they are most satisfied when they are investing themselves in enterprises that build, create, and develop. The creation may be a thing, an object of use or beauty. The development may be of a personal skill, line of communication, or a relationship. We may build houses or ideas. Such self-investment may take place in any institutional role or setting—work, leisure, family, or community. The point is that to be human is to be existential in a social context. Any institutional context that manipulates or coerces us out of that possibility is alienating, dehumanizing, and demotivating. In order to compensate for the lack of real human motivation, those who benefit seek to create substitute motivations—in this case a reward system in which the possession of things symbolizes status and accomplishment. The problem is that such a system is not responsive to the deep strivings of human beings. (Again, note that a philosophical view underlies the argument.) Rather, there will be a continual problem of a lack of productivity and motivation because the system contradicts itself. The basis of the motivation scheme is false.

Fifth, freedom in such an alienating system is lost. It becomes a political slogan rather than a fundamental condition. This is especially acute in leisure, the domain of life in which personal freedom is expected to be maximized. To be free, leisure has to be intrinsic—an end in itself. Play cannot be an instrument, externally controlled for extrinsic ends. Play, to be free and creative, is for its own sake. When there is this protection against manipulation, then play becomes most developmental and productive. It is in such freedom that creation occurs in the interplay of mind, action, and environment. Real play, or leisure, requires openness—a condition in which existential action is possible. Control, whether by coercion or false consciousness, is the negation of leisure and the antithesis of play.

Leisure as Political Freedom. At this point in the argument, two warnings are in order. First, it should be clear that empirical evidence for the argument that has been presented is uneven. There are evident motivation problems, symptoms that something is wrong with the human consequences of the system, and indications that leisure is less than creative for many people. It is clear that the reward system of the society is highly differential and yields vastly different opportunities for self-development. Further, the economic basis of that reward system is well documented. However, much of the analysis is inferential. Direct evidence on the power of economic roles to shape and distort every other domain of life is hard to find. Further, alternative systems of economic organization appear to produce similar results. The argument may or may not be seen as persuasive, but it is certainly not *proven*.

Second, there is a certain romantic or even utopian theme that runs through the analysis. There is the implication that if only we could get the society organized right, then the people in the system would be quite different. It is one thing to find plausible the argument that the system limits and distorts many within it; it is another matter to believe that changing the system would have dramatic effects on the quality of human life—that people themselves would be better. Again, such a premise cannot, by its nature, be proved.

Nevertheless, before going on to the humanistic, or philosophical, presentation of the next chapter, we should look again at the concept of freedom that runs through this entire chapter. Freedom is more than a political dimension, a lack of direct state coercion. Such a political context is a necessary condition of freedom, but it does not exhaust the concept.

Freedom is ontological—a matter of being as well as of knowing. However, the ontology is incomplete—a process rather than a static state. In freedom the human process of becoming can occur. Freedom is more than an idea or an ideal, important as such concepts are. It is more than an awareness of human potential or a lack thereof. Freedom is the existential condition of action that moves from alienation to authenticity. Authentic life is not a gift of the good society, the abundant economy, or even the right philosophy. It is a creation that comes into being through action that uses the condition of social freedom, action that is in Sartre's sense "for itself" (1966).

Freedom, then, encompasses the dialectic of all social action. It is a social condition that enables individuals to act in freedom. Freedom as such a condition is political in providing a context in which self-determining action is possible. It is economic in offering a context for productive and actualizing activity. It is social in its institutional organization that prepares persons for such action. This social context does more than minimize barriers to decisive action; it fosters self-actualization through socialization and action opportunities in which freedom is learned and practiced. Leisure, then, in such a society is the opportunity for decision and action that is primarily for its own sake. Leisure as a social condition is the opportunity structure—time, space, facility, learning, and other elements—for playful engagement that is developmental just because it is oriented primarily toward experience.

The other side of the dialectic of freedom is existential. Freedom is *becoming,* decisive action that transforms the actor. For Marx freedom is not only the condition that supports self-realization but liberating activity as well (Walicki, 1983:52–53). It is action that transcends or controls the environment for human ends. In the *Grundrisse* (1973:599) Marx argues that real leisure is one aspect of such liberating activity:

> Free time—which includes leisure time as well as time for higher activities—naturally transforms anyone who enjoys it into a different person, and it is the different person who then enters into the direct process of production. The man who is being formed finds discipline in this process, while for the man who is already formed it is practice, experimental science, materially creative and self-objectifying knowledge, as he contains within his own head the accumulated wisdom of the society.

Freedom is not separated from institutional opportunity structures, historical culture, or value orientations. They are both objective externalities and internalized beliefs about the world. Freedom takes place within this social and socialized environment. Within that environment there is greater or lesser provision for leisure, in the sense of institutional arrangements that develop capacity for creative activity. Leisure in that social world is made possible by support of activity that *does not have to be done.* Such activity is transforming for those who seize and actualize its potential.

Leisure, then, is more than doing things for their own sake. Leisure is liberation in the sense of action *toward* authenticity. *Alienated leisure* is a contradiction from this perspective. Without the possibility of authenticity, of becoming, then leisure is reduced to nonwork, or discretionary, time—a commodity to be spent or used like other commodities. It can be bought and sold but not realized in activity. Leisure in this metaphor requires piercing any false consciousness to achieve authentic action. Such action results from and at the same time produces a new state of consciousness. It also begins with and is oriented toward social conditions of community rather than alienation.

What has this political metaphor added to what has gone before? First, leisure is existential, action of being and becoming. Even more, it is liberating action that transforms the actor. By acting, we become more authentic, closer to our human nature. The alienating forces around us are pushed back, and we become more actualized. We are able to be more truly productive, creative, and decisive. We become more whole and less fragmented through united action. We act more validly toward others because we are acting *with* rather than against them. In leisure we become more free.

Second, leisure is social—actually, political and economic as well—in requiring a context for actualizing activity. Marxian and other critical approaches analyze how social conditions can distort definitions of self and life, divert action away from authentic becoming into instrumental system serving, and even close fundamental contexts of freedom. Political and economic institutions can combine to be powerfully manipulative as well as coercive in gaining compliance. Freedom as real opportunity is more than designated time; it is openness for creative action. Such openness in leisure enables the actor to choose and carry out activity that is really for its own sake.

Third, the social character of authentic leisure is not limited to the context for action. Although self-realization is at the center of leisure as becoming, such activity is not *against* others. Rather, the exercise of such freedom is also with and for others. One sign of alienated leisure is that it will be carried out even at the cost of the freedom or actualization of others. Authentic leisure, on the other hand, is not alienated from others but encompasses the social as well as existential nature of being and becoming human. For example, alienated leisure may define accomplishment in terms of getting things from others. Authentic leisure uses things *with* others. Things are instrumental; people are not.

The argument developed here has incorporated themes from Marx and a variety of neo-Marxist theorists. However, it is not simply a case for Marxian socialism. Rather, the need to liberate the conditions of modern life from subservience to the means of production and control by any elites with devisive interests is fundamental to developing real leisure. Leisure, like any other part of life, can become an instrument in the hands of the powerful. When this occurs, leisure is alienated from its existential meaning by a twisting of its social contexts.

There is a "liberal" view of leisure that supposes that having the right ideas is all that is necessary to achieve its realization. The problem of alienation is reduced to awareness and may be solved by overcoming the internalized wrong ideas that have been learned. Political theories incorporate this analysis but add the social dimension. The "wrong" ideas have been learned because they reflect the institutionalized values of the social system. Further, those values may serve the interests of only a segment of the society. Therefore, to make the fundamental freedom of leisure possible may require change in the social conditions. To actualize the self, the society may have to change in ways that support authentic freedom. Without such social conditions leisure remains a struggle for a little space in the midst of an environment of control.

References

Andrew, Ed. 1981. *Closing the Iron Cage*. Montreal: Black Rose.

Antonio, R. J. 1983. "The Origin, Development, and Contemporary Status of Theory." *Sociological Quarterly* 24:325–51.

Baxter, Brian. 1982. *Alienation and Authenticity*. London: Tavistock.

Blauner, Robert. 1964. *Alienation and Freedom*. Chicago: University of Chicago Press.

Brantlinger, Patrick. 1983. *Bread and Circuses: Theories of Mass Culture as Social Decay*. Ithaca: Cornell University Press.

Dumazedier, Joffre. 1967. *Toward a Society of Leisure*. Trans. by S. E. McClure. New York: The Free Press.

Ellul, Jacques. 1964. *The Technological Society*. New York: Alfred A. Knopf, Inc.

Ewen, Stuart, and E. Ewen. 1982. *Channels of Desire*. New York: McGraw-Hill Book Company.

Fromm, Erich. 1961. *Marx's Concept of Man*. New York: Frederick Ungar Publishing Co., Inc.

Habermas, Jurgen. 1975. *Legitimation Crisis*. Boston: Beacon Press.

Kellner, Douglas. 1981. "Network Television and American Society." *Theory and Society* 10:265–77.

Kelly, J. R. 1982. *Leisure*. Englewood Cliffs: Prentice-Hall, Inc.

———. 1983. *Leisure Identities and Interactions*. London: George Allen & Unwin Ltd.

———. 1985. *Recreation Business*. New York: Macmillan Publishing Co., Inc.

Kleiber, Douglas, and M. Maehr, eds. 1985. *Motivation and Adulthood*. Greenwich: JAI Press.

Mannheim, Karl. 1951. *Freedom, Power, and Democratic Planning*. Ed. by Hans Gerth and Ernest Bramstedt. London: Routledge & Kegan Paul Ltd.

Marcuse, Herbert. 1966. *Eros and Civilization*. Boston: Beacon Press.

———. 1964. *One Dimensional Man*. Boston: Beacon Press.

Marx, Karl. 1932. *Marx-Engels Gesamtausgabe*. Marx-Engels Verlag. Ed. by D. Rjazonov. Frankfurt.

———. [1867] 1967. *Capital*. Ed. by Frederick Engels. New York: International Publishers.

————. 1970. *Economic and Philosophical Manuscripts of 1844*. Ed. by Dirk Struik, Trans. by Martin Milligan. London: Lawrence andWishart.

————. [c 1859] 1973. *Grundrisse: Foundations of the Critique of Political Economy*. Trans. by Martin Nicolaus. New York: Random House.

Maslow, Abraham. 1976. *The Further Reaches of Human Nature*. Harmondsworth: Penguin.

Neumeyer, M. H., and E. Neumeyer. 1958. *Leisure and Recreation*. New York: The Ronald Press Company.

Sartre, Jean-Paul. 1966. *Being and Nothingness*. Trans. by Hazel E. Barnes. New York: Washington Square Press.

Sennett, Richard. 1978. *The Fall of Public Man*. New York: Vintage Books.

Smith, Adam. [1776] 1902. *The Wealth of Nations*. New York: P. F. Collier.

Thompson, John, and D. Held, eds. 1982. *Habermas: Critical Debates*. Cambridge: The M.I.T. Press.

Veblen, Thorstein. [1899] 1953. *The Theory of the Leisure Class*. New York: New American Library.

Walicki, Andrzej. 1983. "Marx and Freedom." *New York Review of Books*. November 24:51–55.

Weber, Max. [c1930] 1958. *The Protestant Ethic and the Spirit of Capitalism*. Trans. by Talcott Parsons. New York: Charles Scribner's Sons.

Weil, Simone. 1972. *Gravity and Grace*. Glasgow: Collins.

Wigfield, Allan, and L. Braskamp. 1985. "Age and Personal Investment in Work." In *Motivation and Adulthood*. *See* Kleiber and Maehr 1985.

CHAPTER 9

Humanist Theory

What does it mean to "become human"? Both affirming and critical theories of leisure presuppose some answer to this question.

Leisure and creativity should be viewed jointly. Leisure is an openness to seek and create the "not yet," including the developing self. Creative activity is directed toward a realization of potential in the creator as well as in what is being created.

From an aesthetic perspective play may be creative and dialectical activity. Play may create what is new and still be in and of the material world, for its own sake and yet somehow essential. Further, such play is a drama of self-creation just because of its absorption in the process and the material.

Leisure is also a context for social celebrations that are rituals of social solidarity. Yet, such playful re-creations also reveal the fragility of the social order and provide a possibility of criticism.

To become human we need both freedom and community. Becoming has both existential and social dimensions. The theme of humanist theory is that we become human in creative and liberating activity. Such activity is "ex-static" in bringing the "not yet" into being.

Why is leisure significant in this process? Because its products are not prespecified, and its aims and modes of action may be playful.

Leisure, then, requires an environment for creation as well as existential activity. As act, leisure is existential and self-creating. As environment, leisure is a social context in which creative activity is possible.

From a developmental perspective leisure is a context in which we seek and become selves in a cumulative and sequential process. In institutional roles we learn what is expected in stable social situations and how we may take roles in ways that offer some opportunity for growth and expression. Political metaphors offer analyses of the potentially distorting structures of social systems that restrict fundamental freedoms essential to self-development. Implicit in each approach is the possibility that persons have some unrealized potential, that we could become more than we are. However, just what that potential entails is generally left unspecified or suggested in vague slogans. To examine more closely the issue of human potential, we now turn to more philosophical metaphors.

What does it mean to be human? The question is deceptively simple in comparison to the proposed answers. In one sense the entire history of philosophy is an exploration of that question divided into subissues such as those of knowing, being, thinking, communicating, and acting. Much of literature, art, theology, and even odysseys of body and spirit seek to develop answers to the question. And, from classical Greek times on, leisure has been justified as necessary for the search. Leisure is to provide time for exploration and development. It is space for becoming human and creating humanizing opportunities for others.

Underlying the search is the fundamental premise that "being" is incomplete. Human nature is not a given, but a goal; not final, but in process. The essence of being is that it is becoming. This premise turns the question significantly. Rather than "What does it mean to be human?", the question is "How do we become human?" For our purposes, then, the more directed issue is the relationship of leisure to becoming human.

The persistent themes to be presented are those of freedom and community. The contextual requisites of becoming human are freedom to direct life and social contexts of learning and development. Freedom is employed in a directed way toward the realization or fulfillment of one's humanity. Community is not only the context of learning but also offers the possibility of celebrating the cultural realization of meaning.

Focus on *becoming* human does not imply that there is a fixed model to be achieved. Rather, human as well as artistic creation implies that there is always the possibility of something new, a "not yet" that is not just like anything or anyone that has gone before. There is at least a dimension of relativity implicit in the metaphor. Realization of humanity is always a new creation to be celebrated by a community that becomes at least a little different in the event.

In this chapter we examine theories of leisure in relation to becoming human on both the individual and social levels. The exploration will pick up themes and concepts from a wide spectrum of philosophers, artists, theologians, and social theorists. However, development of the themes of freedom and community will be based on the existential and social analyses that have been presented. Humanist metaphors are not a separate and exotic source of insight but have emerged out of the history of ideas with all the conflicts and contradictions that make up the reality of any culture.

Leisure and Creativity ───────────────────────

On an individual level leisure has been identified with the "freedom to become." Leisure involves action directed toward a "not yet" of selfhood. However, it may also involve other kinds of creation in relationships or materials. Leisure has been associated with the arts, creation of new sound or shape or communication. It has been defined as the possibility of meditation or contemplation, the creation of ideas and states of consciousness. Leisure in this sense is a context for creation—oriented toward possibilities for the future.

In the writings of Aristotle there are the two poles of leisure meaning. On the one hand, leisure is a matter of enjoyment. We choose activities and settings because we expect that they will yield pleasure, personal enjoyment. In the *Politics* (pub. 1941), Aristotle argues that "leisure of itself gives pleasure, happiness, and enjoyment of life. . . . But happiness is an end, since all men deem it to be accompanied with pleasure and not with pain." Happiness is not an unworthy outcome but is a guide for choice. Action in accord with nature is most likely to yield pleasure.

On the other hand, such pleasure is not a simple mood or emotion. Rather, satisfaction is produced in a realization—however partial—of one's nature. Pleasure may be seen as one guide toward action that involves becoming. And the becoming is not just any sort of activity. Realization of one's humanity means to "live well" (Wild, 1948:42). In action that comprises some realization of selfhood under the guidance of reason there is found the deepest satisfaction. Happiness, from this perspective, is not just feeling good but is a state of being that stems from becoming. Further, this satisfaction is not transitory, but is given in a life actively directed toward such realization through its course.

What, then, is the place of leisure in this realist metaphor of Aristotle? It is precisely that separation from necessity that is a context for self-directed action. Leisure is an environment for self-actualization. And action directed toward such realization of one's nature is—overall at least—most pleasurable. Further, the separation of leisure from the realm of necessity gives a perspective on all of the life course. As Paul Weiss (1964) wrote, "The good life is a life in which a rich leisure gives direction and meaning to all else we do." Leisure, then, is part of the human and humanizing process of life that is fundamental to the entire life span. Happiness is an affectively perceived state that accompanies this state of becoming human.

The Freedom to Become

The first object of creation in leisure, then, is the self, and this aim is fundamental to the nature of humankind. Johan Huizinga proposed in *Homo Ludens* (1955) that play is rooted in the biosocial nature of the human species. Play is older than civilization. Although forms of play are learned and transmitted socially, playfulness is embedded in animal nature. Pretending, performing, and experiencing of exhilaration and joy are characteristic of animal as well as human play. However, play is more than emotional response and action. "It has a *significant* function—that is to say, there is some sense to it" (Huizinga, 1955:1). There is a possibly indefinable element in play of meaning that is more than instinct if less than teleological. Play is not "nonsense." That is, it is aimed toward something. It is "intentioned," even if the intention is restricted to the moment and the experience. It embodies meaning in at least the limited sense of being communicable.

Play is not quite identical to leisure. However, it is a dimension of leisure—the experiential element that focuses on the action. According to Huizinga, play is voluntary, free, and bounded in time and space and creates its own order. In analyzing leisure, play is the action dimension of the episode or event. If being "leisurely" connotes a freedom from necessity, being "playful" connotes the spontaneity of creation in action that *at that time* is primarily for its own sake.

Play is *fun*—that peculiarly English term (possibly Middle English in origin with a meaning of fooling or deceiving)—in the sense of embodying an experience of immediate pleasure. And yet, fun is more than feeling; it is action-based and implies *doing something*. Play is performing with and toward others, at least in the imagination. Therefore, it has "meaning" or communicable significance even though only within its own boundaries. Insofar as leisure incorporates such an element of action, of fun, it is play. Yet, that element does not preclude meaning such as that proposed by Aristotle. Play may be an immediate and experiential dimension of action that has meaning and is socially constructed. If play has its own order and recognized limits, then it may also have meaning embedded in the nature of the players. It may be part of a larger theme of realization, of meaning based in being and becoming human.

Robert Wilson (1981:288) argues that playful self-creation has a dimension of "letting go" that is different from a calculated program of step-by-step self-improvement. He quotes George Santayana's insistence on the spontaneity of play that is "no longer what is done fruitlessly" (1981:298). The freedom of leisure is not only freedom from constraint but is freedom to "quest"—whether the action is oriented toward self-discovery or toward another person. Wilson proposes that the key to leisure is "courage" rather than withdrawal.

Realization of Potential

If play is an experiential dimension of leisure, what is the other pole of the dialectic? Is it not that the human being has "form" in the sense of a nature to be realized? Just any expression, any emotion, or any action is not "becoming human." Some of the condition of happiness that may occur in leisure is related to nature. It is the nature of the human species to play, to seek and create meaning, to relate to others of the species, and to look forward to fulfillment. We yearn and feel as well as think, seek as well as analyze.

Such becoming presupposes something to become. That potential need not be a detailed blueprint for either the species or the individual. Rather, being human entails having a general form that can be completed in ways that are unique to the individual. However, there may also be violations of that form, actions of becoming that pull or push the self away from its potential. At this point in the argument two requisites for engaging in human action are proposed. The first is freedom that enables action to be directed toward chosen ends. The second is the context of community in which to learn and act. Again, human beings are existential and social in nature so that the two dimensions are inextricably linked (Wilson, 1981:302).

But, what are we to become? What are the ends and acts of realization? And what does leisure have to do with the process?

Creativity: Linking Leisure and Becoming

There is a realm of behavior called aesthetics that involves creation—the production of what does not yet exist. In fact, this realm has been called "playful production" (Hans, 1981:136). For Aristotle (*Poetics,* Ch. 26) art not only imitates what is but creates what "might be" or even "ought to be." Art is more than life in the sense of enhancing what is or envisioning what could be. In this sense, art is always "playful" rather than limited to accepted existence.

And what is necessary for art, for such creation? Is it not leisure, not only as time but as the total environment that enables such playful possibility? Leisure is more than empty time. It is the possibility of creation, an openness toward the "not yet" that can take risks because there is no ultimate failure. Leisure is, after all, for its own sake rather than for survival.

A major figure in the analysis of the aesthetic was the philosopher Friedrich Schiller (1759–1805). Schiller believed that play, aesthetic activity, and creativity were at the heart of being human. "Man only plays when in the full meaning of the word he is man, and he is only completely man when he plays" (*Aesthetic Letters,* number fifteen). In this view creative activity is not a luxury to be added onto life when everything else is completed; it is at the center of what it means to be human. And at the center of creative activity is freedom in the sense of self-determined action.

Schiller was a phenomenologist in his denial that human perception could grasp essential reality. Following Kant, he held that the mind has to construct forms for apprehending what is external to it. Therefore, the mind constructs explanatory schemes to attempt to comprehend experience. As a result, quite diverse accounts of reality may be produced that are consonant with the facts but in conflict with each other. Unlike Kant, Schiller did not posit a consistent human nature that is the foundation of objective knowledge. Rather, the mind structures experience in ways that vary according to modes of cognition, such as those with realist or idealist premises. Realists may construct an image of reality based on information processing and idealists on rational forms. For Schiller the dichotomous approaches are partly reconciled by play that mediates by juxtaposing forms and modes of analysis. The rigidities of the polar positions are softened by the ability to create and juggle other possibilities.

Although Schiller did not develop and offer a systematic epistemology based on this third kind of knowledge, he did place such creative mental activity at the center of acts of knowing. Schiller, often called the "poet of freedom," wanted to liberate humankind from the bondage of industrialized society and from any approach to life that closed opportunities and options. He believed that any formal constructions—philosophical, theological, scientific, or social—that were presented as ultimate and final were an illusion. They were the products of the mind rather than any direct apprehension of reality.

On the other hand, the artist should be free of such illusions by experiencing the act of creation. In order to create, aesthetic activity *plays* with the materials of perception and the mind. In this sense, art is reception, an active engagement with the world, as well as creation. Even the rules of an art are recognized as self-imposed and therefore mutable. For example, the experience of contemplation—requiring freedom from engrossing activity—plays with ideas in ways that may produce combinations that are new to that mind. From this perspective the poet may be more profound than the systematic philosopher. Such creative activity is not trivial or limited in import to the immediate experience. Rather, art creates the concepts that are deemed worthy to be the basis of action, the symbols and ideas on which life may be built. But they should never be cast in concrete, protected from further play.

The influence of Schiller on other thinkers would seem to be less important than the ideas themselves. However, one example may suffice to suggest the extent of his impact far beyond philosophies of aesthetics. A. L. Kroeber (1948), an anthropologist, was referring to mental and aesthetic activity beyond the necessary and outside technology when he wrote that "They rest on the play impulse, which is connected with growth but is dissociated from preservation, comfort, or utility, and which in science and art is translated into the realm of the imagination, abstraction, relations, and sensuous form." Society depends on such activity for the development of discovery and innovation of all kinds.

The aesthetic, then, is both a response to and a heightening of what is perceived. Schiller believed that modern society had become machinelike in its rigidity. Industrialization had taken much of the gentleness and freedom from the daily round of life. The harmony of being human was overpowered by the rhythm of the machine and the timing of the factory. However, Schiller did not argue for a separation or pure privatization of an aesthetic realm. Rather, life must be transformed by the creation of a balanced harmony of the sensual and form. In creative activity, play, form, and beauty may be reconciled.

A further dimension of such activity, reminiscent of Marx, is that it is not possessive. Creative activity, however disciplined to produce something of beauty, is for its own sake. Creation may be shared, appreciated, and allowed to endure, but it is not for the sake of possession. Rather, in the apprehension of beauty we become more human. In a sense, the aesthetic—for the moment at least—possesses us rather than the reverse. Such apprehension requires a freedom from any mechanistic approach to life that closes off the possibility of newness and precludes freedom.

The dialectic of art is that it is both based in and more than the material of the world. Further, art is both disciplined by form and a creation of the "not yet." It is a product of the material, the stuff of existence, and of the nonmaterial, the imagination. Art requires mastery of form to the extent that the artist can play with form in creation. And this dialectic is not limited to activity traditionally labeled aesthetic. There is the possibility of creative activity in thought, conversation, sport, science, and anything else that involves intentioned human action. The dialectic of aesthetics highlights the nature of creative activity for other domains of life rather than limits creativity to a special domain.

Conditions of Creation

For Kant cognitive judgments are constrained by the form of the human mind. Aesthetic judgment, however, is free of such processing form. In his *Critique of Judgment,* Kant argues that such judgment is free both from the forms of reason and of sensory pleasure. Rather, it is playful in being disinterested and transcending definite rules of cognition (*Critique of Judgment* Section 9,52). Creative thought and action require a release from rigid forms in order to be open to novelty. This is the internal, or actor's, side of creative activity.

The environmental side is defined by another philosopher, Josef Pieper. He argues that "Leisure, it must be remembered, is not a Sunday afternoon idyll, but the preserve of freedom, of education and culture, and of that undiminished humanity which views the world as a whole" (*Leisure, the Basis of Culture,* 1963:46). Leisure is freedom, not from culture and its enrichment but for human and humanizing action. Pieper goes further to the proposition that leisure is necessary for the development of culture, not only of the arts but of all the thought and riskful experience that are required for growth and development. Leisure encompasses the individual action of contemplation that explores and plays with ideas. It also encompasses the celebrations of meaning and significance shared by communities.

Leisure, according to Peiper (1963:40–41), is a "mental and spiritual attitude," a "condition" of the mind that lets things happen. Leisure is also "contemplative celebration" that assents to being and affirms creation. As such, leisure stands apart from necessity, from "work." For Pieper (1963:44), in leisure "the truly human values are saved and preserved" in a paradoxical tension between acceptance and ecstasy. The context for this tension is leisure, at the same time a freedom from necessity and an immersion in the universe. Pieper's view, of course, is fundamentally religious. Yet, a secular approach to the same issue could yield the same paradox: leisure is neither freedom from the world nor affirmation of it; it is both. Or, more precisely, it is a measure of freedom within a world that is affirmed but not final.

Another theme in this approach to creative activity is that of *wholeness.* The ancient dualism of body and soul, of mind and spirit, is denied in favor of a fundamentally unified existence. Creation denies that the mental or spiritual is good and the material in some way evil. Existence is not a conflict between mind and matter. Rather, the basic unity of existence allows for creative action to employ material and nonmaterial in a single act. Art, for example, is not subduing the material but working in and with it.

Although dualistic metaphors have been common in religious thought and practice, they are not endemic. Karl Rahner (1968) is one contemporary Catholic theologian who has attacked such spirit-matter models and offers a view of life in its given wholeness. Acknowledging a debt to Heidegger, Rahner has sought to banish "closet Platonism" from Christian theology. All spirituality is material in the sense of being *in the world*. The mind deals with the empirical and cannot transcend itself to grasp some superior world of the spirit. Meaning, then, is found in the world and created out of the material of the world. Religion does not transcend the world but frees the person to live *in* the world. The human being is characterized by an insatiable longing for meaning. This search is more than receiving what is given; it is making meaning out of the stuff of the world.

The Drama of Creation

Creation is not just an individual state or act. Creation is for others as well as for and by the self. Along with the dialectic between freedom and form in creation, there is a dialectic between play and display. The creative activity of play is for itself, not a matter of necessity or seeking extrinsic reward. Nevertheless, there is also a "for others" dimension for such activity. One writes to be read, composes to be played, and paints to be seen. There is the audience or viewer in mind during creation, even though *doing* the act may be so engrossing that any display is forgotten for a period. Creative activity in leisure is for its own sake and yet for others as well. There is a communication element in creation even when concentration on the act is central.

Aaron Copland, who surely composes with the eventual listeners very much in mind, wrote that "I must create in order to know myself, and since self-knowledge is a never-ending search, each new work is only a part answer to the question 'Who am I?' and brings with it the need to go on to other and different part-answers" (1952). He goes on to say that any work of art has a unique life and meaning that would be lost were it not created. Failure to create is loss, to the meaning-discovering process of the creator and to the world of potential receivers.

Creation, then, is by and for the creator in a life journey of self-seeking and development. It is also for others whose own journeys may be enriched by their perceptual reception of the work. What is discovered by the artist about him/herself may contribute to the self-discovery of the receiver. Further, in creation both the producer and receiver may *become* something more than before. That is the production side of creation. At the same time, what is created has its own integrity and meaning. The piece of music, choreography, or lithography makes its own journey in the world. It may stimulate responses quite unintended by its creator as it is merged into the life situations of unknown others. It becomes the object of interpretations unforeseen and of meanings unanticipated. Art, as response to and yet more than the world, participates in freedom both in its creation and reception. There is an openness in its very existence that precludes uniformity and compulsion.

There is even ancient theological warrant for such a metaphor. The poem of creation in the first chapter of Genesis is divided into periods (days) in which the Spirit of the Creator pauses to contemplate what has been done, pronounces it good, and then goes on to the subsequent act. Creation is a process of activity. In the process the "Spirit of God *played* over the face of the waters" (Genesis 1:2, King James Version). And some theologians would argue that in the playing out of creation the creating Spirit comes to a greater self-knowledge. In any creative activity the creator becomes something more than prior to the act.

There are, then, a series of dialectical elements in creative activity:

- Creation is at the same time free in its act and constrained by form.
- Creation is at the same time open to the imagination, or creating spirit, and composed of the materials of the world and culture.
- Creation is an act with its own meaning and integrity and yet an offering to others for their free reception.
- Creation is always new and unique and yet communicated in ways that can be comprehended and interpreted by others.
- Creation is based in the perceived world and yet has dimensions that heighten or re-form that world.
- Creation is immersion in a contemporary act for its own sake and yet yields something new with a thrust toward the future.
- Creation is self-contained in the playful act and yet becomes for others.
- Creation is self-discovery and yet may stimulate the self-knowledge and development of others.
- Creation is a consummate paradox: for itself and yet the basis of all that moves life forward in experience and understanding.
- And, finally, creation is the freedom that is necessary in being and becoming human—in both the personal and social journeys of existence.

The exploration of creative activity and the context of leisure may begin with individuals who create. However, we are soon led to social dimensions. Leisure is, at least, a social space of relative freedom that makes creative activity possible. Further, creation is out of the stuff of the culture and its forms as well as oriented toward the future and the "not yet." And, creation presupposes that others will receive the offering of the creator. What, then, does it mean for creative activity to be social?

Leisure and Celebration

Culture may be understood as the shared symbols and meanings of a society. These meaningful symbols are communicated and learned by those who interact in the social system and are accepted as the way things are. In the process, they come to carry value as well as meaning. Such symbols and meanings are the nonmaterial side of social structure—the persistent institutional arrangements of the system.

This culture is more than a language-embedded set of symbols. It is the way of life in and out of which we construct our own life journeys. It is not only material which we employ but is the multidimensional context in which we formulate and realize what we seek to become. And, the culture is not neutral! As introduced in previous chapters, throughout a culture are pervasive concepts of what it means to be human, how human beings should relate to each other, and what it all may mean.

One of the functions of leisure is to afford opportunity to *celebrate* the meanings of the culture. In both religious and secular festivals and events people gather to dramatize and reinforce the symbols of meaning that are central to a social system. In feast and festival they dramatize the values that support the system and "play out" the meanings of the culture.

Ritual and Re-creation

Johan Huizinga (1955) was presenting his view that there is a ludic, or play, element in culture when he analyzed ritual. He suggests that there is a "re-presentation" of events in various social rites. Through participation in those rites the individual identifies with the event. It is more than imitation. The participant—worshipper, celebrant, actor, or even spectator—is a part of the re-creation of the event. And the event symbolizes some meaning integral to the culture. Ritual may take many forms, but the substance is that of a celebrative re-creation that draws people into its meaning and thus solidifies the society.

The nature of such celebration is "play" (Huizinga, 1955:15). The celebration is nonserious in its boundedness; it is not the event itself.

Nevertheless, feast and festival are meaning-laden and intended to draw members of a social group into an affective demonstration of what binds them together. Whether the celebration is of a wedding or a war, the rite reinforces the commitment of all participants to the value system represented. Leo Frobenius takes an anthropological stance in arguing that in such rites humans are actually "playing at nature" (Huizinga, 1955:16). All social order, institutions, and common interpretations of existence are in some ways "played" in common celebrations. The images may mix metaphors as they draw on the mythic elements of the culture to dramatize meaning. Social solidarity, from this perspective, is not just "taught" to children as fact and then accepted. Rather, it is reinforced and even reconstituted in the recurrent rituals of the common culture.

In this view there are ludic dimensions to much of the culture. As examples, various writers point to the re-creation of war and the rehearsing of adult roles in the games of children and youth. Gender differences in games may be based on differing social expectations and related values. In some cultures males have been led into organized contests simulating combat, whereas females have engaged in play rituals of nurturance and interpersonal communication. The point is that such rites are not just done; they are *believed*. Their images and symbols are recognized as unreal and yet are the bearers of the meaning of social bonding. The temporary event bounded in time and space—play—represents the most central and sacred meaning of the community.

Threats to Solidarity

Huizenga argues that belief is necessary for play. The common arena of play is a fabrication, an illusory world. And yet, to join in the game requires a suspension of "reality" and an acceptance of that fabrication. In fact, in some contests, one who violates rules and gets away with it—the cheat—is tolerated or even admired. However, one who challenges the game itself by pointing out that it is just a construct—the spoilsport—is universally condemned and subsequently excluded. The suspension of the reality question for the time and place of the game is a prerequisite of participation and acceptance.

Harvey Cox makes an intriguing proposal in his book *The Feast of Fools* (1969). He describes this rite in which the normal order of the social system is overturned for one brief period each year. Rather than celebrating the order to strengthen commitment, the ritual dramatizes that the order is a fragile creation. In the festival one person of a low position is rendered homage as "King." The drama reconstructs order in such a way that it becomes play. Within the limits of the play episode, it is clear that things might be different. Of course, it is possible that the rite may ridicule change and solidify the way things are. On other hand, the play shows that even sacred and unassailable order rests on agreement rather than a given structure.

A festival may be a "sacra-ment"—a sacred thing to be respected and honored. Nevertheless, it is also from the culture, usually incorporates folk elements, and can be shown to have changed over time. A historical analysis of celebrations in urban Brazil demonstrates how change came about through imposition by the dominant social classes (de Moraes von Simson, 1983). First, folk festivals became "carnivals" in which the bourgeois exhibited their level of luxury in costumed parade. Lower classes were allocated a place in the festivities that was both expressive and entertaining. Since 1930 relative homogeneity was developed through mass media. The "samba schools" became both a marketable product to be exhibited for tourists and a regulated part of the parade. What began as popular culture in rural festivals had been transformed into a market product to be consumed both on site and through the medium of television. The forms of the festive "play" are reshaped by cross-class adoption, market forces, mass media, and economic interests. Over two centuries rites that rose out of folk culture with sacred meanings came under the control of the dominant social forces of succeeding periods. Folk culture gave way to the rising bourgeoisie. Bourgeois control was lost in turn to commercial interests using the media to re-create carnival as a product.

The implication is that the play of cultural celebration is more than just an expression of the common life. Rather, both the content and the symbolic meanings of festival are shaped by many social forces. Social play is indeed a construct and subject to change. However, the change is more than a reinforcement of a single set of values. Political, economic, and other institutional factors as well as the common culture may influence or dominate festival.

A common anthropological view has been that festival is designated and institutionalized play, a kind of leisure. This play arises out of and expresses fundamental meanings of the culture—symbols of social coherence and of existence. A more sophisticated view would be that such celebration is subject to multiple and even conflicting forces, especially in a complex social system. In a conflict metaphor festival may even become an instrument of manipulation by those with power to shape means of symbolic communication such as media, the arts, the school, and religion. Humans may "play the order of nature." However, they may also be led to "play" out the interests of ruling classes.

Huizinga (1955:17) wrote of being "seized" by the experience of celebration. A dramatized re-creation may be so gripping that participants are caught in its meaning. The affective dimensions overcome any rational skepticism or disbelief to carry those involved into an immersion in the cultural meanings of the rite. At this point what has been defined as "play" has quite *serious* outcomes. Especially when such celebration is manipulated to advance the interests of one or more powerful social segments, the essentially benign view of celebration may be questioned.

There have been proposals to renounce control by the symbols and stories of the past developed in the name of "freedom." One such was that of the theologian Dietrich Bonhoeffer (1959), who wrote from his cell as a prisoner of Hitler during World War II. He proposed the possibility of a "world come of age." Such a world would no longer be bound by the traditional myths of the past. Rather, even theology would be released from its ancient bonds to become an instrument of liberation in which human beings would now take responsibility for their own lives. They would recognize themselves as actors in a world that was still in process of becoming. Rather than seeking the dominance of the supernatural, they would create new meanings of faithfulness and responsibility *in the world*. Such a formulation is, of course, also "play" in which a radical openness is set before human actors. In this view the "not yet" is defined as a possibility for new creation, both individual and social. The idea of a "world come of age" is one in which the celebration is of the future rather than the past. The past is desacralized to make way for a new creation.

Consensus and Criticism

In *The Social Construction of Reality,* Peter Berger and Thomas Luckman (1966) analyze how symbols are communicated in ways that give the appearance of being "real." Explanations that are constructed, usually by those with interests at stake, become accepted as "givens"–unassailable realities of existence. What is in reality a constructed drama—a metaphor—comes to be accepted as is. Radical critical analysis is suspended and replaced by "tinkering" with peripherals. The "hardware" of the system is in place and only the "software" subject to change.

Celebration, whether or not it has emerged out of folk roots deep in the consciousness of the community, has become a factor in consensus and solidarity. Assent is not strictly intellectual. The exact formulations of value systems may be questioned on an intellectual level. They may produce some uneasiness when received and interpreted literally. However, in festival they are affirmed in common acts of ritual celebration. Together a people may sing the creed and dance the culture that may be received with ambivalence on a more rational level. Leisure, especially the special and set-apart events of religious and patriotic significance, serve to provide a context for such consensual rites.

Yet, Berger and Luckman argue that even such rituals may indicate the fragility of the consensus. The world views that undergird the affirmations of institutionalized values are fundamentally faith-based. Even the scientific premise of the knowability of a structured existence requires a decision of faith. Perhaps in the need to celebrate our cultural metaphors and myths we reveal the fragility of their "giveness." And in counterthemes within the festivals—the "feast of fools" and juxtaposition of contradictory elements—we remind ourselves that our culture is not ultimate or final.

After all, we know that we do not live in just any culture. We are culture-specific—ethnic to the core. And to live within that ethnic context requires some provisional acceptance of its ways. To require that every decision involve a radical reexamination of basic presuppositions or to make every ordinary act follow a thoroughgoing critical analysis would make life impossible. To a greater or lesser degree, we all go along with the consensus, even when we know its contradictions and groundless items of faith. One solace in this acceptance is the view that the world we know is still in process. There is no given or unchangable nature enforced by some supernature. Although few are able to have dramatic influence on a culture, we are able to add some small weight to strands of change in the process.

There is always a dialectic in the play of leisure. On the one hand, cultural celebrations are an instrument of social bonding and sometimes of social bondage. On the other hand, in the same celebrational acts we may experience their openness to change. When we can play with culture, sing and dance value systems, and celebrate commonalities, then such celebrations are also revealed as less than permanent. As the mythic elements in history and the affective themes in common celebrations are recognized, then we may be enabled to deal with the culture for what it is—a complex and only partly integrated system of public values and underlying views that is never final. The symbols are understood as representing deeper and often inconsistent themes and orientations by which social life is organized. Then, in this awareness, we may participate in the creative and re-creative process in which a society becomes more than it is.

Cox suggests that life is a mixture of fact and fantasy (1969:69f). In a varying rhythm humans focus on the empirical in one context and imaginative constructs in others. There is often, for example, a religious tone to dealing with ordinary problems of life. In the study of adult life in Peoria, religious concepts and orientations were frequently employed in formulating "philosophies of life" by those who seldom or never participated in organized religion (Kelly, in press). At one moment, we examine the elements of a decision with logical precision. At another, we respond to a mythic interpretation or an imprecise emotion that we label "love." Most often, we mix such elements.

We create as well as celebrate a mytho-poetic world in which we try to live. When "hard facts" threaten the construct, we may ignore, reinterpret, or fight them. Sometimes we even change our myths of meaning. More often, we return to the celebrations that reinforce them in time of stress. We seek reassurance more than critique. And yet, in this process there is also the possibility of play that is open to alteration. There is the possibility of creation of new interpretations, of new myths that are more adequate to the task of making sense of the present and giving hope for the future. We live in a dialectic of celebration and critique that finds a crucial context in the relative openness of playful leisure.

A Metaphor of Being Human ───────────────

A number of themes have been introduced thus far in this chapter: enjoyment, creativity, aesthetics, self-realization, critique, celebration, consensus, myth, and play. All have in common the dialectic of being and becoming, of form and freedom. This exploration of what it means to be human may have begun with the requisites of freedom and community, but has also explored several approaches to *becoming human* through creative activity. The fundamental argument of this chapter is this: that we become human by exercising our freedom in acts of becoming. Such creative activity—for which the arts are a model and arena but not *the* domain of action—takes the stuff of what is and seeks to form what is "not yet."

Leisure, from this perspective, is both activity and a context for activity. It is intentioned action that brings into being something—an aspect of self, mode of communication, presentation, artifact, concept, relationship, or other outcome—that in that context is new. Leisure is the act and possibility of creation, if usually on a very limited scale. It may be a moment of humor, a solution to a room decoration problem, or a transient tactic in the midst of a game. But it is in its own frame of meaning something new. And in the creation the self becomes something more and the community is enriched, if infinitesimally.

Leisure and the Making of Meaning

If leisure is such creative activity, then can it be distinguished from work? Is is not possible to act and create as well as enjoy and find personal growth in the realm of work? The answer is, of course, "Yes." Only one dimension differentiates leisure and work, and it is so imprecise as to leave a wide latitude for blurred distinctions. It is the element of necessity on both the individual and social levels. For the actor leisure is not done primarily to meet self or social needs but for its own sake. There is no necessary consequence or product. And in this relative freedom from necessity, there is a world of difference! It is precisely this lack of external requirement that infuses leisure with play—the possibility of openness and novelty.

Even the experience of leisure may be almost indistinguishable from work. One possible model will illustrate. Leisure activity in its self-containment may yield enjoyment. That enjoyment would seem to be most intense when the actor is fully absorbed in the action, in the state of flow, and it is in such absorption that the heightened intensity of exitement called ecstasy may be experienced. It would be in error to argue that such high intensity can be found only in activity that is clearly noninstrumental. However, it is possible to argue that full concentration on the creating action is enhanced by separation from the constraints of necessity.

One possibility is that too much attention has been given to defining leisure and distinguishing it from other life domains, especially work. A more fundamental issue is the question of what happens in those times and places that are relatively free from necessity and can be oriented more toward the experience. However, even then there is the tendency to focus on the *experience* of leisure and the *products* of work. Further, leisure may be approached as individual activity and work as a social construct. James Hans (1981) seems to be arguing for a more unified approach. Why speak of joy in relation to leisure, ecstasy in creative activity, and satisfaction for work? Is it not more accurate to see beauty, truth, harmony, grace, joy, and even ecstasy as elements in human action? Further, activity that is "ex-static" (Hans, 1981:133) is oriented toward change and novelty. It is creation in some sense and therefore production. Ecstasy is not just immersion in activity but an affective state most likely to occur when "something happens." That something is a creative act, when there is some novel and effectual result from our action.

What is harmony or grace but the bringing together of materials into a realized form? What is beauty but the perception of such realized grace? Whether the stuff of such creation is material or ideas is not crucial. Whether the setting is home or factory or studio is beside the point. What is crucial is that a human actor or community of actors has completed an act of creation. In this act expressing the freedom of the self the emotion of ecstasy is a by-product of the action.

Insofar as humans are a meaning-oriented species, then any act has the dimension of seeking and producing meaning. When this meaning has a material form, we call it a product. When it is immaterial, we refer to it as fantasy or imagination. It may be concrete or symbol, affective or rational, private or communicated, representative or novel. In any case, the actor is not only expressing the self but seeking the self, not only being but becoming. And in such action we are and become human. Only when we refuse to act and deny the possibility of creation do we alienate ourselves from our humanity. Only when such action is denied us are we alienated by external forces. Work and leisure are not opposing domains but distinguishable environments for human action. And such action seeks and produces meaning.

When Marx divided the social world into realms of necessary production and the freedom of leisure, he was responding to the manifest bondage of the new industrial world. However, Marcuse (1969) was more responsive to the modern world when he proposed their interdependence. He saw the negative side. Alienation in work can be intensified by socialization in which meaning and fulfillment come to be defined by the accumulation of commodities. The workplace loses any meaning of useful production or community. In a like manner, leisure also becomes commodity-intensive and evolves into an inhuman reward. Marx seemed to believe that the world of necessity could not be infused with enough freedom to transform fully its drudgery. The world of freedom, on the other hand, was to be completely free from any compulsion of discipline or long-term development.

Marcuse (1969:21) argued that in a socialist society there could be an "ingression of freedom into the world of necessity." Consistent with those who find the possibility of creative activity in production as well as in expression, Marcuse saw life as more of a whole. Leisure could be alienated and alienating in a condition of false consciousness and commodity fetishism. Necessary production, however, might have some elements of real community and freedom. In a different society there would be the possibility of voluntary engagement with productive activity that was needed by the society. In short, both work and leisure—at least in a utopian context—can be human and humanizing. Any domain of life could become what Rene Dubos (1965:313–14) described as one "maintaining the human qualities of life (as) an environment in which it is possible to satisfy the longing for quiet, privacy, independence, initiative, and some open space." The "open space" of physical and social environments lost in a social system that seeks overall dominion over lives may be regained in a society designed for the fullness of human life.

For Marcuse becoming human requires more than a change of aim or consciousness. "Awareness" and programs to reorient the value systems of the self are not enough. Further, social programs that concentrate on the realm of necessity, the workplace, are also inadequate. Simply transferring ownership and control of the "means and mode of production" will not transform alienation into freedom. Rather, true liberation requires a more total integration of the possibilities of becoming human with social contexts that allow for and foster human becoming.

In his *An Essay on Liberation* Marcuse wrote that the rationality of the "Performance Principle" had so infiltrated modern capitalist and socialist systems that both systems stifled the development of human consciousness and activity. He proposed a different basis for social organization, one that would create an "aesthetic rather than repressive environment" (1969:90). There would be openness in the social and physical environment. Parks would take precedence over parking lots, areas for privacy over mass amusement, and exploratory sensual engagement over manipulation. The real achievements of the industrial society would be utilized as an economic base for a society seeking grace more than possessions and play more than production. The massive self-propelling power of modern society would be tamed and diverted to re-create environments on a human scale that enable creative activity. From this perspective the internalization of a new consciousness requires a new society. The individual and social dimensions of change require each other rather than develop independently.

Negation of Creativity

The foregoing analysis suggests two main kinds of negation. The first is that of false consciousness. Immersion in a culture that extols freedom and some modest creativity may become deceptive. We may believe in the reality of such openness because the symbols are celebrated when, in fact, truly creative action is penalized. Certainly when such action becomes revolutionary, in ideas as well as politics, repression is more likely than applause. Humanist metaphors may be employed as euphemisms that screen the social forces concentrated on conformity. Slogans may substitute for action and consciousness for change. Believing we are free to create may be false consciousness unless the conditions that foster creative action are present.

The second negation of humanist metaphors is in the perpetual philosophical danger of elitism. Not only in Plato's *Republic* but also in more modern thought, meditations and celebrations on creativity may have meaning only for a small proportion in any society. Whether or not a society is clearly stratified in a way that purchases transcendence from toil for a few at the price of economic bondage for the masses, self-creating action may require resources and conditions available only to a few. Casually suggesting that leisure is a state of being rarely achieved and impossible for the masses (de Grazia, 1964:5–7) does not avoid the humanist issue of universality. If leisure is required to engage in becoming human, then it cannot be limited to any elites.

Freedom and Leisure

What, then, is freedom today? It is the existential realization of self-directed life. It is also the political and social space to engage in re-creative activity. Marcuse argued for a humanizing principle for action (1969:31–32):

> The aesthetic universe is the *lebenswelt* on which the needs and faculties of freedom depend for their liberation. They cannot develop in an environment shaped by and for aggressive impulses, nor can they be envisaged as the mere effect of a new set of social institutions. They can emerge only in the collective *practice of creating an environment* level by level, step by step—in the material and intellectual production, an environment in which the nonaggressive, erotic, receptive faculties of man, in harmony with the consciousness of freedom, strive for the pacification of man and nature. In the reconstruction of society for the attainment of this goal, reality altogether would assume a *Form* expressive of the new goal. The essentially aesthetic quality of this Form would make it a work of *art,*
> . . .

The aesthetic imagination would be applied to more than what has been designated as art. Creative activity would be applied to more than the traditional materials of music, drama, dance, graphics, ceramics, and so on. Individuals and social organization would also be new creations. Physical and social environments would be transformed according to the principles of grace and harmony. Coercion and repression would be replaced by openness and access to richness of resources. What Schiller referred to as a harmony of energy and form (Hans, 1981:113) would be applied to the reconstitution of life in human terms. The existential dimension of creation and the social dimension of community would be united in bringing the "not yet" into being.

Here many of the themes of previous metaphors and theories share in the images of what it means to be human. Because the aim of life and of leisure is not self-expression but *self-creation,* life itself is seen as creative activity. Aesthetic principles may help direct the existential striving to *become.* At the same time, the structures of the social system are to be re-created to provide a context for this humanizing activity. And one model for this context is *leisure*—the open space for individual and common activity that is most significant just because it is beyond necessity.

Becoming human means:

- Being free from necessity.
- Transcending false consciousness to gain some vision of being human.
- Taking decisive and directed action toward becoming.

- Exploring principles of harmony and grace to direct energies of action.
- Accepting the unity of life in its rational, sensual, material, and spiritual dimensions.
- Acting with others to transform the environments of life into contexts that stimulate and facilitate free and self-creative activity.
- Seeking to become human, not according to some exact image, but in activity that builds community and develops selves of wholeness, grace, and the capacity to love.

Leisure, then, from this humanist perspective is more than an individual state of consciousness or a social condition. It is a total environment in which creation is possible. It is separation from necessity but not from the production of all that contributes to the fulfillment of human existence. It is aesthetic and yet more than narrowly defined art. It is freedom, not *from* but *for* others. It is the openness to re-create the world without the drive to destroy in the process. Leisure is also creative activity in that environment. It is the risk of becoming as well as the grace of at least partial realization of the nature of the human actors.

References _____

Berger, Peter, and T. Luckmann. 1966. *The Social Construction of Reality*. New York: Penguin.

Bonhoeffer, Dietrich. 1959. *Letters and Papers from Prison*. Edited by Eberhard Bethge. London: Fontana.

Copland, Aaron. 1952. *Music and Imagination*. Cambridge: Harvard University Press.

Cox, Harvey. 1969. *The Feast of Fools*. New York: Harper Colophon.

de Grazia, Sebastian. 1964. *Of Time, Work, and Leisure*. Garden City: Doubleday & Co., Anchor Book.

de Moraes von Simson, Olga. 1983. "Cultural Changes, Popular Creativity, and Mass Communication: The Brazilian Carnival over the Past Two Centuries." *Leisure Studies* 2:317–26.

Hans, James. 1981. *The Play of the World*. Amherst: University of Massachusetts Press.

Huizinga, Johan. 1955. *Homo Ludens*. Boston: Beacon Press.

Kant, Immanuel. [1892] 1964. *Critique of Judgment*. Trans. by J. Bernard. New York: Hafner.

Kelly, J. R. (in press). *Peoria Wintor: Later Life Styles and Resources*. Lexington: Lexington Books.

Kroeber, A. L. 1948. *Anthropology*. New York: Harcourt, Brace.

Marcuse, Herbert. 1969. *An Essay on Liberation*. Boston: Beacon Press.

Pieper, Josef. 1963. *Leisure: the Basis of Culture.* New York: New American Library, Mentor Books.

Rahner, Karl. 1968. *Spirit in the World.* Trans. by W. Dych. New York: Herder and Herder.

Schiller, Friedrich. 1954. *On the Aesthetic Education of Man.* Trans. by R. Snell. New Haven: Yale University Press.

Weiss, Paul. 1964. "A Philosophical Definition of Leisure." In *Leisure in America: Blessing or Curse?* ed. J. C. Charlesworth. Washington D.C.: American Academy of Political and Social Science.

Wild, John. 1948. *Introduction to Realistic Philosophy.* New York: Harper & Row, Publishers.

Wilson, Robert N. 1981. "The Courage to Be Leisured." *Social Forces* 60:282–303.

CHAPTER **10**

Dialectical Theory: A Synthesis

The play of theories has taken a dialectical form in which theory building is a reflexive process rather than a final product.

Retracing the spiral from the bottom up moves from immediate experience to creative activity without losing contact with either the existential or social dimensions of leisure.

Leisure is a social creation, of its culture and yet re-creating the culture. In the cultural context leisure is relative openness, situated freedom, and social space.

All leisure is not existentially creative. Yet, there is always the freedom *for* creating the "not yet," in possibility if not realization.

Leisure is dialectical: necessary because it is free, productive because it is immediate, and creative because it is self-contained.

In the dialectic of creation leisure is action that overcomes environment and environment that permits action. It is engagement with doing and becoming.

The *social existentialism* of this action-structure dialectic is a metaphor that unites being and becoming—in all life as well as in leisure.

From the perspective presented in the first chapter, theory construction is a creative process. It is play with metaphors and models that encompass only parts of the entire phenomenon to be understood. Such an approach is no excuse for failing to develop propositions that are as systematic as possible. Nor should empirical evidence, both supporting and conflicting, be ignored or left unweighed. However, carrying out the implications of a theoretical metaphor and relating it to other metaphors may be a better test of its value than simply listing research results selected to support elements of its overall formulation.

In the analyses of the previous eight chapters some of the most relevant and well substantiated research on leisure has been included. It should be evident that when research is designed on the premises of a type of theory, there is a good likelihood that the results will in some way support or advance the model. Less often has research been designed or interpreted in ways that may offer possibilities for the reconstruction of theory. The tendency in doing "normal science" (Kuhn, 1970) is to remain comfortably within the accepted issues and methods of the normative theoretical model. As a consequence, empirical research usually is cited and incorporated in a discussion only as it supports or raises questions *within* the overall metaphor. In the previous chapters, some research has been lifted out of its customary habitat and placed in the analytical world of another kind of theory.

The title of Chapter 1 suggests that theory building may be a kind of play. That is, it takes materials not usually found on the same intellectual shelf and attempts to discover what may be created out of them. Even in this process we tend to be limited to known and available materials. Further, we find our creation biased by the language forms we use and the cultural assumptions that we are unable to suspend. From this perspective, the development of theory—about leisure or anything else—is itself a metaphorical process. The process is more than an exercise in constructing a logical system with propositions of the "known." There is considerable playing with "if-then" analysis. For example, "If weekend leisure is more active and energy-intensive and uses blocks of time, then weekday leisure may be constrained by economic roles in both energy levels and time sequences." Evidence is assembled and weighed. Then, implications for institutional-functional theory and for political-critical theory may be assessed in ways that amend or support either or both. Theory building is made up of an endless pursuit of such items that may be utilized in the development of explanatory metaphors.

Play is not without its form and precedents. The form of this attempt to build a framework for leisure theory is that of the dialectic. The thesis-antithesis-synthesis process is taken to be ongoing and cumulative rather than once-and-for-all. Even such a far-ranging project as this is recognized as selective and partial. It is an insertion into the process that may alter future analysis and building. However, it is only part of the processual play of theory.

The Dialectical Spiral: A Review

Before going on with an attempt at synthesis, we review the dialectical process in its eight steps and in its experience-based order. Then, the spiral will be inverted and compressed to extract and meld some of the major themes and issues. The form adopted begins with this metaphor: "Explanatory theory is developed in a dialectical process beginning with what is 'known' or generally supported. This thesis statement is challenged by counterargument and evidence in order to test, amend, and possibly reject it." In the case of leisure, the first thesis was that of documented immediate experience. Then, each of seven succeeding theses was challenged in a way that seemed to lead to another metaphor:

1. The immediate experience of leisure—characterized by relative freedom and immersion in the activity—is challenged by its own processual nature. Leisure is not static or an abstracted mental state but an experiential process.
2. The action nature of leisure involves existential decision that produces meaning. However, such decision and action are always limited by situational factors and the acceptance of limits as final.
3. Longer-term outcomes for leisure are located in the developmental aims of actors through the life course and in decisions that lead to personal "becoming." Yet, such development may be stunted and distorted when inauthentic images of a closed world and static self are adopted.
4. Personal and social identities provide continuity to the process of becoming in its social settings. The openness of the process is challenged when actors are led by the instruments of mass society to use their freedom merely to become like others.
5. In social interaction contexts we learn and demonstrate who and where we are in the social system. However, the process is not linear or conflict-free, as seemingly problematic outcomes may be determined by others for their own ends.
6. The social system is an institutional context in which we take and enact roles. In the complex of role sequences through the life course leisure may provide a balance to other outcomes and associations. However, when leisure roles are secondary and determined in situations of unequal power, functional leisure may lose its existential freedom.
7. In a closed social system leisure is determined by the economic and political interests of those in control. The exercise of power may be masked in the nurture of a false consciousness in which freedom to become is surrendered to marketplace consumption.
8. Leisure is creative action in an environment that makes possible its actualization and celebration. However, creative activity may be reduced to a celebration of the given in acquiescence to a closed future. In a humanistic metaphor the crucial element of leisure is the creative exercise of freedom.

The eight steps do not yield a tight sequence of propositions that can be scrutinized for logical consistency. However, they are intended to provide a framework that is coherent enough to challenge and examine for major flaws. Each step has its own internal weaknesses and external challenges. Each is not only partial but imperfect. And, each seems plausible enough not to be rejected in its entirety.

There are a number of problems with undertaking a critical review. The sequence moves from one level of analysis to another, making data comparisons difficult. Seldom have lines of research been reflexive as well as cumulative in ways that yield their own corrections. Further, the various disciplines employed in the process have different rules of evidence as well as conventions of presentation. Therefore, a summary becomes more like the analysis of the ebb and flow of a basketball game than of the wiring diagram of a microcomputer.

Further, all this takes place in a historical context composed of countless specific events and an accretion of views and values. There is no ahistorical theory construction that transcends the shaping forces and factors of era and culture. Even the age-cohort history of the theorist has its impacts on the process. Theory building is a process that ends only when the subject becomes irrelevant and is discarded.

In this perspective and in a slightly playful spirit we now take the "bottom up" spiral and reenter it from the top down. The reformulation integrates the eight-part dialectic into two more general sections. One deals with leisure as social and the other with leisure as existential. Then, the two major segments are juxtaposed in a dialectic directed toward an integrating synthesis.

Leisure: A Social Creation _____

Anthropological, historical, and sociological perspectives on leisure presume that it is always in and of its particular culture. Leisure forms, interpretations, and orientations are learned in the culture. The common means of transmitting that culture are through the institutions of the society as well as the auxiliary devices of mass media, economic marketing, and common wisdom that permeate the system. In some societies the state may employ leisure policy and provisions for political ends. In some, leisure becomes a major factor in attachment to the system and its rewards. Leisure as time and access to resources may come to be accepted as the reward over and above the package of basic goods—housing, transportation, education, health care, food, and clothing—that yields acceptance of the system and its requirements.

Whether leisure is an integrating or a liberating element in the social system, it offers its meanings within a culture and employs the material of that culture. As such, it is learned by individuals. Further, it is given form and content by the "stuff" of the culture—its symbol system, institutional role sets, socialization processes, and layers of formal and informal organization.

Leisure Re-creating the Culture

While leisure is always in and of the culture, it is more than product. The other side of the dialectic is the possibility of leisure becoming a factor in social change. If it is accepted that leisure *may* be the least predetermined kind of social activity, then the possibility of change-oriented action may be enhanced. When the role requirements and productive purposes of so much organized behavior—in work, family, or community—are undertaken with comprehensive expectations for outcomes and behavioral styles, leisure may be the domain in which there is the greatest openness to novelty. In play we may be able to try out new forms and try on new behavioral styles.

As analyzed in Chapter 9, the relative openness of leisure and its less-consequential outcomes provides a context for playing with the given forms and meanings of activity. Such a style of action makes possible creation in the arts, virtuosity in sport, and humor in communication. It is the openness of form and outcome that creates and re-creates the activity itself in the action process. In the play of leisure, we may try the novel and risk the problematic. We enter into the possibility of the realization of the "not yet," of creation.

Although some leisure may be constructed to celebrate the consensus of a social system, there is also the alternative possibility. Even when historical events are dramatized and central values re-presented and cheered, the fact that they are re-creations is also evident. However deep in the culture a celebration may be rooted, it is not the "real thing." Rather, symbols and stories are extracted from the known history to take symbolic contemporary meaning.

In such re-creation the "social construction of reality" is demonstrated (Berger and Luckman, 1966). In a social event of manifest symbolic meaning the most basic values and world views of the culture are revealed as constructs. They are "givens" only in the sense of being fundamental to the tradition-based value consensus holding the society together. The consensus may be presented as sacred and above question but without fully submerging the playful element of celebration that permeates the event. When the play of re-creation is recognized, then the possibility of directed change may counter the solidarity aims.

In the arts we take up the materials of the art as part of the discipline of creation. In sports we agree to the forms of the activity in order to discover and develop new levels of skill. In conversation we may suspend the serious in order to weave a fanciful created language for fun, excitement, or metacommunication. We employ form and material for creative ends. In much the same way, we may employ the rituals and dramatizations of our culture toward new ways of bonding, communicating, producing, and even governing.

Structure and Creation

In social contexts we both create and are created. This dialectic is fundamental to the development of both self and society. The revelation of the social construction of society does not imply that social structure is in some way secondary to action. Not even the most open activity is without its own form as well as existing in a culture with a full set of norms, conventions, rules, and expectations. "Roleless" activity is difficult to locate.

On the one hand, we are products of our history and culture. At an extreme, we may be so cut off from freedom to determine our own actions that we are alienated from this requisite of humanity. We are controlled in action and consciousness in a system constructed to further the interests of others. Some segment in the system has the power to make things come out their way and the authority to legitimate such control. Such an elite may even control socialization agents in the system so that those being used in alienating ways believe that their interests are being served. This false consciousness can turn even the relative freedom of leisure into an instrument of control.

On the other hand, structure is endemic to any social action and interaction. Leisure is *relative* openness, not total lack of form. Leisure is *situated* freedom, and in the situations there is a history of previous behavior and meanings that sets the stage for the next performance. Leisure is a *social space,* not a vacuum.

The openness of leisure is its dimension of play in a milieu that is fluid enough to permit change of direction. It is action in an environment with the potential of re-creation. It is the possibility of rebuilding the structure, not the absence of structure. For this reason there is always a potential element of revolution in play. In leisure that retains the creative and critical dimensions of play there may be the seed of radical change. The accepted foundations of a culture, especially one that is repressive, may be undermined by play that explores and develops alternatives. There may be other ways of seeing the world, defining the self, relating to others, and completing lines of action. Life may be seen in the metaphor of game as well as that of given and necessary structure. And the rules of a game are subject to negotiation!

Structure is not in and of itself a denial of freedom or of leisure. Only when it loses its openness and historical relativity to the interests of entrenched power or of fearful acceptance does structure become alienating. However, the existential side of the dialectic is just as crucial. Without freedom there is no leisure. Without the consequence of creation there is no real decision.

Leisure: An Existential Creation

As presented in a variety of ways in the previous chapters, leisure also has a defining existential dimension. Leisure, from this perspective, is *action*. It is deciding and doing as well as feeling. In the sense of intentioned action, leisure is activity. Such decisive action produces meaning. Leisure does more than reflect the cultural meanings attached to certain symbols and settings. It creates meaning whenever the decision is real and the action carried out. In the process of enactment, there is at least the infinitesimal seed of novelty. The manifest consequences of the action may be fully contained in the situated event, but the latent consequences have the potential of boundary-breaking creation.

Doing Leisure

Why do we engage in leisure activity? Generally, we choose or respond to opportunity anticipating the renewal of some previous experience. Leisure is seldom a strategy of self-development or creation to the exclusion of the immediate experience. What is argued here is that it is just this focus on the immediate that frees leisure for its potential of creation and change. Because we are not compelled to do something and because the outcome is open to action, we can take existential action. We can create.

The traditional Aristotelian theme of freedom *from* necessity remains relevant. As analyzed in Chapters 2 and 3, leisure may have a full range of levels of intensity and engagement. Disengagement in the sense of separation from role requirements and longer-term aims is a part of leisure. Relaxation from bodily, social, and mental disengagement is legitimate leisure, not second-rate. The "balance" model does describe patterns of leisure choice. Leisure includes activity that is solitary as well as social, disengaging as well as demanding of high investment, and conditioned by previous activity intensity as well as autonomous. Being entertained may be as much a part of the balance as creative action. However, the overall "shape" of leisure is more than momentary in meaning. It is part of a whole in which social and high-investment activities tend to be valued most by those who have not surrendered their existential freedom.

One orientation of this "creation" is toward the self. We are interested in becoming more than we are in some critical dimensions. We would like to change in some significant ways. Or we may have begun a process of becoming that we want to carry further. In any case, there are aspects of personal identity that are incomplete or less than satisfactory. One orientation of leisure is to inaugurate and carry out lines of action that promise to enhance development. And some of the positive affect in the immediate experience is derived from the sense of such development. A sense of competence and self-creation, especially when recognized by significant others, may be central to satisfaction within the episode. -

A second orientation is social. In leisure we may not only create a somewhat different self, but we may create community. As previously analyzed, community requires a risk of communication and trust. There is an openness in community—whether in a growing friendship or the sharing of intimacy—that requires decision. We have to decide to risk honesty and openness as the bases for community. We have to forego manipulated outcomes and risk the problematic in order for relationships to grow. We have to take action that may result in altered social identities if we are to join in common lines of action with others. There is risk in any interaction process that we do not control. Yet, part of our humanity is to seek such community. Again, leisure *may* offer the social space for such action; we may create community in the relative openness of leisure.

There is this paradox possible in such leisure: that it is most consequential in its results just when it is least focused on results. When the outcome is not predetermined, we may invest ourselves most fully in the process. When we are fully engrossed in the action rather than meeting product expectations, we may be most creative—of self, community, and even material product.

This does not mean that there is no form or discipline in leisure. On the contrary, the freedom of leisure is freedom *for* real action, not freedom *from* form. Therefore, leisure *is* creation, not always realized but always in possibility. Because it is primarily for its own sake, it may be most fully creative.

The Dialectic of Meaning

On the one hand, leisure is action with its own meaning. On the other, it is action that may be most creative. Further, without the freedom for creation, leisure loses its necessary intrinsic meaning. It becomes another instrument of external interests.

Leisure, then, is

- oriented toward the action experience and yet self-creating,
- self-contained and yet productive,

- not required and yet significant,
- self-oriented and yet of social value,
- most free and yet central to the necessary process of social change.

Leisure, just because it is relatively free, is necessary for social criticism and change and for personal development. Whether the existential freedom of leisure is located in separate and designated times and places of play is a secondary issue. What is necessary is that the opportunity for such action exist.

Without the existential freedom to decide there is no becoming. Without freedom for intimacy there is no community—only "I-it" relationships. Without existential freedom, the risk of becoming and relating is a sham. The issue is not whether this action context is called "leisure" but that it be supported and realized in the social context in which we make our life journeys.

The Dialectic of Creation

A dialectical model permits a theoretical construction to encompass divergent elements without discarding each. However, the inclusion of such differences comes at a price. It allows for no neat formula that can be passed on to generations of willing recipients as the final truth. A dialectical formulation can serve as the basis for many varieties of research but makes the sequential propositions of logical positivism impossible.

The Process of Leisure

Further, a dialectic cannot be reduced to an either/or or a both/and model. Leisure, in this metaphor, is process with both existential and social dimensions—sometimes in conflict. Leisure is not either/or: decision or a state of being, immediate experience or personal development, relaxed or intense, flow or creation, separate or engaged, problematic or structured. Leisure is act and an environment for action, of the culture and creating the "not yet," developmental and community-building. Sometimes one dimension is dominant in a particular decision or episode. A dialogue may be silly and unrelated as well as a deep exploration of meanings and relationships. An event may be relaxing and have a minimal intensity of involvement as well as strenuous with maximum intensity. Often in a given leisure episode there is a sequential development of the action that moves to one pole of the dialectic and back.

Nevertheless, the both/and connection is as inaccurate as the either/

or. Leisure, from a dialectic perspective, is not just an inclusive blob of elements. Rather, it is process that may require struggle to assert the existential in the midst of social structure. Or it may require a decisive act to extend intimacy in the midst of conflict or competition. A social consensus on the forms and meanings of a leisure event or setting does not preclude extra-official activity. Often we seek to maintain some autonomy in a structured environment, some creativity amid rigid expectations, and some separation in a social world of overlapping roles and relationships. Leisure is a dialectic process in its actualization as well as its theoretical formulation.

The Dialectic of Creation

There is a theory of creativity that is based on fantasy and romanticism. Its various versions presume that there is some ideal environment for creative activity, secluded from the struggle and confusion of ordinary life and dedicated to noble aims. This Shangri-la of creativity is alleged to be an emotional haven for those who are waiting to take the risk of decision and action. Further, leisure may come to be identified with this environment of protection and special purpose. The common justification for failing to engage in creative risk is that one does not have the necessary leisure, the separated time and place.

Of course, we know that if Bach or Mozart had waited for such leisure in which to compose, the world of music would be infinitely diminished. Rather, theirs and most creative activity has taken place in the midst of responsibilities, relationships, and conflicts that could not be shut out in some sanctuary. Creation is not produced by any environment, however designed. Creation is existential action in environments that do not absolutely prevent a necessary degree of autonomy and authentic action. Creation occurs when action overwhelms environment, not when the environment is perfect. Leisure, then, is not some perfect realm of creativity but is relative openness for existential action.

Creativity does not require a perfect environment, nor does it produce perfection. Rather, in this metaphor, creation is also a process in which there is a decision to risk a product. However, that process is a dialectic in which act struggles with material, the novel with the form, and the authentic with the accepted. There may be perfect creations somewhere according to some incomplete criteria, but most creation is bringing into being the less-than-perfect and then presenting it to others. It is more likely a recognition of imperfection than a presumption of finality. In one sense, perfection means completion, and in life the only completion is death. Creation is the engagement of life with doing and becoming, not finishing for all time some product beyond criticism. Creation is process that presumes further possibility.

The dialectic of creation begins with risk in the face of openness, of action before indeterminacy. If we *knew* the outcomes of our action, there would be no creation, only repetition. Whether the creative act is aimed toward an artistic product, a useful tool, an expanded relationship, or a family, there is no surety of result and no protection from critique. It is a dialectical process in which the creator decides to exhibit the product, not as perfect but as worth the risk of sharing.

The dialectic of creation, then, is more than theory. It is a fundamental process of life. In creation there is a dialectic of myth and reality in which an aesthetic vision may be expressed. There is a dialectic of the authentic and the distorted, both within the creator and in the learned views and values that shape action. There is the dialectic between what is—the culture—and what might become.

Leisure is no guarantee of creative action; it is a possibility of situated freedom. That possibility may be oriented toward a product, artifact, or act. It may be oriented toward the self, a developmental self-creation of competence or attitude. It may be oriented toward relationships, intimacy, and community. Or leisure action may be oriented away from creation and toward an inner mental state or fundamental state of being. In any case, it is freedom for such action.

Leisure may also be twisted and distorted so that its possibilities become inhuman and alienated. We may deny our freedom in favor of prescribed conventions. We may avoid risk by seeking a static state of being. We may forfeit the process of becoming in an attachment to what is. We may so fear conflict and critique that we pull back from any moment of presentation or exposure. We may prefer the "bad faith" of denying decision to go along with every signal of what others want and expect. We may even engage in activity that places others in alienating contexts in which they are denied access to self-determining action. We may be among the manipulators as well as the manipulated.

Creation, then, is not finality but existential activity. Leisure is not seclusion but possibility. And becoming is not a gift but a consequence of risk. All this is not intended to imply that the relative self-containment of leisure is not conducive to many kinds of creation. Nor does it suggest that the relative openness and concentration on the immediate process that we call "play" are not essential to creation. However, no attitude or environment can ensure creative action or playful orientations.

Social Existentialism as Theory ⸻

The central theme of social existentialism is the dialectic between action and structure, between self-determination and social forces. The foregoing analysis of leisure leads to the premise that there is no state of freedom that is asocial and no social context that totally precludes existential decision. The relative freedom of leisure is found to be thoroughly social, however uncomfortable we might be with the concept of leisure roles. On the other hand, in even the most structured and predetermined setting there is at least the possibility of a momentary playful attitude or definition of the situation. The situated character of human action and interaction places life into the existential/social dialectic.

Within this context there is also the continual interpretive process of cognition and signification. As actors we continually read the situation, place it into some context of previous experience or a schema of meaning, and take action out of our interpretation. The perceiving and meaning-giving process is the basis for action, both immediate and oriented toward the future. The only "hard facts" are those we choose to interpret as immutable and given. (Of course, some are harder than others in the sense of being resistant to our action.)

Social existentialism, then, is the metaphor of synthesis chosen to represent an overall interpretation of the dialectical spiral. It does not answer all questions or incorporate every tangent or loose end. It does, however, give at least partial coherence to the overall argument analyzing leisure as a human phenomenon. It is a framework for tying together elements of decision and determination, creation and form.

Further, this metaphor is not a final synthesis. Rather, the dialectical process of theory building goes on—and should! Insights are omitted, evidence is unrecognized or misunderstood, and connections are garbled and vague. The questions are not those to be addressed to perfection. They are those that come out of the process: What is omitted from the dialectical spiral that might redirect the analysis? Are there overriding factors that have been given too little weight in this process? Most important, where does the theory-building dialectic go from here?

Leisure: To Be and To Become

As context or possibility, leisure is the *freedom to be*. It is an environment for self-determining action, the possibility of situated freedom. Again, this context is not itself the actualization of leisure, nor is it simply a social or political arrangement. Rather, it is a sociocultural environment in which decisive action without predetermined outcomes is possible. It is opportunity for creation, identity development or revision, and exploration and building of relationships *for their own sake*.

As situated action, leisure is the *freedom to become*. It is a process, not a completed act or final product. In leisure existential action can bring into being what does not yet exist—a dimension of the self, community, or object. Leisure does not happen to us. We create leisure by acting in the realm of possibility. This action is directed toward the experience and what may occur in that experience. The problematic element of leisure is the basis of becoming. As with intensity, that element varies in range of possible outcomes as well as in its immediacy of experience. Nevertheless, it is essential to leisure. Without the possibility of becoming there can be no decision. Without decision there is no riskful engagement. Without such risk there is no creation.

As environment, leisure is the possibility of becoming—sometimes enhanced by structure and sometimes focused on indeterminacy. As act, leisure is existential—taking action without having the outcome fixed. As learning, leisure is social—profoundly of the culture. As creation, leisure is free—when something new emerges in the process.

Life as Existential and Social

At this terminal point, one other question can be addressed: Is all this just about leisure? Can other domains of action and interaction also be understood in the metaphor of social existentialism?

The obvious answer is "Yes". Leisure may be more conducive to play than other contexts, but it holds no exclusive rights to freedom, expression, involvement, creation, intimacy, or risk. Leisure may be *relatively* open, developmental, expressive, intrinsic in aims and outcomes, and supportive of creative activity. It may have a special place of significance in a society just because of the relative openness that is most likely to foster riskful and playful creation, but these dimensions can be found almost anywhere in greater or lesser degree.

In fact, we can argue that these dimensions need to exist in all human settings. There are no tasks that might not benefit from some play. There are no relationships that do not gain from concentration on the interaction for its own sake rather than getting something from the others present. There are no efforts to create that cannot be enriched by riskful decision. There is no state of being that cannot be extended into personal growth and development by decisive action. All life is, indeed, existential and social.

This means also that all the negations of leisure can be found in the rest of life. False consciousness, bad faith, alienation, control, focus on possession, reduction of freedom to market choice, acquiescence to the given, and manipulation of others in an intimacy-denying contest are all possible in work or family or community. The predetermined outcomes of work or the responsibility requirements of the family neither eliminate all freedom nor guarantee meaning. The dialectic of human existence between the existential and the social is endemic to all life.

Life is becoming—a process. It may be creating whenever freedom is not surrendered to security. Life is action amid dilemmas—developmental and social. It may be alienated and lonely or supported by community, but the journey of life knows only one final end to its movement into the future.

In human life leisure does have a special place. However defined and supported by the culture, leisure is more than nonwork or leftover time. Leisure is more than freedom from requirement. It is freedom *for* being and becoming—for the self and for society.

References

Berger, Peter, and Thomas Luckman. 1966. *The Social Construction of Reality*. New York: Penguin Books, Inc.

Kuhn, Thomas. 1970. *The Structure of Scientific Revolutions*. Chicago: University of Chicago Press.

Annotated Bibliography

This listing includes only books that have leisure as their primary focus. Not included are most textbooks on recreation and its various subfields. The list does include most of the books currently available in English that have had the most influence on the contemporary study of leisure.

Cheek, Neil H., Jr., and William R. Burch, Jr. 1976. *The Social Organization of Leisure in Human Society*. New York: Harper and Row, Publishers.

An argument for the significance of leisure in a modern society. Regularities and differences in behavior are analyzed in relation to age, gender, and social position. Primary relationships are fostered in leisure's expressive environment in ways that contribute to social bonding.

Csikszentmihalyi, Mihaly. 1975. *Beyond Boredom and Anxiety*. San Francisco: Jossey-Bass, Inc.

An analysis of intensity and involvement in activity. A fit between challenge and ability avoids the boredom of too little challenge and the anxiety produced by too much. The optimal "flow" experience yields meaning for the ordinary. Both freedom and environment are found related to such involvement.

de Grazia, Sebastian. 1962. *Of Time, Work, and Leisure*. Garden City: Doubleday & Co., Anchor Books.

A now-classic argument for leisure as a rare state of being that may be destroyed by the modern preoccupation with activity, possession, and social timetables. The Aristotelian ideal of contemplation that is enobling and fulfilling is presented in modern terms accompanied by an appendix of dated but interesting statistical tables.

Dumazedier, Joffre. 1967. *Toward a Society of Leisure*. Trans. by S. McClure. New York: The Free Press.

With an interesting introduction by David Riesman, this pioneer volume was the most influential book in leisure studies for the 1960s. Dumazedier, a French sociologist, explores with both critical and functional premises the meanings of leisure in relation to work, family, social policy, and community. From an empirical base in the study of workers in an industrial town, issues of relative freedom, popular culture, and planning for the future are treated from sociological perspectives.

Dumazedier, Joffre. 1974. *Sociology of Leisure*. Trans. by Marea McKenzie. Amsterdam and New York: Elsevier Scientific Publishing Co.

A historical as well as sociological analysis of the development of leisure in Western societies. Embedded in social structures, leisure also has influenced social institutions and the orientations of ordinary life. French and Soviet leisure development are compared.

Godbey, Geoffrey. 1985. *Leisure in Your Life: An Exploration*. State College: Venture Publishing.

An introduction to the study of leisure that combines social science with a personal approach. It includes exploration of the life cycle, religion, sexuality, education, and institutionalized recreation.

Hans, James. 1981. *The Play of the World*. Amherst: University of Massachusetts Press.

A recent study of play as desire and production. Employing poststructural European philosophical concepts and methods, Hans argues that play is an essential element in any life and society that is not closed to change and creation.

Huizinga, Johan. 1955. *Homo Ludens: A Study of the Play Element in Culture*. Boston: Beacon Press.

Probably *the* classic in the field. Huizinga explores history and ideas around the theme of "man, the player." Dimensions of play as voluntary, free, secluded, ordered, and nonserious are examined. With philosophical understanding, the author finds play *in* life and the culture rather than peripheral.

Iso-ahola, Seppo, ed. 1980. *Social Psychological Perspectives on Leisure and Recreation*. Springfield: Charles C. Thomas, Publisher.

A collection of papers written for this volume that offer a basis and directions for the application of social psychology to the study of leisure. A significant agenda-setting effort in this developing area.

Kando, Thomas. 1980. *Leisure and Popular Culture in Transition* 2d ed. St. Louis: The C. V. Mosby Company.

A sociology of leisure emphasizing cultural and social changes that have influenced leisure and popular culture. Particular attention is given to mass media, sport, and the arts.

Kaplan, Max. 1979. *Leisure: Lifestyle and Lifespan*. Philadelphia: W. B. Saunders Company.

With his groundbreaking first book long out of print, this approach to leisure and gerontology is the best introduction to Kaplan's thought and insights. His analysis of adult roles leads to life-styles, environments, and activities in which creativity may be expressed.

Kelly, John R. 1980. *Leisure*. Englewood Cliffs: Prentice-Hall, Inc.

A multidisciplinary general introduction to leisure in contemporary life.

Kelly, John R. 1983. *Leisure Identities and Interactions*. London and Boston: George Allen & Unwin Ltd.

A symbolic interaction approach to leisure with attention given to life-course role sequences, development, and identity formation and expression.

Neulinger, John. 1974 (2d ed., 1983). *The Psychology of Leisure*. Springfield: Charles C. Thomas, Publisher.

A groundbreaking beginning in the application of social and personalistic psychology to leisure. Initial research efforts are mixed with an advocacy of leisure as essential to being and becoming human.

Parker, Stanley. 1971. *The Future of Work and Leisure*. New York: Praeger Publishers, Inc.

Presents models of the work-leisure relationship that have been standard for subsequent discussions. Parker tends to see work as the dominant context of life in society, with leisure emerging as increasingly salient to modern life.

Parker, Stanley. 1983. *Leisure and Work*. London and Boston: George Allen & Unwin Ltd.

Includes some research and issues that have emerged since the 1971 volume. Attention is given to unemployment, women's work environments, and impacts of the electronic technologies. However, the basic perspective of the earlier book is reaffirmed.

Pieper, Josef. 1963. *Leisure: The Basis of Culture*. Trans. by Alexander Dru. New York: Random House, Inc.

A traditional formulation of leisure as a condition of freedom of mind and soul that fosters the development of culture and contemplation. As such, leisure is seen as necessary for a living culture.

Rapoport, Rhona and Robert N. 1975. *Leisure and the Family Life Cycle*. London: Routledge and Kegan Paul, Ltd.

Brings together developmental approaches to the life course with family and leisure sociology. The first major work to break out of the work-leisure dyad and investigate the relationship of leisure to ongoing life in school, family, peer group, and community. Important also for its attention to women as well as men.

Roberts, Kenneth. 1978. *Contemporary Society and the Growth of Leisure*. London: Longman Group Limited

As in his small earlier book, Roberts employs the concepts and knowledge base of mainstream British sociology in analyzing the social nature of leisure in relation to changing social institutions. Leisure is seen in a reciprocal relationship with economic, family, and other social roles.

Roberts, Kenneth. 1983. *Youth and Leisure*. London and Boston: George Allen & Unwin Ltd.

The special conditions and preoccupations of youth are examined in the context of employment issues, sexuality, social class, and ethnicity.

Smigel, Erwin, ed. 1963. *Work and Leisure: A Contemporary Social Problem*. New Haven: College and University Press.

The book that provided most of the agenda for the sociology of leisure in the 1960s. Especially chapters by Bennett Berger, Robert Dubin, and Harold Wilensky have provoked innumerable responses in theory and research.

Indexes

Author Index

Subject Index _____